Seventeenth Century Contexts

SEVENTEENTH CENTURY CONTEXTS

by

GEORGE

WILLIAMSON

Revised Edition

THE UNIVERSITY OF CHICAGO PRESS

Library of Congress Catalog Card Number: 71-75137

THE UNIVERSITY OF CHICAGO PRESS, CHICAGO 60637
Faber and Faber Limited, London W. C. 1, England

Contents

★

Preface

★

My acknowledgements are due to *ELH: A Journal of English Literary History*, *English Studies*, *Modern Philology*, *Philological Quarterly*, *Reveiw of English Studies*, and *Studies in Philology*, in which most of these essays originally appeared. Since the value of the essays now reprinted is partly historical, their dates of publication have been supplied in the table of contents. The others are unpublished. Together these essays acquire new meaning from the variety of their contexts.

G.W.

I

Mutability, Decay and Jacobean Melancholy

★

I see the world grows old, whenas the heat
Of thy great love once spread, as in an urn
Doth closet up itself and still retreat,
Cold sinne still forcing it, till it return,
And calling Justice, all things burn.

(G. Herbert's *Decay*)

Some years ago I ventured to call a peculiar intensity of feeling in Donne the 'metaphysical shudder'. Now I should like to discuss the 'metaphysical' concept which was largely responsible for that feeling, and which may be said to have 'brought death into the world' of early seventeenth-century thought. This is the ancient idea of the decay of the world, which grew particularly strong with the waning of the Middle Ages, but perhaps never acquired such powers of disturbing the soul as came with the astronomical study of the late sixteenth century. One of the momentous effects of the Renaissance, when men had turned their eyes to the things of this world, was to give new life to the idea of the decay of the world by planting mutability in the heavens and by stimulating admiration for Antiquity. The stout declaration of Ben Jonson in his *Discoveries* bears witness to

9

the force of this idea: 'I cannot think Nature is so spent and decayed that she can bring forth nothing worth her former years. . . . Men are decayed, and studies: She is not.'

Although various explanations have been given for seventeenth-century melancholy, none has considered seriously enough the concept of the Decay of Nature, which surely every reader must have felt in the mood of writers from Spenser to Milton. It is this concept which illuminates the 'valley of dry bones' in seventeenth-century thought, and turns a feeling about the afternoon of time into the moral that is too late to be ambitious. Without pretending to exhaust the subject, I shall indicate the power of this concept both as theme and as mood in the period between *Two Cantos of Mutabilitie* and *Urn Burial*. But first it will be necessary to outline some of its astronomical, philosophic, and religious connections at the close of the sixteenth century.

I

The old idea of the mutability and decay of the world was metamorphosed by the new astronomy following Copernicus. In 1572 a brilliant new star appeared in the constellation Cassiopeia and disappeared sixteen months later. After taking careful observations without finding any parallax, Tycho Brahe assigned it to the region of the fixed stars. 'To us of to-day this result may appear fairly commonplace, but most astronomers of the time held so firmly to Aristotle's doctrine that the heavens generally, and the region of the fixed stars in particular, were incorruptible and unchangeable, that new stars were, like comets, almost universally ascribed to the higher regions of our own atmosphere.'[1] The Comet of 1577 Tycho likewise placed far beyond the moon, and thus dealt another blow to this popular belief.[2] But in his account of the new star, published in 1573, Tycho remained a man of his time, for he 'dealt at some length with

[1] Arthur Berry, *A Short History of Astronomy*, London, 1898, pp. 131–2. Thomas Digges published his important work on this star, *Alae seu Scalae Mathematicae*, at London in 1573.
[2] Ibid., pp. 135 ff.

the astrological importance of the star, and the great events which it foreshadowed'.

What Tycho began, Galileo confirmed and completed. When in 1604 a new star suddenly appeared in the constellation Serpentarius, Galileo made his first contribution to astronomical discovery by showing that it was at least more distant than the planets: 'a result confirming Tycho's conclusions that changes take place in the celestial regions even beyond the planets, and are by no means confined—as was commonly believed—to the earth and its immediate surroundings.'[1] In *The Sidereal Messenger* (1610) Galileo announced his observations of the moon; apart from details, the really significant result of his observations was 'that so far the received doctrine of the sharp distinction to be drawn between things celestial and things terrestrial was shewn to be without justification'. But the most striking discovery announced in the *Sidereal Messenger* was that of the satellites of Jupiter, which 'shewed the falsity of the old doctrine that the earth was the only centre of motion; it tended, moreover, seriously to discredit the infallibility of Aristotle and Ptolemy'.[2] Finally, in 1612 Galileo revealed his discovery of spots on the sun. 'The presence on the sun of such blemishes as dark spots, the "mutability" involved in their changes in form and position, and their formation and subsequent disappearance, were all distasteful to the supporters of the old views, according to which celestial bodies were perfect and unchangeable.' Thus the new astronomy introduced corruption and change into the most retired regions of the incorruptible and unchangeable heavens. And Tycho Brahe was instrumental in upsetting these received opinions, although (and even more because) he did not accept the Copernican theory but compromised with the Ptolemaic.[3]

[1] Ibid., p. 149.   [2] Ibid., p. 152.

[3] For the full significance of Tycho in sixteenth-century astronomy, see J. L. E. Dreyer, *Tycho Brahe*, Edinburgh, 1890, especially Chaps. I, III, & VII. As for astronomy in England, the mathematician Thomas Harriot (1560–1621), who was an associate of Marlowe and Ralegh, was one of the first to use the telescope for astronomical purposes, being among the earliest to observe the spots on the sun (cf., Berry, op. cit., pp. 150 and 154).

Mutability, Decay and Jacobean Melancholy

If we feel these remarks to be the reflections of a modern rather than a seventeenth-century mind, we may turn to Burton's 'Digression of Air' in the *Anatomy of Melancholy*. There we shall find a useful résumé of the work of the new astronomers, such as Tycho, Rothmann, Kepler, and Galileo, who were, as Burton suggests,[1] 'exploding' the old doctrine of the heavens set forth by Aristotle and Ptolemy. In Burton we find most of the discoveries and consequences that we have noticed, together with many others, and something of the uncertainty of mind which they produced.[2] Burton is engaged in explaining the variety of climate and weather over the earth, for which he examines the various theories of astronomical influence:

'The Philosophers of *Coimbra* will refer this diversity to the influence of that *Empyrean* Heaven: for some say the *eccentricity* of the Sun is come nearer to the earth than in Ptolemy's time; the virtue therefore of all the vegetals is decayed, men grow less, &c'.[3]

Others, he says, observe the mutability of the heavens by reason of their new motions, new stars or comets, and conclude that from those motions proceed 'divers alterations'. In connection with the new stars, the question arises 'whether there be generation and corruption, as some think, by reason of aethereal Comets'. Burton notes that 'the fixed stars are removed since Ptolemy's time', and raises the question 'whether there be such a precession of the Æquinoxes, as *Copernicus* holds, or that the eighth Sphere move'.[4] In connection with the theory that every star has an 'intelligence', he includes Kepler among those who have in part

[1] *Anatomy of Melancholy*, ed. Shilleto, (Bohn ed.), 2. 57–8. The alteration of the Aristotelian heavens aggravated the feeling about the decay of the world, belief in which taxed the faith and motivated the melancholy of a man like John Norden (cf. *Vicissitudo Rerum*, 1600, sts. 38 ff.).

[2] Ibid., Part II. Sect. II. Mem. III., especially pp. 54–67. On the satellites of Jupiter Burton adds this note: 'Some of those above Jupiter I have seen myself by the help of a glass eight feet long' (ibid., p. 62, note 6).

[3] Ibid., 2. 54.

[4] Ibid., pp. 54 and 59. Although genuine 'Copernicanism' was impossible before the work of Tycho, Galileo, and Kepler, the new tables of Reinhold showed men how the new ideas altered their calculations of the celestial bodies.

revived the opinion of Averroes, Plato in his *Timaeus*, and others that the earth is animated and that the souls of men derive therefrom and return hence.

But to omit all smaller controversies, Burton hastens to 'examine that main paradox, of the Earth's motion, now so much in question'. Here he reviews the opinions of those who discuss the theory of 'a plurality of worlds'; he refers to 'Brunus' infinite worlds', and cites Nicholas Hill as one who publicly defends the theory which Pythagoras, Epicurus, Democritus, and others had maintained.[1] Yet the notion of an infinite universe seems to have become associated with the Copernican theory in the English mind through the influence of Thomas Digges, who anticipated Bruno in this respect. To the *Prognostication euerlastinge* (1576) Digges contributed *A Perfit Description of the Caelestiall Orbes according to the most aunciente doctrine of the Pythagoreans, latelye reuiued by Copernicus and by Geometricall Demonstrations approued*, in which he incorporated the idea of the infinity of the universe, placing the stars at varying distances throughout infinite space.[2] Although Digges probably did not accept literally the rigid Aristotelian distinction between the mutable sublunar realm and the immutable superlunar realm, he did retain this distinction in his diagram as well as register his emotions in phrases involving the received opinion:

'The Globe of Elements enclosed in the Orbe of the Moone I call the Globe of Mortalitie because it is the peculiar Empire of death. For aboue the Moone they feare not his force but as the Christian Poet sayth. . . . In the midst of this Globe of Mortalitie hangeth this darcke starre or ball of earth and water. . . .'[3]

---

[1] Ibid., p. 63. Hill's *Philosophia Epicurea, Democritana, Theophrastica, proposita simpliciter, non edocta*, Paris, 1601, defended the atomistic theories of Epicurus and Democritus. Burton often cites Bruno, and seems to be the first English writer upon whom Bruno made a verifiable impact.

[2] Cf. F. R. Johnson and S. V. Larkey, 'Thomas Digges, the Copernican System, and the Idea of the Infinity of the Universe in 1576', *Huntington Library Bulletin* 5 (1934). 69–117.

[3] Ibid., pp. 80–1; cf. pp. 101–2.

Factually the earth was for him one of the planets, and the sun and fixed stars were fixed; emotionally the earth was 'this litle darcke starre wherein we liue'. But even for this emancipated Copernican the earth, as opposed to the heavens, was still confined to the realm of mutability and death, subject to the vicissitude of the four elements. Digges did not yet dare openly to attack the 'incorruptibility' theory as Galileo did later in his *System of the World*.

Burton mentions Digges several times in connection with the Copernican theory, including him among those who defend in sober sadness the opinion that 'the earth is a planet, moves, and shines to others, as the moon doth to us', and who hold 'that the moon is inhabited'.[1] He concludes that 'if it be so that the earth is a moon, then are we also giddy, vertiginous and lunatick within this sublunary maze'. Another side of the controversy over the new astronomy is brought into our view when he remarks:

'Others freely speak, mutter, and would persuade the world (as *Marinus Marcenus* complains) that our modern Divines are too severe and rigid against Mathematicians, ignorant and peevish in not admitting their true demonstrations and certain observations, that they tyrannize over art, science, and all philosophy, in suppressing their labours (saith *Pomponatius*) forbidding them to write, to speak a truth, all to maintain their superstition, and for their profit's sake.'[2]

Burton observes that in all these controversies 'the World is tossed in a blanket amongst them, they hoise the Earth up and down like a ball, make it stand and go at their pleasures.' Thus he returns to the satiric vein in which he treated the Centre earlier, when he alluded to Donne by calling Hell '*Ignatius*' Parlour'.[3] Although Burton verifies the impetus which the new astronomy lent to the idea of

[1] Op. cit. 1. 86.
[2] Ibid., 2. 64.
[3] Ibid., 2. 49. Burton decides to await God's solution of these matters, but meanwhile his love of paradox induces him, though more superficially than Donne, to prove a sceptic in Browne's sense 'and stand like Janus in the field of knowledge'.

mutability and decay, he does not sound its emotional
depths; that office fell chiefly to the preachers and poets.

II

In seventeenth-century England the ideas of mutability
and mortality unite in the quarrel about the decay of the
world. We can best understand the case for the decay of the
world by considering the most formidable answer to that
view which appeared in this time. Its author was Dr. George
Hakewill; his formal opponent was Dr. Godfrey Goodman;
and his answer was the same as Nature's reply to Mutabilitie
in Spenser's *Two Cantos*.[1] The case for the decay of the
world was most completely stated by Goodman in *The Fall
of Man, or the Corruption of Nature Proved by Natural Reason*
(1616) relating, as Anthony Wood remarks, 'to the eternity
of the World, or for the universal and perpetual decay
thereof, whereby *Goodman* would prove the fall of Man'.
Goodman finds that man, the animals, nature generally, and
even the heavenly bodies are subject to decay; he argues
decay upon the assumptions that the creature becomes more
and more imperfect as it departs farther from the first mould,
and that since parts of the world experience decay, the whole
must experience it as well. He often falls back upon the
analogy with man's life, in which the decay of the microcosm mirrors the decay of the macrocosm. For support in
his argument Goodman cites passages from Scripture and
St. Cyprian, which are the main religious props for his
view.[2]

To this view Hakewill opposed his *Apologie or Declaration
of the Power and Providence of God in the Government of the
World, Consisting in an Examination and Censure of the Common Errour Touching Nature's Perpetual and Universal Decay*
(1627), which reached a third edition in 1635. When Hake-

[1] This quarrel has been described, in connection with the quarrel of the
ancients and moderns, by R. F. Jones in 'The Background of the *Battle of the
Books*', *Washington University Studies* 7 (1920). 104–16.
[2] For an excellent statement of his position see R. F. Jones, op. cit., pp. 106–7.

will's reply finally captured the imagination and emotions of the seventeenth century, the days of Jacobean melancholy were over and the idea of progress passed into the ascendancy.[1] But our concern is not with Hakewill's answer, but rather with the case which he had to answer. We ought, however, to know so much of his answer as we find in 'The Argvment of the Front and of the Worke':

'Although the Creator and Disposer of all things hath left all Particulars and Individualls, under the circle of the *Moone*, to the stroake of *Time* and *Death*; yet by His powerfull Hand He holdeth backe the Sythe of *Time* from destroying or impayring the Vniverse: Though the same Hand shall at last destroy the Whole by *Fire*.

'In the meane time, he hath so ordained that the Elements, of which all sub-lunary bodies are composed, doe so beget one the other, and are againe so begotten, each from other; that while they seeme to dye, they become immortall. For as *Earth* is resolved into *Water*, the *Water* rarefied into *Ayre*, and the *Ayre* into *Fire*, in the way of their ascension; So in their descending down-ward, by a mutuall Compensation, the *Fire* becommeth *Ayre*, the *Ayre* thickneth into *Water*, and the *Water* againe into *Earth*.

'And as a *Ship* which rideth at Anchor is tossed to and fro by the Windes and Waves, and yet cannot move beyond the length of his Cable, but is carried about in a Round, still mooving yet never remooved.

'Or as a *Wheele*, at every turne, bringeth about all his Spoakes to the same places, observing a constancy even in turning.

'So though there be many changes and variations in the World, yet all things come about one time or another to the same points againe.

'And there is nothing new under the *Sunne*.'[2]

This discovery of constancy in mutability, for which Hake-

---

[1] Cf. R. S. Crane, 'Anglican Apologetics and the Idea of Progress, 1699–1745', *Modern Philology* 31 (1934). 279–83.

[2] In Hakewill this Pythagorean doctrine of change is supported by Ovid and others; it constantly appears in arguments on mutability and decay. For Hakewill this 'change' was Pythagorean rather than Heraclitean.

will goes back to Philo and Ovid, is precisely the answer
which Nature makes to Mutabilitie in Spenser's *Two
Cantos* (7.7.58):

> *I well consider all that ye haue sayd*
> *And find that all things stedfastnes doe hate*
> *And changed be; yet being rightly wayd*
> *They are not changed from their first estate;*
> *But by their change their being doe dilate:*
> *And turning to themselues at length againe,*
> *Doe worke their own perfection so by fate:*
> *Then ouer them Change doth not rule and raigne;*
> *But they raigne ouer change, and doe their states maintaine.*

Moreover, Hakewill finds this argument of constancy in
change not only in Philo and Ovid, but also in Plato's
Timaeus and in Du Bartas, whom he quotes at length on the
Pythagorean doctrine of change.[1] From Philo, in the passage
quoted, Hakewill probably gets the figure for his idea of
circular change, by which he refutes the decay of the world;
this figure is 'the circle of the yeare' or *anni circulus*. Of
course the idea is found in the Pythagorean Fifteenth Book
of Ovid's *Metamorphoses*, which serves as one of the chief
texts in the quarrel of mutability and decay. But we shall
find this 'circle' used on the other side of the argument as
well, especially by Lipsius, whom Spenser approaches in
his suggestion of 'fate'.

Hakewill indicates the prevalence of the idea of decay in
his opening sentence: 'The opinion of the Worlds decay is
so generally receiued, not onely among the Vulgar, but of
the Learned both Divines and others, that the very com-
monness of it, makes it currant with many, without any
further examination.' This opinion was supported by the
popular paradox 'that the present time is the real antiquity',
from which Bacon could draw an optimistic conclusion
favouring the moderns.[2] For Bacon the excessive admiration

---

[1] *Apologie*, Second Edition revised, Oxford, 1630, pp. 113–14.
[2] Cf. *The Physical and Metaphysical Works*, ed. J. Devey, London, 1904, pp.
417–18 (*Novum Organum*).

of Antiquity was an error of learning, from which another
error proceeded: 'a distrust that anything should be discovered in later times that was not hit upon before. . . . For
thus we seem apprehensive that time is worn out, and become unfit for generation.'[1] But most of Bacon's contemporaries were left with the apprehension rather than the
optimism which he gave to the paradox. The reasons for
this apprehension Hakewill enumerates as 'the weake
grounds which the contrary opinion of the Worlds decay is
founded vpon'.[2] The fictions of poets 'first gaue life vnto it';
above all, the pretty invention of the four ages of the world
—gold, silver, brass, and iron—made such an impression on
the minds of men that it could hardly be rooted out. This
opinion was also furthered by the morose and crooked disposition of old men, who always decry the present in
favour of the past. And the excessive admiration for
Antiquity completed the argument.

But the most imposing arguments which confront Hakewill come from the 'new philosophy' and are answered by
him in Book II under 'the pretended decay of the Heavens
and Elements'. Because he accepts the notion of sympathy
and correspondence between the heavens and the sublunar
bodies, he is forced to meet the arguments which point to
decay in the heavens; and consequently we find him trying
to answer the implications of the astronomical discoveries
which we have noticed.[3] He argues that discoveries made by
the telescope do not prove that the things discovered 'were
not before in being'. While he does not deny that the new
star in Cassiopeia was a true star and among the fixed stars,
he takes it to have been not the effect of nature, but the
miraculous work of God; and hence it cannot be inferred
that the heavens are composed of a corruptible matter,
naturally subject to impairing and fading, or that their
motion is irregular.[4] 'That which touches neerer to the
quicke,' says Hakewill, 'and strikes indeede at the very

[1] Ibid., p. 49. Cf. *Advancement of Learning* (Everyman ed.), pp. 31-2, for the
earlier version of this passage.
[2] Op. cit., pp. 24-5.   [3] Ibid., pp. 70-1.   [4] Ibid., p. 81.

throate of the cause, is an opinion of very *many*, and those
very *learned* men, that the *Body* of the *Sunne* is drawne
nearer the Earth by many degrees then it was in former
ages, & that it dayly makes descents & approaches towards
it, which some ascribe to a deficiencie of strength in the
Earth, others in the *Sun*, most in *both*.'[1]

He then quotes Bodin out of Copernicus, Reinoldus, and
Stadius, to the effect that since Ptolemy's time the sun has
come much nearer to the earth. Another argument he sums
up in these words:

'As some haue inferred a diminution in the Heavenly
warmth from a supposed neerer approach of the Sunne to
the Earth, so haue others (at leastwise in regard of the Earth)
from the removall thereof more Southerly then in former
ages.'[2]

Both arguments, he answers, are grounded upon differences
among astronomers rather than upon any certain and infallible conclusions. And he wonders at our late learned Dr.
Case, 'who in his *Lapis Philosophicus lib. 8.* among other
weake arguments for the *worlds decay*, makes the *irregularitie*
of our late *Eclypses* to be one'.[3] It is important to notice the
emphasis given to the new astronomy in Hakewill's
Apologie, because this emphasis measures the new impetus
and argument which that astronomy imparted to an old
idea.

When Hakewill considers the decay of the elements, he
finds his sources in Antiquity. Lest he should seem to fight
with shadows, he 'unbowells' the state of the question,
declaring:

'It is then agreed on all hands, that all subcoelestiall bodies,
individualls, I meane, vnder the circle of the Moone, are
subject not onely to *alteration*, but to *diminution* and decay. . . .'[4]

[1] Ibid., p. 99. Bodin's *Methodus ad Facilem Historiarum Cognitionem* (cap. 8)
presents this and other arguments for the decay of the world.
[2] Ibid., p. 101.
[3] Ibid., p. 153. Case's *Lapis philosophicus seu commentarius in 8. lib. phys.
Aristot.*, Oxon., 1599, was a commentary on Aristotelian physics, and reached
another edition in 1612. [4] Ibid., p. 30.

But, he argues, there is in this alteration and diminution in the sublunar world always a keeping of due proportion between parts. He quotes the Pythagorean discourse in Ovid's *Metamorphoses* (15. 252–58) on the eternal flux of form in which 'all things in their sum total remain unchanged'.[1] As for the heavens, although they are not made of the elements, they are made of the same matter as the elements, but have a form which differs from 'the *formes* of all corruptible Bodies'.[2] The first matter, says Hakewill, 'cannot by the force of nature bee destroyed', but only by God;[3] in support of this idea he quotes Lucretius (2. 1002–7), beginning with the line,

nec sit interemit mors res ut materiai corpora conficiat,

which leads to the famous figure of the letters of the alphabet. Although Lucretius believed in the decay of the elements and the dissolution of the world, this passage develops a theory of the eternity and mutability of atomic matter similar to that of the elements in Ovid. On the 'foure Elements of the World' and their 'reciprocall vicissitude' Hakewill quotes Philo (*Liber de Mundi incorruptibilitate*) and finds similar doctrine in Plato's *Timaeus*, Aristotle's *De Mundo*, Ovid's *Metamorphoses* (15. 245–51), and Sylvester's Du Bartas, 'touching severall prints stamped vpon the same lump of waxe'.[4] In the passage from Du Bartas there are borrowings from the First Book of Lucretius,[5] upon whom Hakewill also has drawn for similar material on the vicissitude of things. In short, for Hakewill the Pythagorean philosophy of change confirms the theory of mutability and decay in the parts, but not in the whole of the sublunar

---

[1] Ibid., p. 47.

[2] Ibid., p. 73.

[3] Ibid., p. 45.

[4] Ibid., pp. 113 ff. This material is reproduced in the 'Argvment of the Front and of the Worke'.

[5] On the same passage see C. T. Harrison, 'The Ancient Atomists and English Literature of the Seventeenth Century', *Harvard Studies in Classical Philology* 45 (1934). 15–16. Du Bartas reacted vigorously against both the Epicureans and the Copernicans.

world; from the reign of mutability the heavens are still excepted.

For the idea of the decay of the world itself Hakewill blames chiefly St. Cyprian and Lucretius, not forgetting the apocryphal Esdras; except perhaps for Lucretius, these writers are common to the argument about the decay of the world. As Hakewill says, in arguments drawn from religious authority, 'the testimonie most of all stood vpon, is that of S. *Cyprian*'.[1] Hakewill censures Cyprian for ascribing plagues to 'the old age and naturall decay of the world', and asserts that Pammelius, his annotator, excuses him by saying 'that therein he alludes to the opinion of the ancient *Philosophers & Poets*'; Hakewill adds, 'perchance thereby intending *Lucretius* the great admirer and sectary of *Epicurus*, who of all the Poets I have met with hath written the most fully in this argument'.[2] Whereupon he quotes the splendid final passage from Book II of Lucretius on the outworn earth 'wasting away and going to the tomb'. Nor is this surprising, for of all the poets Lucretius had written not only the most fully but also with the greatest power on this argument; while he had taught the mutability and eternity of atomic matter, he had preached (5. 235–46) that decay in the parts, the elements, necessitates mortality in the whole.

What has deceived many into believing in the decay of the world, remarks Hakewill again, 'is that *idle tale* and *vaine fancie* forged by *Poets*, & taken vp by some *Historians*, & beleeued by the *vulgar* of the *foure ages of the world*'.[3] This 'idle tale' is then quoted from Ovid's *Metamorphoses*, followed by what Hakewill calls Boethius's borrowing, and later by Juvenal's Thirteenth Satire, all deploring the world's degeneration from the golden age; it is capped by Bodin's assertion that what 'they call the *Golden age* being compared with ours, may well seeme but *iron*'.[4] With the implicit

---

[1] Op. cit., p. 56.
[2] Ibid., p. 59.
[3] Ibid., p. 323.
[4] Ibid., p. 324. Cf. Harvey's reply to Spenser's 'bill of complaynte' over the decay of the world, *Letter-Book of Gabriel Harvey* (Camden Society, 1884), pp. 82–8; Harvey's reference (p. 86) to Bodin in refutation of Spenser is no doubt

moral of the golden age, we reach the end of the main body of argument which confronted anyone who sought to oppose the idea of the decay of the world; yet not even Hakewill countered with the explicit idea of progress, but only with circular change—at most, 'a kinde of circular progresse'. Bacon alone seems to have risen to the clear conception of progress as power acquired over nature, and round this idea grew up the 'climate of opinion' which eventually subdued the vapours of melancholy that rose from a decaying world.

In the course of his argument Hakewill often refers to the *De Constantia* of Justus Lipsius, which provided a neo-stoic formulation of the mutability and decay theme. Published in 1583, this work was translated into English in 1595 by John Stradling, who says that it came into his hands 'about ten yeares past, being a student in Oxford'.[1] The part of *De Constantia* with which Hakewill is most concerned is Chapter 16 of Book I, dealing with 'Instances of Necessary Mutation and Death throughout the whole World'. Here again we meet the argument that 'the Heavens and Elements change, and', Lipsius concludes, 'shall pass away'. Commenting on 'certain new kinds of Motion and Starrs' that have been discovered of late, he says:

'There arose a Starr in this very year, whose increment and decreases were thoroughly observ'd; and we then saw (what will scarcely be believ'd) that in Heaven it self, there may be something Born and Dye.'[2]

This, one of the great arguments for decay, we have seen

the same as Hakewill's—that is, '*Method. Hist. c. 7*'. Obviously the 'complaint' treated of matters which trouble Spenser in the prologue to Book V of the *Faerie Queene*, and which are answered in the *Two Cantos of Mutabilitie*; these matters had been discussed by Bodin in *Methodus ad Facilem Historiarum Cognitionem*, 1566, before the full impact of the new astronomy. Harvey's argument (p. 87) for 'appetite' and inconstant Nature anticipates the sceptical 'naturalism' and heresy of change which Jack Donne opposed to the orthodox constancy.

[1] *Two Bookes of Constancie*, London, 1595, sig. A2v. *De Constantia* was a popular work and received two other English translations in the seventeenth century, one by R. G. in 1654, and one by Nathaniel Wanley in 1670, from which I shall quote.

[2] *A Discourse of Constancy*, London, 1670, pp. 89–90.

Hakewill attempt to answer. For Lipsius, increase or de-
crease in the parts argues that the whole will totally perish,
and hence the conclusion of mutability in the elements is
decay in the world. Both by human analogy and by analogy
with the great bodies of nature, he concludes that cities and
countries have their youth, maturity, old age, and death.[1]
But the grand finale of his argument is this:

'That which we may more (though never sufficiently)
wonder at; this World which hath been inhabited this Five
thousand and Five hundred years, doth now grow old, and
that we may again applaud, the old exploded Fable of
Anaxarchus; there arise now elsewhere, and are born new
Men, and a new World. O the wonderful and incompre-
hensible Law of Necessity! All things turn about in this
Fatal Circle of beginning and ending: and there may be
something in this whole frame that is long liv'd; but nothing that is Eternal.'[2]

Hakewill, who also uses the figure of the circle, modified
Lipsius to his purpose by quoting him thus: 'This circle and
ring of things returning alwaies to their principles will never
cease as long as the world lasts';[3] and thereby got rid of the
'fatall Necessity' which, he declared, the Stoics stiffly maintained 'not only in the events of humane actions, but in the
actions themselues, as thereby they blunted the edge of all
vertuous endeavours, and made an excuse for vicious
courses'.[4] For Lipsius, Stoicism was the only answer to the
despair induced by this world view; for Hakewill no such
answer was possible; only the refutation of this view could
bring hope. Although each translation of *De Constantia*
offered itself as consolation to the distressed, the world view
which it represented seems to have been the chief source of
Jacobean melancholy.

Constancy, with the various changes rung upon it,
appears to have provided the usual answer to this view of
things. If change ruled the world, constancy ruled change,

[1] Ibid., p. 92.
[2] Ibid., pp. 94–5. The argument of Lipsius is Lucretian as well as Stoical.
[3] Op. cit., p. 41.   [4] Ibid., p. 320.

and there was no 'universall and perpetuall decay': thus Hakewill gave the common answer to an argument which was far more often concluded in the decay of the world. By 'common' I mean that it was the usual answer of the few who felt able to reply; most did not, and only Bacon replied with the idea of progress, although Hakewill caught something of his spirit. We are now in position to understand the 'metaphysical shudder' or melancholy which the idea of the decay of the world provoked in the literature of the early seventeenth century.

III

Dr. Johnson seems to have been the first to appreciate something of the force of this idea in the seventeenth century. Writing of Milton, he remarks:

'There prevailed in his time an opinion that the world was in its decay, and that we have had the misfortune to be produced in the decrepitude of Nature. It was suspected that the whole creation languished, that neither trees nor animals had the height or bulk of their predecessors, and that every thing was daily sinking by gradual diminution. Milton appears to suspect that souls partake of the general degeneracy, and is not without some fear that his book is to be written in *an age too late* for heroick poesy.'

To feel oneself born in 'an age too late' was the great emotional aftermath of the Renaissance. It is in this mood that Spenser made a genuine and profound communication with the Jacobean age, which in part rejected him. Although Dr. Johnson finds a suspicion of this feeling in Milton, it is well known that Milton wrote a Latin poem, 'Naturam non pati senium', in support of Hakewill's thesis at the Cambridge Commencement of 1628. But Spenser's yearning for the golden age was an expression of this feeling, and the notion of the decay of the world is the most significant idea that he shared with the seventeenth century. In holding to this belief, however, Spenser would not have felt himself guilty of a Lucretian heresy.

24

Mutability, Decay and Jacobean Melancholy

In the current dispute over Spenser's *Mutabilitie* cantos, two arguments have, in the light of our investigation, special weight. They are Professor Greenlaw's argument for a Lucretian influence and Professor Cumming's argument for an Ovidian source.[1] For Spenser's immediate source Professor Cumming has the stronger case, but in allowing for the complexities of the problem Professor Greenlaw has the advantage, since he has more regard for the confusion of philosophies in a mind like Spenser's. And yet not even he makes a sufficient allowance, if Hakewill may be a case in point. After quoting Philo on the reciprocal vicissitude of the four elements of the world, Hakewill remarks:

'Hitherto *Philo*, wherein after his vsuall wont he *Platonizes*, the same being in effect to bee found in *Platoes Timaeus*, as also in *Aristotles* booke *de Mundo*, if it be his, in *Damascene*, and *Gregory Nyssen*. And most elegantly the wittiest of Poets'.[2]

Whereupon he quotes Ovid's *Metamorphoses* (15. 241-51) on the mutation of the elements. From this instance it would appear that Spenser could have felt that he was still Platonizing rather than introducing discordant Lucretian factors when he argued the case of mutability. But Hakewill then adds a passage from Du Bartas developing the Pythagorean philosophy of change, which here involves the elements, their combination in a harmony like music, the Lucretian figure of the alphabet to explain the diverse objects of the world, and finally the Ovidian lump of wax with its mutation of shapes. Other arguments from Lucretius in this passage show how easily Du Bartas, Hakewill, or Spenser could mingle or confuse the Lucretian theory of mortality with the Pythagorean philosophy of change. In the perception of a Lucretian feeling for mortality in Spenser, Professor Greenlaw comes closer to the truth than Professor Cumming, for Ovid's Pythagorean discourse never arrives

[1] Cf. Edwin Greenlaw, 'Spenser and Lucretius', *Studies in Philology* 17 (1920). 439-64; and W. P. Cumming, 'The Influence of Ovid's *Metamorphoses* on Spenser's "Mutabilitie" Cantos', *Studies in Philology* 28 (1931). 241-56.

[2] Op. cit., p. 113.

at the idea of the decay of the world, and this is precisely where Spenser does arrive.

But both Professor Greenlaw and Professor Cumming miss the effect of the new astronomy in reinforcing this idea in Spenser, and the new astronomy is not to be discounted because its case was still incomplete when the Cantos were published. The decay of the world is set forth most explicitly by Spenser not in the *Mutabilitie* cantos themselves, but rather in the prologue to Book V of the *Faerie Queene*. Here Spenser develops the theory of decay by means of arguments which we have observed in Hakewill. He laments the degeneration of the world from the golden age, remarking (st. 4):

> *Ne wonder; for the heauens reuolution*
> *Is wandred farre from where it first was pight,*
> *And so doe make contrarie constitution*
> *Of all this lower world, toward his dissolution.*

The theory of the influence of the heavens upon the sublunar world, which has already been noticed in Burton and Hakewill, was not immediately rejected by the new astronomy. For Spenser mutability has ascended to the heavens, and not the least evidence for this is the declination of the sun—an argument that Hakewill felt obliged to meet and that Spenser accepts (st. 7):

> *For since the terme of fourteene hundred yeres,*
> *That learned* Ptolomaee *his hight did take,*
> *He is declyned from that marke of theirs,*
> *Nigh thirtie minutes to the Southerne lake;*
> *That makes me feare in time he will vs quite forsake.*

In this prologue, published in 1596, Spenser certainly subscribes to the idea of the decay of the world, and registers his disquiet with astronomical reasons.

In the *Mutabilitie* cantos themselves, published in 1609, 'the thesis of Mutabilitie', as Professor Cumming has remarked, 'is that all things in the universe are subject to the rule of Change'; and the argument is developed under the three main heads of 'the mutation of the four elements, the change of the seasons, and the inconstancy of the moon and the planets'.[1] With the cogency of these lines of argument for the decay of the world we are already familiar. And even of 'the Earth (great mother of vs all)' the Titanesse argues that although she alone seems not to be in thrall to *Mutabilitie* (7. 17),

> *Yet is she chang'd in part, and eeke in generall.*

This statement reminds us that Hakewill had to meet the Lucretian argument that change in the parts implied decay in the whole. But the climax of Mutabilitie's argument comes in the stanza which she addresses directly to Jove, wherein she celebrates mutability's invasion of that last stronghold of constancy, the heavens (7. 54):

> *Then are ye mortall borne, and thrall to me,*
> *Vnlesse the kingdome of the sky yee make*
> *Immortall, and vnchangeable to bee;*
> *Besides, that power and vertue which ye spake,*
> *That ye here worke, doth many changes take,*
> *And your owne natures change: for, each of you*
> *That vertue haue, or this, or that to make,*
> *Is checkt and changed from his nature trew,*
> *By others opposition or obliquid view.*

The force of this argument of mortality and change in the heavens came from the new astronomy, and carried with it strong implications in the general notion of the decay of the world. However, 'the legend of Constancie' is justified by Nature's reply to Mutabilitie, in which she declares constancy the final victor over mutability (7. 58); thus Spenser anticipates the answer which Hakewill gave. But the two stanzas of Canto VIII show that Spenser was still troubled by Mutabilitie, for 'though she all vnworthy were of the Heav'ns Rule', yet the truth is,

[1] W. P. Cumming, op. cit., p. 254. See John Norden's *Vicissitudo Rerum* for a similar thesis and argument, and Gabriel Harvey's *Marginalia* (p. 161) for Spenser's admiration of Du Bartas's astronomical book.

In all things else she beares the greatest sway.

His final recourse is, in the mood of prayer, to fall back 'vpon the pillours of Eternity' and the rest of God.

It must not be forgotten, however, that at the beginning of the *Mutabilitie* cantos Spenser asserts that mutability first upset the order and broke the laws of Nature, bringing death into the world (st. 6),

> *Since which, all liuing wights haue learn'd to die,*
> *And all this world is woxen daily worse.*
> *O pittious worke of* Mvtabilitie!
> *By which, we all are subject to that curse,*
> *And death in stead of life haue sucked from our Nurse.*

And this is the chief root of seventeenth-century melancholy, for mutability, augmented by the Renaissance, plunged to new depths of melancholy in the idea of the decay of the world. To redeem the time and to sharpen the edge of virtuous endeavour, there was need of a Hakewill and of a *Paradise Lost*. Neither should it be forgotten that it was quite orthodox for Spenser, caught between the love of this world and the desire for an abiding state, to conclude that God was the only refuge from the sway of mutability. To call his belief in the decay of the world 'medieval' is to neglect one aspect of the Renaissance in a religious mind.

The fictions of the golden age, remarked Hakewill, were fashioned by the poets and taken up by the historians. Of the historians it is Spenser's friend, Sir Walter Ralegh, who disturbs Hakewill most, for he marvels that a man of such piercing wit and clear judgment 'in many places positiuely defends *Nature's universall decay*'.[1] The only explanation, concludes Hakewill, is 'that as others he tooke it vp vpon trust'. Certainly the theory of the decay of the world intensifies the melancholy eloquence of Ralegh's *History of the World*. Published two years before Goodman's *Fall of Man*, it employs the same arguments to prove the corruption of nature in 'this decrepit age of the world'. For instance,

[1] Op. cit., p. 49.

when Ralegh seeks to explain the long lives of the patriarchs, he argues, like Goodman, that they were nearer to 'the first and purest seed'; in other words, his assumption is the same as Goodman's, that the farther generation gets from the first mould the more degenerate the creature becomes.[1] His second argument is that 'the earth itself was then much less corrupt'; and this argument could be found, as Hakewill knew, in the close of the Second Book of Lucretius. Then Ralegh launches into a sentence that is full of the sombre eloquence and reason which the decay theme provoked in a Jacobean mind:

'And as all things under the sun have one time of strength and another of weakness, a youth and beauty, and then age and deformity; so time itself (under the dreadful shade of whose wings all things decay and wither) hath wasted and worn out that lively virtue of nature in man, and beasts, and plants, yea the heavens themselves, being of a most pure and cleansed matter, shall *wax old as a garment*; and then much more the power generative in inferior creatures, who by the ordinance of God receive operative virtue from the superior.'[2]

Not only did men in the younger age of the world have longer lives, but they were greater in wisdom and achievement: 'Likely it is that their works excelled all whatsoever can be told of after-times, especially in respect of this old age of the world, when we no sooner begin to know, but we begin to die.'[3] Then, before corruption had set in, men were stronger and more beautiful than now. Since 'both nature and the heavens wax old', it is inevitable that degeneration should appear in 'the bulks and bodies of men which are now born in the withered quarter and winter of the world'.[4] In the golden age 'the law of nature was the rule of man's

[1] Cf. Ralegh's *Works*, Oxford, 1829, 2. 149. This argument depends on the theory that souls are transmitted by the parents rather than infused by God at each birth; the orthodox theory was that of infusion by God, but Milton and Browne both held to the other theory.

[2] Ibid., 2. 149–50.

[3] Ibid., 2. 157–8.

[4] Ibid., 2. 162.

life';[1] the ancient simplicity and temperance had not then been corrupted by luxury and sin. Although the fall of the angels first brought degeneration into the world, man's 'defection and falling away from God' brought on the corruption of the golden age;[2] and so the fall of man was associated, for Ralegh and Goodman, with the decay of the world. Consequently Ralegh's great peroration on *hic jacet*, 'O eloquent, just, and mighty Death!' becomes a kind of organ close to the idea of the decay of the world—the coda to his earlier digressions on mortality; like the greatest eloquence of its time, it is played upon a keyboard and with stops which can be fully understood only in the light of our study.

Perhaps no writer in the early seventeenth century reminds us of the changing astronomical views more often than Donne. Copernicus, Tycho Brahe, Galileo, and Kepler, or the 'new philosophy', are never very far from his thoughts when he turns from the microcosm to the macrocosm. It was the fascinating equivalence of the microcosm and the macrocosm which gave Donne many of his characteristically 'metaphysical' figures as well as the occasion for his metaphysical shudder at decay.[3] With Donne we find that the poet was again before the historian in marking the decay of the world from a golden age, for the *First Anniversary* develops the same idea of the decay of the world that we find in the *History of the World*—from the fall of the angels to signs of degeneration in the heavens. In *Biathanatos*, while scoring obstinacy in opinion for which there is no longer any reason, he declares St. Augustine's disciples as stubborn as those of Aristotle, 'who defending the Heavens to be inalterable, because in so many ages nothing had been observed to have altered, his Schollers stubbornly maintain his Proposition still, though by many experiences of new

[1] Ibid., 2. 347.

[2] Ibid., 2. 163 ff.

[3] For a view of Donne to which this article offers objection, see Merritt Y. Hughes's 'Kidnapping Donne', *Essays in Criticism: Second Series*, Univ. of Calif. Press, 1934, p. 61–89.

Stars, the reason which moved *Aristotle* seems now to be utterly defeated.'[1]

He annotates this passage by a reference to '*Kepplerus de Stella Serpent*', and thus specifies the 'experiences of new stars' which had recently been altering the unchangeable heavens of received opinion.

In a sermon preached at St. Paul's on Whit Sunday, 1625, Donne describes the decay of the world which fastened itself upon the seventeenth-century imagination:

'As the world is the whole frame of the world, God hath put into it a reproofe, a rebuke, lest it should seem eternall, which is, a sensible decay and age in the whole frame of the world, and every piece thereof. The seasons of the yeare irregular and distempered; the Sun fainter, and languishing; men lesse in stature, and shorter-lived. No addition, but only every yeare, new sorts, new species of wormes, and flies, and sicknesses, which argue more and more putrefaction of which they are engendred.'[2]

Referring to St. Cyprian, Donne reminds us that the early seventeenth century also attributed plagues to the decay of the world; and quoting Cyprian, he draws the melancholy conclusion that 'we do not die old, and yet we are borne old' because there is 'a sensible decay and mortality of the whole world'. The implications of this passage carry us back to the various sorts of evidence for the decay of the world which we have examined. In his funeral sermon on faith and imperfect knowledge, preached for Sir William Cokayne, 12th December 1626, he reverts to the mutability theme in connection with the 'new philosophy':

'I need not call in new Philosophy, that denies a settlednesse, an acquiescence in the very body of the Earth, but makes the Earth to move in that place, where we thought the Sunne had moved; I need not that helpe, that the Earth it selfe is in Motion, to prove this, That nothing upon Earth

---

[1] Facsimile Text Society's replica, New York, 1930, p. 146. Other uses of the new astronomy and decay appear in his *Verse Letters*, *A Funerall Elegie*, and *Ignatius his Conclave*.

[2] *Complete Poetry and Selected Prose*, ed. J. Hayward, London, 1930, p. 619.

is permanent; The Assertion will stand of it selfe, till some man assigne me some instance, something that a man may relie upon, and find permanent. . . . In the Elements them-selves, of which all sub-elementary things are composed, there is no acquiescence, but a vicissitudinary transmutation into one another; Ayre condensed becomes water, a more solid body, And Ayre rarified becomes fire, a body more disputable, and in-apparent. It is so in the Conditions of men too. . . .'[1]

And Donne, who celebrated a philosophy of change in his early poetry, when he opposed a libertine inconstancy to the orthodox constancy, found that Pythagorean change invades the most sacred precincts of love, as the *Second Anniversary* reveals:

> *Poore cousened cousenor, that she, and that thou,*
> *Which did begin to love, are neither now;*
> *You are both fluid, chang'd since yesterday;*
> *Next day repaires, (but ill) last dayes decay.*
> *Nor are, (although the river keepe the name)*
> *Yesterdaies waters, and to daies the same.*
> *So flowes her face, and thine eyes, neither now*
> *That Saint, nor Pilgrime, which your loving vow*
> *Concern'd, remaines; but whil'st you thinke you bee*
> *Constant, you are hourely in inconstancie.*[2]

Feeling now the melancholy of mutability, as Spenser had before him, Donne discovered, at least before ordination, that 'our best firmament and arrest' is faith in God's word.[3] In his *Devotions* he makes decay the very centre of the universe:

[1] Ibid., pp. 674–75. This sermon contains strong reminders of Montaigne's *Apologie of Raymond Sebond*, in which Montaigne also 'Pyrrhonizes' over Copernicus while he defines the scepticism of the age: 'So when any new doc-trine is represented unto us, we have great cause to suspect it, and to consider, how, before it was invented, the contrary unto it was in credit; and as that hath beene reversed by this latter, a third invention may paradventure succeed in after-ages, which in like sort shall front the second' (Everyman ed. 2. 285 ff.).

[2] Ibid., p. 225. Pythagorean change also supplies the framework for his satiric *Progresse of the Soule*.

[3] *Essayes in Divinity*, London, 1651, p. 20.

Mutability, Decay and Jacobean Melancholy

'This is *Natures nest of Boxes*; The Heavens containe the *Earth*, the *Earth*, *Cities*, *Cities*, *Men*. And all these are *Concentrique*; the common *center* to them all, is *decay*, *ruine*';[1] 'only that is *Eccentrique*, which was never made'; only that light in which the Saints shall dwell and be apparalled, 'only that bends not to this *Center*, to *Ruine*'.

But it is in *An Anatomie of the World* ('The First Anniversary') that Donne employs the decay of the world with the most startling effect, as the 'fundamental brainwork' of a poem. Here the world nears the end of its degeneration, which began with the fall of the angels; here we find the common arguments for decay: shortness of life, smallness of stature, corruption in physical nature, the moral world, and even the heavens.

> *And new Philosophy calls all in doubt,*
> *The Element of fire is quite put out;*
> *The Sun is lost, and th'earth, and no mans wit*
> *Can well direct him where to looke for it.*
> *And freely men confesse that this world's spent,*
> *When in the Planets, and the Firmament*
> *They seeke so many new; then see that this*
> *Is crumbled out againe to his Atomies.*[2]

With this final Lucretian touch, Donne goes on to draw the deformed heavens which have been revealed by the 'new philosophy', touching on the inability of the sun to perfect a circle and concluding that,

> *seeming weary with his reeling thus,*
> *He meanes to sleepe, being now falne nearer us.*[3]

This theory, one of the chief arguments for the decay of the world, we have already met in Burton and Hakewill.

---

[1] *Complete Poetry and Selected Prose*, ed. Hayward, p. 523. And now his first words are, 'Variable, and therfore miserable condition of Man' (ibid., p. 507).

[2] Ibid., p. 232; cf. Grierson ed. 2. 189–90, on the element of fire. Donne, like most Englishmen after Digges, associates the plurality of worlds with the Copernican theory; Montaigne, in his *Apologie of Raymond Sebond*, associates the idea with Democritus, Epicurus, and Lucretius (ed. cit. 2. 230 ff.).

[3] Ibid., pp. 203–4.

C

Mutability, Decay and Jacobean Melancholy

Formerly 'spring-times were common cradles, but are tombes' now; and out of decay in the earth new worms are engendered,[1] as new creatures arose in strange disguise in Spenser's *Mutabilitie* (7. 18). For a world in decay, Elizabeth Drury—'the Idea of a Woman'—could have done much more than she did,

> But that our age was Iron, and rustie too.

And so the poetic fiction of the four ages is used to round off the decay of the world as a hyperbolic elegy for a young lady, who provided the occasion but not the theme of the *First Anniversary*. In these examples we have observed enough to understand the emotional depths to which the idea of the decay of the world penetrated Donne's imagination, its religious significance in relation to the fall of man, and its power to deepen mutability into the great *memento mori* of the seventeenth-century sermon.

Between *An Anatomie of the World* and *Urn Burial*, we ought to comment on several rather interesting works which are definitely oriented by the ideas of mutability and decay. The first is a book of verse called *Visiones Rerum*, written by John Hagthorpe and published in 1623. 'Fearing a wrong starre', Hagthorpe dedicates his work to Charles, Prince of Wales, and describes himself as 'ignorant of all planetarie revolutions and eccentricities: and in this Age of doubtfulnesse, where the most certaine things are most subject to question, seeing least reason (with *Copernicus*) to beleeve, that which strives most to enforce the sense'.[2] Of the four poems in this book the first, which is expressly upon our subject, carries the title: 'Principium & Mutabilitas Rerum, or *The beginning and Mutabilitie of all things*'. Hagthorpe explains that 'the first shewes, how *Folly* first entertaines us at our entrance into the house of *Time*, deluding us with a more certaine assurance of things most incertaine untill *Reason* approaching, brings us truer releation, shewing the Mutabilitie, uncertainti and change of all things'.[3] While his

[1] Ibid., p. 207; cf. p. 619.
[2] *Visiones Rerum*, London, 1623, sig. A2ᵛ.   [3] Ibid., sig. A3ʳ.

34

book has a strong tinge of the medieval, Hagthorpe serves to remind us of the connection between mutability and sceptical thought at this time.

William Drummond's *Cypresse Grove* (1623), which borrows so much from Donne,[1] is another work that emerges from the melancholy born of mutability and decay. This famous and characteristic work of the seventeenth-century sensibility again connects the mortality theme with the 'new philosophy' found in Donne:

'The Element of Fire is quite put out, the Aire is but Water rarified, the Earth is found to moue, and is no more the Center of the Vniuerse, is turned into a Magnes; Starres are not fixed, but swimme in the etheriall Spaces, Cometes are mounted aboue the Planetes; Some affirme there is another World of men and sensitiue Creatures, with Cities and Palaces in the Moone; the Sunne is lost, for, it is but a Light made of the conjunction of manie shining Bodies together, a Clift in the lower Heauens, through which the Rayes of the highest defuse themselues, is obserued to haue Spots; Thus, Sciences by the diuerse Motiones of this Globe of the Braine of Man, are become Opiniones, nay, Errores, and leaue the Imagination in a thousand Labyrinthes. What is all wee knowe compared with what wee knowe not?'[2]

This is the disorder in nature which argued the decay of the world in Donne's *First Anniversary* and which added a modern character to the mutability theme of the Middle Ages. It was this that gave a sceptical turn to the seventeenth-century mind and left its 'imagination in a thousand labyrinths'. It is unnecessary to point out how much of the new astronomy is represented in this passage, but it should be observed that the thought is common to Donne's *Anniversaries* and to Montaigne's *Apologie of Raymond Sebond*.

Even literary criticism in this time felt the weight of the

[1] Cf. G. S. Greene, 'Drummond's Borrowing from Donne', *Philological Quarterly* 11 (1932). 26–38.
[2] *Poetical Works*, ed. L. E. Kastner, Manchester, 1913, 2. 78.

decay of the world. Henry Reynolds, accounting for the decay of poetry, finds it necessary to begin his *Mythomystes* (1633), with this declaration:

'I haue thought vpon the times wee liue in, and am forced to affirme the world is decrepit, and, out of its age & doating estate, subiect to all the imperfections that are inseparable from that wracke and maime of Nature, that the young behold with horror, and the sufferers thereof lye vnder with murmur and languishment. Euen the generall Soule of this great Creature, whereof euery one of ours is a seuerall peece, seemes bedrid, as vpon her deathbed and neere the time of her dissolution to a second better estate and being; the yeares of her strength are past, and she is now nothing but disease, for the Soules health is no other then meerely the knowledge of the Truth of things.'[1]

Where Jonson laid the decay to men and studies, Reynolds lays it to nature. And Reynolds felt that even his friend Drayton suffered from the effects of 'this declining state of the world'. It is safe to say that there were few departments of life over which the theory of the decay of the world did not cast its shadow at this time, and few themes sank so deep into the sensibility of the age as the theme of mutability and decay.

In 1649 Thomas Forde made a sketch of the mutability theme in his time. Writing in Civil War days, Forde felt that his subject was justified by the event, and so his book is entitled: '*Lusus Fortunae:* The Play of Fortune: Continually Acted by the Severall Creatures on the Stage of the World. Or, A glance at the various mutability, inconstancie, and uncertainty of all earthly things. *From a consideration of the present Times.*' There is nothing novel in the title, but in the book itself names like Hakewill and Copernicus indicate a particular orientation of an old theme, while a reference to Spenser's *Two Cantos of Mutabilitie* suggests its seventeenth-century character. In the English writers most frequently quoted by Forde we may trace the course of the theme of mutability and decay; among these writers we find Donne,

[1] *Critical Essays of the 17th Century*, ed. J. E. Spingarn, Oxford, 1908, I. 144.

Mutability, Decay and Jacobean Melancholy

Hakewill, Browne, and Cowley. In the last name we encounter a rather different connection for the mutability theme, joining the heresy of inconstancy in the early Donne rather than penetrating the depths of feeling associated with decay.

While Forde spends much of his time upon the mere play of fortune or chance, bidding us remember (out of *Religio Medici*) 'that it is the providence of God which our blindnesse hath nick-nam'd Fortune',[1] yet he does not fail to note the relevance of Pythagorean change, for he sets the theme by quoting Ovid:

> *So change our bodies without rest or stay,*
> *What we were yesterday, or what today,*
> *Shall be to morrow.*[2]

He extends the theme by again quoting the *Religio Medici*:

'The *lives*, not only of *men*, but of *Commonwealths*, and the whole World (says that incomparable Physician) run not upon an *Helix*, that still enlargeth, but on a circle, where arriving to their Meridian, they *decline* in obscurity, and fall under the *Horizon* again.'[3]

This offers Forde a moral which applies to the decline of his own country. In support of the rise and fall of nations, he refers to Hakewill's *Apologie* on the passage of learning from East to West, and on 'a Vicissitude of virtues and vices'.[4] Like Burton, he concludes:

'All creatures in the world may be said to be *Lunaticks*, for their mutability, as if they would out-vie the *Moon*. I might run over the several *Planets*, and their courses, but I forbear, lest I should *toto caelo errare*: It shall suffice, that we can finde no place free from the rule of this *Titanesse* (Spencers Fayry Queen. Canto *last*), as she pleads her power in our English Virgin.'[5]

Like Donne, though in allusion to Cowley, he declares, 'And that is the absolute condition of the world, whose

---

[1] *Lusus Fortunae* (Printed for R. L., 1649), p. 40.
[2] Ibid., p. 24.   [4] Ibid., pp. 77 and 79.
[3] Ibid., p. 74.   [5] Ibid., p. 82.

37

constancy is altogether *inconstancy*'. To Forde the theme of mutability, it would appear, runs back to Spenser for its seventeenth-century English root. And he believes the heavens to be 'the only *Seat and Center of rest*', for he says: 'I will not here maintain, that disputable opinion of *Copernicus*; but only make thus much use of it, That it is in *Heaven* only where we must respect a *rest*; for here on *earth* is no place to fixe our eyes, or mindes upon.'[1] Like many others who wrote on the mortality theme, Forde reminds us of the famous Sixteenth Chapter in Book I of Lipsius's *De Constantia*, which he quotes: 'Kingdoms & Commonwealths must needs be subject to the like mutability, and corruption, as the *men* are of whom they are *compounded*.'[2] Although Forde fears that he will be counted a pedant for quoting so many authors, his pains in this respect help us to discover who were significant to one writing on mutability at this time.

Before *Urn Burial*, that great funeral sermon on the decay of the world, Sir Thomas Browne wrote several passages in his *Religio Medici* relative to mutability and decay. Besides the passage already quoted by Forde, he gives, for instance, this open statement of his view:

'I believe the World grows near its end, yet is neither old nor decayed, nor shall ever perish upon the ruines of its own Principles. As the work of Creation was above Nature, so is its adversary, annihilation; without which the World hath not its end, but its mutation.'[3]

Browne agrees with Hakewill that the world will be destroyed by fire at the hand of God; but although he denies its decay, he believes that it approaches its end. 'That general opinion that the World grows near its end,' he admits, 'hath possessed all ages past as nearly as ours';[4] and yet he feels this general opinion too strongly to indulge in any optimism about the future. He is no Bacon, nor is he ready with Hake-

[1] Ibid., p. 104.
[2] Ibid., p. 73.
[3] *The Religio Medici and Other Writings* (Everyman ed.), p. 50.
[4] Ibid., p. 52.

will to enjoy the prospect of the world's mutation. And neither is he as yet sufficiently 'dampt with the necessity of oblivion' to break into the sonorous melancholy of *Urn Burial*.

In 1658, when it was almost too late for the melancholy born of the decay of the world, Browne published the supreme expression of the mortality theme in which seventeenth-century melancholy culminated. Men who acted 'before the probable Meridian of time' had some reason for ambition, mused Browne, but 'in this latter Scene of time' we cannot expect to outlast our monuments.

' 'Tis too late to be ambitious. The great mutations of the world are acted, or time may be too short for our designes. To extend our memories by Monuments, whose death we daily pray for, and whose duration we cannot hope, without injury to our expectations, in the advent of the last day, were a contradiction in our beliefs. We whose generations are ordained in this setting part of time, are providentially taken off from such imaginations; And being necessitated to eye the remaining particle of futurity, are naturally constituted unto thoughts of the next world, and cannot excusably decline the consideration of that duration, which maketh Pyramids pillars of snow, and all that's past a moment.'[1]

No doubt Browne felt at times, with Hakewill, that the better part of religion prohibited belief in the decay of the world, but this did not prevent his pen from writing 'mutation' and 'corruption', or his mind from thinking that he lived in the 'setting part of time'. And yet he seems to have stuck to the conclusion of the Pythagorean philosophy of change, that things are 'durable in their main bodies, alterable in their parts':

'In vain do individuals hope for Immortality, or any

---

[1] Ibid., pp. 133–4. In 1657 an English translation of John Johnston's *Naturae Constantia* (1632) had appeared under the title, '*An History of the Constancy of Nature. Wherein by comparing the latter age with the former, it is maintained that the World doth not decay universally, in respect of it Self, or the Heavens, Elements, Mixt Bodies, Meteors, Minerals, Plants, Animals, nor Man in his Age, Stature, Strength, or Faculties of his Minde, as relating to all Arts and Science.*'

patent from oblivion, in preservations below the Moon:
Men have been deceived even in their flatteries above the
Sun, and studied conceits to perpetuate their names in
heaven. The various Cosmography of that part hath already
varied the names of contrived constellations; *Nimrod* is lost
in *Orion*, and *Osyris* in the Doggestarre. While we look for
incorruption in the heavens, we finde they are but like the
Earth; Durable in their main bodies, alterable in their parts:
whereof beside Comets and new Stars, perspectives begin to
tell tales. And the spots that wander about the Sun, with
Phaetons favour, would make clear conviction.'[1]
But here Browne recognizes that corruption has entered
the heavens, that the new astronomy has destroyed the received distinction between the heavens and the earth or the
'Globe of Mortalitie'. And this brings us back to the point
from which we began and to which we have so often
returned—the significance of the 'new philosophy' or
astronomy in relation to mutability and the decay of the
world. For Browne, as for so many religious thinkers, 'the
Metaphysicks of true belief' found its stay in a future life,
another world; but the disturbing metaphysics of the new
astronomy disclosed 'the Globe of Elements' extending its
'peculiar Empire of death' into the hitherto incorruptible
heavens.

<h1 style="text-align:center">IV</h1>

If mutability was sometimes answered by the theory of
constancy in mutation, or circular change, it was more often
concluded in the idea of the decay of the world. Even if,
like Browne, one admitted mutability but denied decay, one
did not therefore escape the melancholy of living in the
afternoon of time; if the end of the world depended not
upon decay, but upon God, still it was not remote. In
theory Browne could partly agree with Hakewill, and yet
fail to share his mood; Spenser could anticipate Hakewill's
answer, and yet not escape the melancholy to which he
replied. Men's emotions and imagination were still involved

[1] Ibid., pp. 136–7.

in a Ptolemaic universe, in which the new astronomy had destroyed the distinction between the Globe of Mortality and the immutable Heavens, thereby accelerating the decay of the world. Even for a Hakewill the new astronomy was more of a denial than a challenge; not even a Bacon associated his idea of progress with the new cosmic scheme; while an ardent Copernican like Digges still left the earth hanging in the globe of mortality, with the 'orbe of starres fixed infinitely vp'. If the new astronomy lent an impetus to the relativity of thought, it brought the final proof of the mutability of things; if it left the mind without 'ends', it seemed to bring the world to an end. The old order was cracking up; it was the decay of Nature, not the beginning of a new order, so far as the imagination and emotions of men were concerned. As Drummond remarked, the chaos which brought scepticism to their reason left their 'imagination in a thousand labyrinths', and their emotions, like Hamlet's, to feed on mortality. Mutability and decay compelled the deepest tremor in their emotions, the greatest flights of their imagination; the prospect of infinite worlds affected them less than the decay of their world. If they did not quite feel, with Pascal, the terror of the infinite, they did feel a metaphysical shudder at decay passing from the microcosm to the macrocosm. In this concept we may recognize not only the chief source of seventeenth-century melancholy, but also the sounding-board for the finest eloquence of the time.

II

The Libertine Donne

✱

The tender and paradoxical regard which Donne felt, even after ordination, for his greatest paradox, *Biathanatos*, has not been enough to save it from such grudging encomiums as 'a literary curiosity' or 'an exercise in casuistry'. As 'a Book written by Jack Donne', he had sent it to Sir Robert Ker, with the hint that its few particular readers had responded 'that certainly, there was a false thread in it, but not easily found'; and he had enjoined Ker to 'publish it not, but yet burn it not'. Another manuscript copy had gone into the library of Lord Herbert of Cherbury, 'where Authors of all complexions were preserved', with the comment, 'If any of them grudge this book a room, and suspect it of new or dangerous doctrine, you who know us all, can best moderate.'[1]

Finally, *Biathanatos* was published by his son in 1646, nearly forty years after its composition; because, says the younger Donne in his dedication, it was threatened by two dangers: 'a danger of being utterly lost, and a danger of being utterly found', and fathered by the atheists. If it escaped the first danger by its publication, it did not altogether escape the second. But, however he may have tried to guard its secret, certainly Donne hoped that his book might not be utterly lost.

---

[1] Did Donne know that Lipsius's defence of suicide *Thraseas*, even though destroyed in MS., had attained a dangerous notoriety?

42

The Libertine Donne

The knowledge that *Biathanatos* did not evade the danger of being utterly found is provided by the publication of John Adams's *Essay concerning Self-Murther* in 1700.[1] The heading of the fifth chapter of this book tells us, '*Who they are chiefly that maintain this Act to be Lawful: The Stoicks, the Author of Biathanatos.*' On his title-page, however, Adams had already given pre-eminence to *Biathanatos*, which, he now tells us, 'by the great Character of the Author, rais'd afterwards upon *better* Grounds, by the Agreeableness of the Argument to the present Age, and by its having passed some Years unanswer'd (as far as I can understand) has been highly esteem'd by *some·People*'.[2] As Adams makes abundantly clear in the course of his *Essay, some People* were the Libertines. In short, the general tenor of Adams's book indicates that *Biathanatos* became a libertine document in the latter half of the seventeenth century.

For *Biathanatos* Donne certainly did everything to provoke the curiosity of posterity, and in this paradox, to my mind, he made his most complete philosophical statement. Adams's *Essay* affords us the opportunity to examine the associations which *Biathanatos* made in a mind at the end of the century, and, if we may accept Adams, the associations which it made in other minds as well. Adams centres his attack upon self-murder round the interpretation of the 'Universal Law of Nature' descended from the Stoics, or the 'eternal and immutable Law of Nature' as opposed to 'natural' liberty. In attacking Donne on this ground, Adams

---

[1] Various books against suicide appeared both before and after Adams. One might list George Strode, *The Anatomie of Mortalitie*, 1618 and 1632; (Sir William Denny), *Pelecanicidium: or the Christian Adviser against Self-Murder*, 1653; Charles Moore, *A Full Inquiry into the Subject of Suicide*, 1790. Strode treats suicide in one chapter and probably did not know Donne; Denny seems to have been inspired by Donne's paradox; Moore, like Adams, is largely occupied with Donne and his interpretation of the Law of Nature; in short, he declares that 'to combat Donne therefore is in fact to answer almost all the material arguments that have been used by modern defenders of suicide' (Vol. II, p. 6). Keynes's *Bibliography of Dr. John Donne* (Cambridge, 1932) notes on p. 70 that 'another treatise was written, but never saw the light'; and quotes *Hearne's Collections*, under the date 14th November 1705, about a certain Mr. Kannell's 'short Discourse against *Self-Murther* in opposition to Dr. *Donne*'.

[2] *An Essay concerning Self-Murther*, London, 1700, p. 41.

has to meet not the bold and frank rebel of the love poetry,[1] but a subtle fencer who mixes conviction with charity, dissimulation, and the sharpest reason.

We may well ask why self-murder could be regarded as in particular repute at this time. To answer this is to consider some aspects of contemporary libertine thought. While Adams believes that the most 'Universal Law of Nature' is self-preservation, 'as is confest by the Stoicks especially', he declares that it must be subservient to and consistent with the end of life, which is 'the following Reason by Virtue'.[2] And although he seizes upon an inconsistency between suicide and self-preservation in Stoic doctrine, he is in the main really in agreement with Stoic ethics. But Hobbes had introduced a libertine interpretation of this universal Law of Nature, against which Adams complains:

'Indeed that unbounded Authority which Mr. Hobbs (Leviath. Part I. Chap. 14) gives to what he calls Right of Nature, under which Self-preservation is included, opens a very wide door to the worst consequences of Knavery or Cowardice; *For*, he says, *that this is the Liberty each Man hath to use his own Power as he will himself for the preservation of his own Nature; that is to say, of his own Life; and consequently of doing any thing, which in his own Judgment and Reason he shall conceive to be the aptest means thereunto.* This Latitude of Right of Nature in order to Self-preservation seems to be the ground of most of his Errours concerning Civil Society, and may well be the occasion of the basest Actions.'

This is Hobbes's definition of *Jus Naturale*; and this, says Adams, leads either to a miserly overvaluing or to a prodigal undervaluing of life itself; not to its true value in proper use, but rather to 'that *Contempt of Life*, which is so very much affected by some People'. It is those who despise reason and 'depend only upon the gross Enjoyment of the present Moment' that find life worthless when they meet with dis-

---

[1] For an admirable discussion of Donne's love poetry in relation to the libertine blend of scepticism and naturalism exemplified by Montaigne, see L. I. Bredvold, 'The Naturalism of Donne', *Jour. of Eng. and Ger. Phil.*, XXII (1923), 471–502.

[2] Op. cit., pp. 30–2.

appointment.[1] In this connection he attacks 'the Unreason-
ableness of several Passages which are frequently to be met
withal in the Writings of *the Stoicks and Epicureans*, and which
have been received with much applause by some People; who
are pleas'd to see Life represented as a *dull Business*, not
worth a Man's *Care*'.[2] In a later chapter Adams explains that
Epicurus advanced 'a new Principle of Morality, and indeed
a very strange one, as commonly understood; which was
Pleasure: And conformably to this he new dress'd up the
Systeme of *Democritus*, and us'd the Gods *worse* by his
manner of *owning them*, than *Anaxagoras* had done by *dis-
carding them entirely*: In all Ages the *Natural Systeme* has been
fitted to the *Moral one*, and where-ever you find *Libertinism*
encourag'd, under the popular pretence of asserting the
right of *humane Reason*, there you will meet with a *world
ready made to the purpose*, and *God*, and *Providence excluded*,
for fear of being injurious to the *Liberty* and *Property of
humane Nature*.'[3]

But in his earlier reference to the Epicureans, Adams concludes by quoting against contemporary Libertines 'a Person, who is very much esteem'd by the Gentlemen who are
chiefly concern'd in this matter'—Montaigne. Perhaps
enough has been said to show the confluence of Epicurus,
Hobbes, and Montaigne in Restoration libertinism, which,
Adams felt, produced a contempt of life.

Long before Adams 'Libertine' had become a word and
thing thoroughly familiar to English thought. In Thomas
Blount's *Glossographia*, first published in 1656, we find it
defined as follows: '*Libertine* (*libertinus*) a free-man, one first-
born or made free. Also one of loose life, or careless of

---

[1] Ibid., pp. 34–6. Adams also inveighs against injudicious poets who support a
false notion of magnanimity by portraying 'a Hero strutting and ranting against
Life'. All of this makes an interesting comment on the Heroic play.

[2] Ibid., p. 160. How this discovers the tone of Temple's great sentence!
'When all is done, Human Life is, at the greatest and the best, but like a froward
Child, that must be Play'd with and Humor'd a little to keep it quiet till it falls
asleep, and then the Care is over.'

[3] Ibid., p. 160. Cudworth, of course, had connected Hobbes and the Epicurean
system in 1678; and in 1670 Eachard had called this period 'the Reign of
Atoms'. Lucretius was much read.

Religion.' And *Libertinism* is defined as 'Libertinage, or
Libertinity (*libertinitas*) the state of him that of Bond is made
free; Licentiousness, Epicurism. In Divinity it is thus defined.
Libertinism is nothing else but a false liberty of belief and
manners, which will have no other dependence but on particular fancy and passion. It is a strange monster, whereof it
seems *Job* made description under the figure of *Behemoth*; as
much as to say, as a creature composed of all sorts of beasts,
of which it bears the name.' The last definition was used by
Edward Reynell in his *Advice against Libertinism* in 1659.[1]
And as a thing *libertinism* had penetrated the English mind
through numerous issues of Montaigne and of his disciple,
Charron, who was still more popular and perhaps more in-
sidious because of his religious tinge.[2] Nor can we forget the
great influence of Donne's libertine love poetry, which
could persuade by its matter after its style had been condemned.[3] By the time of Adams one does not have even to
use the word to be understood perfectly. To quote Cicero
on the Eternal Law which is Reason itself, rising from the
very Nature of Things and prompting us to Good, in
refutation of the asserters of 'Natural Liberty', is to be
understood as replying to the Libertines.[4] It is into these
associations that the author of *Biathanatos* enters as the main
concern of Adams.

II

Before Adams comes to his chief argument against Donne,
he finds no lack of occasion for effective thrusts that define
his position. He observes, for instance, that Donne admits
self-preservation to be a natural law, yet one so general that

[1] London, 1659, pp. 27–8.
[2] The British Museum Catalogue lists 5 issues of Montaigne's *Essais* in translation during the seventeenth century, 1603, 1613, 1632, 1685–6, 1693; and 7
issues of Charron's *Of Wisdome*, 1608, 1615, 1620, 1630, 1640, 1658, 1670.
[3] See Dryden's (or Tonson's) *Miscellany* (1684–1709), in which many of
Donne's love poems are reprinted in 1716, and observe the marks of that libertine philosophy which Donne introduced into English love poetry.
[4] See Adams, op. cit., pp. 306 ff. Hobbes, though unnamed, is the chief
opponent in this passage, which does not omit his followers, the Wits.

it extends more to beasts than to men;[1] to which Adams replies that man, being qualified 'to follow Reason by Virtue', is the more obligated.[2] He points out as a crucial argument in Donne the notion that 'Self-preservation is not of so particular a Law of Nature, but that it is often transgress'd Naturally'.[3] And he finds Donne guilty of opposing 'God's Propriety of Humane Life' indirectly in his argument that though man has not the 'dominion' of life, he has the 'use' of it.[4] In this connection he quotes a passage from Montaigne's essay on 'The Custom of the Isle of Cea'.[5] It is from this essay that Adams makes his chief quotations from Montaigne; and it ought to be added that this essay offers a good many parallels to *Biathanatos*, beginning with the 'key' as a symbol of suicide. While most of these parallels are natural to the subject and one cannot conclude that Donne is indebted to Montaigne, in no other instance with which I am acquainted do they approach each other as closely. But opposed as he is to suicide, Adams subscribes in general to the Stoic Law of Nature, and at times kindles with the Stoic spirit.

The brunt of Adams's attack upon Donne really falls upon the relativistic philosophy which supports his interpretation of natural law. Adams gives a fair summary of Donne's position in the following passage:

'*No Law is so Primary and Simple, but that it fore-imagines a Reason upon which it was founded; and scarce any Reason so constant, but that Circumstances may alter it; in which Case a private man is Emperour of himself*, sui juris. *And he whose Conscience is well temper'd and dispassion'd assures him, that the Reason of Self-Preservation ceases in him, may also presume, that the Law ceases too, and may do that then which otherwise were against the Law.*

---

[1] *Biathanatos*, London (1646?), pp. 44–5. Adams uses the 1648 issue of *Biathanatos*, not the edition of 1700; his references will apply equally well to the first issue.

[2] Op. cit., p. 43.

[3] Ibid., p. 45. Cf. Donne, p. 56.

[4] Ibid., pp. 50–1. Cf. Donne, p. 112.

[5] Ibid., p. 56. Cf. the Cotton translation, Bk. II, ch. 3.

'*Self-preservation which we confess to be the foundation of general natural Law, is no other thing than a natural Affection and Appetition of Good, whether true or seeming.—Now since this Law of Self-preservation is accomplish'd in attaining that which conduces to our Ends, and is* (i.e. *seems*) *good to us.—If I propose to my self in this* Self-homicide, *a greater Good, though I mistake it; I perceive not wherein I transgress the general Law of Nature, which is an affection of Good, True or Seeming; and if that which I affect by Death be truly a greater Good, wherein is the other stricter Law of Nature, which is rectified Reason, violated.*'[1]

Before making these statements, in which Adams sees a dangerous substitution of private reason and appetite for Law, Donne comments upon the difficulty of understanding 'this terme the law of Nature' or of lighting upon any constant meaning for it, remarking, 'Yet I never found it in any sence which might justifie their vociferations upon sinnes against nature.'[2] He concludes that if it means anything, it must mean *recta ratio*; but this, he says, 'is with most authors confounded and made the same with *jus gentium*', which is whatever is 'practised and accepted in most especially civil'st nations'.[3] To Donne and his libertine tendency to reduce 'natural Law' to 'custom', Adams opposes this interpretation of the Law of Nature:

'The Word *Nature* is sometimes a very general Term, and signifies that Order which the great Creator put the *whole*

---

[1] Ibid., pp. 73–4. Cf. Donne, pp. 47–50. It is noteworthy that in 1695 Gildon defended both the doctrine and suicide of his master, Charles Blount, on the very grounds set forth by Donne in such passages as this. Significantly, he connected the idea of *sui juris* with the right to withdraw 'Consent to any Government' (Locke?), and clinched his argument by declaring, 'For every man is in this, what *Almanzor* tells *Boabdelin*,

I my self am King of Me."

This fragmentary line from Dryden's *Conquest of Granada* (Part I, Act I, Sc. i) is, in the play, connected with an assertion of the primitive rights of man; moreover, Almanzor is troubled by problems raised by Hobbes. For the *locus* of this pretty tangle of seventeenth-century thought, and a real occasion for Adams's book, see the prefatory 'Account of the Life and Death of the Author' in *The Miscellaneous Works of Charles Blount, Esq.*, especially sigs. (A6–A9.)

[2] *Biathanatos*, 1646?, p. 36.

[3] Ibid., pp. 39–40.

World to move in; sometimes, in a more limitted sence, it signifies that Rule which he gave *each* Creature to follow, for the fulfilling of that *particular End* for which it was made, in proper Harmony and Consent with the Universe; so that the Word *Nature* rises in its signification according to the several Degrees of the Creation; and by following Nature must be meant, the *obeying it according to that particular Power which distinguishes one Creature from another.* This Beasts do by Sensation, this Man shou'd do by Reason: That great, that God-like Faculty which is given us to discern Good and Evil, and to regulate our Passions and Appetites by Virtue accordingly. Wherefore for *Man to follow Nature*, is the very same, with the End of Life, to which Self-preservation is subservient, as has been shown, namely *the following of Reason by Virtue*.'[1]

Of course the elements are the same as in Donne, but not the direction. The chief support for this interpretation Adams finds in the Stoics, and what he has to say on this subject provides an interesting commentary on neo-classical doctrine.

Adams is next concerned with Donne's objection that 'some things are natural to the Species, and others to the particular Person; and therefore when Cicero consulted the Oracle, he had this Answer, FOLLOW YOUR OWN NATURE'. To this Adams replies, 'That to follow *ones own Nature* cannot be any *Exemption* from what was said before'; and that the phrase must mean 'the being the same in Opinion, Humour, Manners, the having ones Life *all of a Piece*, whatsoever comes to pass; which they also call'd *Decorum*'.[2] Yet, says Adams, 'this must still be grounded upon the former Universal Maxim, the living *according to Nature*, as *Humane* and *Reasonable*'. To Donne's covert plea for 'particular reason' and the 'privilege of judging for oneself', Adams replies vigorously:

'A Man cannot *do so safely, without some Rule*, and that Rule must be *universal publick Reason*; and unless every private Man's Reason be squar'd accordingly, it can never

[1] Op. cit., pp. 79–80.   [2] Ibid., pp. 82–3. Cf. Donne, p. 45.

be right; but if it be squar'd accordingly, then it ought not to be contended for as private Reason.'[1]

To introduce 'seeming Good' and 'seeming Evil' as the rule of human action is to Adams the last straw, which a puff of private reason will blow into the 'primrose path' of libertinism.[2] It is to make the ground of General Natural Law 'nothing but the appetition of Good, True, or Seeming'; in short, to subvert all law. Adams cannot make it too strong:

'In a Word, to give a Man up to act by *seeming Good* and *seeming Evil*, is to let him loose to his own *Will* and *Pleasure*, to grant him *Wildness* instead of *Liberty*, and to make Life depend upon this, is to tell him he may destroy *himself whenever he thinks fitting.*'

And this, as Adams said of Hobbes, 'opens a very wide door to the worst consequences of Knavery or Cowardice', but it is a conclusion that Donne did not contemplate in this light.[3] If we find ourselves hesitating to push Donne's ideas to the conclusions to which Adams pushes them, we must remember that no contemporary of Adams would have shared our hesitation. Certainly Adams is right in detecting a naturalistic bias in Donne's interpretation of the Law of Nature, and a bias which is supported by a sceptical and relativistic philosophy.

It would be more tiresome than illuminating to follow the whole of Adams's argument against Donne, but it will be worth our while to notice occasional points. Adams finds Donne making this statement in effect:

'That the *General Concurrence* of Nations in any Law proves a *General Inclination* in Mankind to the *committing* of the thing *forbidden*; and therefore that that thing is Natural.'[4]

[1] Ibid., p. 90.

[2] Ibid., pp. 92 ff.

[3] Charles Moore (op. cit., II. 9) says: 'It will then be found however in the examination of the book itself, that his arguments tend to overthrow all the principles and laws on which the general guilt of suicide is established; and that therefore if valid, they open the way to a much more frequent commission of the crime than Donne himself thinks allowable.' Adams did not allow Donne this mitigation.

[4] Op. cit., p. 114. Cf. Donne, pp. 94-5.

'This,' says Adams, 'is very strange'; but in Donne it is merely a statement of the difficulty of declaring anything to be a sin because of its 'having by custome onely put on the nature of law'.[1] Quoting Donne's argument that universal inclination proves suicide not to be against the Law of Nature, and that 'both express Litteral Law, and Mute Law, Custom hath Authorized it', Adams proceeds to show that 'there is no way of Arguing so *fallacious* as that which depends upon *Example*'.[2] In picking examples one must distinguish between nations, 'many being so *Ignorant* and so *Savage* that it would be very strange to fetch the Principles of right Reason from among them'; and one 'ought to en-quire carefully into the ground and occasion of the Custom which is pleaded; whether it be founded upon some *Religious* or *Superstitious* Principle, or encouraged by some *Political* Consideration; any of which if it be, it ought not to be alledg'd as meerly Natural'. This, one might add, is to make Natural Law less immutable. Adams then proceeds to consider examples offered by Donne, Montaigne, and the Stoics. In Chapter X he considers the doctrine of the Stoics, 'whose Books falling often into our Hands when we are young, and leaving lasting Impressions upon many People, require a particular Examination'. He finds self-murder to be inconsistent with the other principles of 'this Wise and Virtuous Sect'. But in all these instances, as elsewhere, Adams shows a nice concern for the immutable Law of Nature which derives from the Stoics and which is con-stantly threatened by a naturalistic substitution in the argument of Donne.

Against the promptings of extravagant notions of honour as a motive to suicide, Adams quotes Montaigne and Mackenzie's *Moral Gallantry* with approval; of the former he writes, '*Montaign* says very well, that *the Virtue of the Soul does not consist in flying high, but in walking orderly.*'[3] Beside

---

[1] Cf. Donne, p. 91.

[2] Op. cit., pp. 132–3.

[3] Ibid., p. 232. Whenever possible, Adams quotes Montaigne against the Libertines.

this we may put Adams's notion of 'Liberty, the last Plea for Self-murther', recalling that Donne dissimulates any 'darke and dangerous Secessions and divertings into points of our Free-will, and of God's Destiny':

'But *Man's Liberty*, is very *different*, as he is a *finite Creature*; it can be perfect only according to its *measure*, and that measure must be *proportionable* to his *particular Nature*.'[1]

That nature, as Adams has made clear, is rational, and so his liberty must conform to *recta ratio* or the Law of Nature. It is perhaps unnecessary to remark again the interesting connections which Adams has with neo-classical doctrines. The problem of liberty, however, leads Adams directly into a definition of libertinism:

'Can any Man pretend to be *Free* while *his Reason* is made to *Serve*? And does it not *serve most basely* in such People, at the beck of every Lust and Passion; is it not forc'd to fetch and carry in more and more of the vicious Object; to be drudging always to Sensation; to provide to glut this or that Appetite, or to administer to this or that Passion; this is the glorious End of that Liberty of *following their own Reason*; which is so much affected by many People, who will be *riding* over Hedge and Ditch, rather than be *impos'd upon by a beaten Road*, and throw away their *Rudder* and their *Compass* in order to *Sail freely*.'[2]

The end of this course is that 'these *free thinking* Gentlemen . . . being weary of a Life which they have so miserably misus'd, they as miserably destroy it'.[3] But where they declare, 'Who has the Property of my Life but my self? And what does Property signifie if I may not have the Liberty to do what I will with my own?', Donne had claimed not 'property', but 'use'. While this must be said, it must also be said that Adams is perfectly right in discovering attributes of 'property' in Donne's 'use', and in detecting the *tendency* to libertinism which the early readers of *Biathanatos* called 'a false thread'.

As Donne had considered the occasions on which the liberty of destroying himself may devolve upon a man,

[1] Ibid., p. 263.   [2] Ibid., p. 267.   [3] Ibid., p. 270.

The Libertine Donne

Adams also considers them; and his general answer is that no occasion can abrogate the immutable character of the Law of Nature. Milton is cited for making the first man argue against self-murder from the Light of Nature; but once before Milton is mentioned as a case in which 'the World had lost that *admirable Poem*', had he taken advantage of a Stoic occasion for suicide.[1] It is striking and even significant, to find Milton thus lined up against the 'liberty' of Donne; but there are other ways in which Milton and Adams agree, not to mention Belial as one sort of libertine. Thus Adams bears witness that *Biathanatos* did not escape the second danger with which the younger Donne felt it to be threatened: that 'of being utterly found; and fathered, by some of those wild Atheists, who, as if they came into the World by conquest, owne all other mens Wits, and are resolved to be learned, in despite of their Starres'. While the younger Donne had made sure that *Biathanatos* bear the name of Donne, Adams tried to make sure that it be stamped for what it was in his day, a libertine document, in which he attempted to nullify the insinuation of its learning.

III

The relativistic philosophy from which this insinuation draws its cunning informs the most eloquent passage in *Biathanatos*. While this philosophy had supported the naturalism of Donne's youth, it now began to give structure to his emergent need of religious faith. I quote from the opening of the third part, 'Of the Law of God':

'That light which issues from the Moone, doth best represent and express that which in our selves we call the light of Nature; for as that in the Moone is permanent and ever there, and yet it is unequall, various, pale, and languishing, So is our light of Nature changeable. For being at the first kindling at full, it wayned presently, and by departing further and further from God, declined by generall sinne, to almost a total Eclipse: till God comming neerer to us, first

[1] Ibid., pp. 313 and 111.

53

by the Law, and then by Grace, enlightned and repayred it
againe, conveniently to his ends, for further exercise of his
Mercy and Justice. And then those Artificiall Lights, which
our selves make for our use and service here, as Fires, Tapers
and such resemble the light of Reason, as wee have in our
Second part accepted the Word. For though the light of
these Fires and Tapers be not so naturall, as the Moone, yet
because they are more domestique, and obedient to us, wee
distinguish particular objects better by them, than by the
Moone; So by the Arguments, and Deductions, and Conclusions, which our selves beget and produce, as being more
serviceable and under us, because they are our creatures;
particular cases are made more cleare and evident to us; for
these we can be bold withall, and put them to any office,
and examine, and prove their truth, or likeliehood, and
make them answere as long as wee will aske; whereas the
light of Nature, with a solemne and supercilious Majestie,
will speake but once, and give no Reason, nor endure
Examination.

'But because of these two kindes of light, the first is to
weake, and the other false, (for onely colour is the object of
sight, and we not trust candlelight to discerne Colours) we
have therefore the Sunne, which is the Fountain and Treasure of all created light, for an Embleme of that third best
light of our understanding, which is the Word of God.
Mandatum lucerna, & Lex lux, sayes *Solomon*. But yet as
weake credulous men, thinke sometimes they see two or
three Sunnes, when they see none but Meteors, or other
apparance; so are many transported with like facilitie or
dazeling, that for some opinions which they maintaine, they
think they have the light and authority of Scripture, when,
God knowes, truth, which is the light of Scriptures, is
Divine truely under them, and removed in the farthest
distance they can bee.'[1]

It is evident that Donne regards the Law of Nature as too
weak a guide, especially since it speaks but once and admits
no interrogation; but for that good domestic, 'our discourse

[1] Ed. cit., pp. 153–5. Cf. the opening of Dryden's *Religio Laici*.

54

and ratiocination', he has a sneaking fondness, though he calls her false. And yet even the Word of God, the 'best light of our understanding', is liable to human error; which, in this case, is to be prevented by numerous authorities, subject of course to interpretation by the 'discourse' of Donne. Thus, all three lights are associated with error in man, and cast a sceptical shadow beyond the object which they reveal; their truth is, in short, relative to the deficiencies of man. But even here in 1608 the 'best light' to Donne is the light of God, and its superiority rests upon the defection of the Law of Nature and the uncertainty of reason. In other words, the scepticism that supported the naturalism of his youth now lends support to the reliability of divine light, which becomes deceptive only when it is associated with 'our discourse and ratiocination'. In *Biathanatos* the naturalism of his youth is expressed chiefly in his scepticism of the Law of Nature, which manifests itself in a tendency to substitute a libertine nature for the ethical nature of the Stoics.

Biathanatos reveals a crucial point in the progress of the soul which converted Jack Donne into Dr. Donne, for it marks the end of his naturalistic journey. It is clear that Adams regards self-murder as the probable end of all naturalistic progresses, that he believes Donne to have made a dangerous defence of this end, and that he attacks this defence mainly on the ground of the Law of Nature. It is equally clear from the eloquent passage which I have quoted that Donne regards the Law of Nature as faint and 'changeable' until 'repayred' by the Law and Grace of God. From a philosophy of change based on a libertine nature, Donne is brought to the admission that the flickering light of ethical nature can be made steady by grace, and this admission comes at the end of that last argument in a libertine philosophy of nature—suicide. In my long quotation from the Donne of 1608 we find all the elements which compose his mature religious view, or his last mystical reliance upon faith and grace, together with the scepticism which induces and supports that reliance. How these elements arrange themselves, with the shift in emphasis which completed his religious progress, may be seen in a sermon preached on Christmas Day, 1621, in which subtle correspondences carry us back to the eloquent passage written in 1608:

'In all philosophy there is not so dark a thing as light; as the sun, which is *fons lucis naturalis*, the beginning of natural light, is the most evident thing to be seen, and yet the hardest to be looked upon, so is natural light to our reason and understanding. Nothing clearer, for it is clearness itself, nothing darker, it is enwrapped in so many scruples. Nothing nearer, for it is around about us, nothing more remote, for we know neither entrance, nor limits of it. Nothing more easy, for a child discerns it, nothing more hard, for no man understands it. It is apprehensible by sense, and not comprehensible by reason. If we wink, we cannot choose but see it, if we stare, we know it never the better. No man is yet got so near to the knowledge of the qualities of light, as to know whether light itself be a quality, or a substance. If then this natural light be so dark to our natural reason, if we shall offer to pierce so far into the light of this text, the essential light Christ Jesus (in his nature, or but in his offices), or the supernatural light of faith and grace, . . . if we search farther into these points, than the Scripture hath opened us a way, how shall we hope to unentangle, or extricate themselves? They had a precious composition for lamps, amongst the ancients, reserved especially for tombs, which kept light for many hundreds of years; we have had in our age experience, in some casual openings of ancient vaults, of finding such lights, as were kindled, (as appeared by their inscriptions) fifteen or sixteen hundred years before; but, as soon as that light comes to our light, it vanishes. So this eternal, and this supernatural light, Christ and faith, enlightens, warms, purges, and does all the profitable offices of fire and light, if we keep it in the right sphere, in the proper place, (that is, if we consist in points necessary to salvation, and revealed in the Scriptures) but when we bring this light to the common light of reason, to our inferences, and consequences, it may be in danger to vanish itself, and perchance extinguish our reason too; we may search so far, and reason so long of faith and grace, as that we may lose not only them, but even our reason too, and sooner become mad than good.'[1]

This passage would repay minute comparison with the one from *Biathanatos*. The least we can notice is that natural light is stronger here, but still 'enwrapped in so many scruples', and just as difficult of interrogation; that passionate affirmation is given to 'the supernatural light of faith and grace', only suggested in the former passage as capable of restoring natural light; and that reason, which retains its sceptical aura, not only imperils, but is imperilled by, this supernatural light. If possible, the latter passage is more paradoxical than the former; certainly, Donne's intensely mystical and quizzical faith rests upon the same paradox of sceptical reason. Even the altered relations in the symbols are suggestive; the result is that natural light is both stronger and darker, while supernatural light is smaller, more remote, and yet more powerful. The paradox has deepened, but the religious feeling has grown more passionate, more anxious.

The full significance of *Biathanatos* cannot be appreciated without some notion of the state of Donne's mind during those middle years. No greater travesty upon Donne has been written than Professor Elliot's essay dealing with the same years;[2] for correction one should turn to Professor Bredvold's *The Religious Thought of Donne*.[3] The gospel of doubt is so central to Donne's thought that we must observe its expression at different stages of his career. We find it first in his 'Satyre III':

> *doubt wisely; in strange way*
> *To stand inquiring right, is not to stray;*
> *To sleepe, or runne wrong, is.*[4]

This satire, in which Donne condemns suicide, cannot be overvalued as a reflection of the serious thought of the early

---

[1] Alford, V. 55.
[2] See *The Bookman* (American), June 1931, pp. 337-46.
[3] See *University of Michigan Publications*, Lang. and Lit., Vol. I.
[4] *Complete Poetry and Selected Prose*, ed. Hayward, p. 129.

Donne. Even when he knew 'Flesh (it selfes death) and joyes
which flesh can taste,' he knew much more, for the next
lines tell us that it is the soul 'which doth give this flesh
power to taste joy'. Here is early recognition of the necessity of that progress of the soul which he describes in *The
Second Anniversary*. His next expression of the sceptical mode
of thought comes in his cynical *Progresse of the Soule:*

> *Ther's nothing simply good, nor ill alone,*
> *Of every quality comparison,*
> *The onely measure is, and judge, opinion.*[1]

This, in 1601, immediately suggests Hamlet's 'there is nothing either good or bad, but thinking makes it so', or
carries us back to Nashe, who says ten years earlier, 'So that
our opinion (as *Sextus Empiricus* affirmeth) giues the name of
good or ill to euery thing.'[2] And this should remind us that
Donne was also expressing the sceptical thought of his day.
As we have already seen this relativistic philosophy operative in *Biathanatos*, we may observe it next in *The Second
Anniversary*:

> *Be not concern'd: studie not why, nor when;*
> *Doe not so much as not beleeve a man.*
> *For though to erre, be worst, to try truths forth,*
> *Is far more businesse, than this world is worth.*[3]

In the time of his deepest gloom the world seemed hardly
worth scepticism, and this was in 1612. In the *Essayes in
Divinity*, written just before his ordination, faith has definitely become the superstructure of scepticism, for his
mind now affirms that 'our best firmament and arrest will be
that reverent, and pious, and reasonable credulity, that God
was Author of the first of these books, the Decalogue'.[4] In
these essays Donne refers to the Pyrrhonian philosophy as
'having invented a way by which a man should determine
nothing of every thing';[5] and in his great sermon on faith

[1] Ibid., p. 272.
[2] *Works*, ed. McKerrow, III. 332.
[3] *Ed. cit.*, p. 216.
[4] London, 1651, p. 20.
[5] Ibid., p. 56.

and imperfect knowledge, preached at the funeral of Sir William Cokayne on 12th December 1626, he brings this progress in scepticism to its conclusion:

'One philosopher thinks he has dived to the bottom, when he says, he knows nothing but this, that he knows nothing; and yet another thinks, that he hath expressed more knowledge than he, in saying, that he knows not so much as that, that he knows nothing.'[1]

For the imperfection of things, even spiritual things, there is now but one answer; for the 'fluidness, the transitoriness' of things, which the 'new philosophy' only corroborates, there is now but one 'best firmament and arrest'. Nature still pleads inconstancy, but with a moral different from that of his youth; his deep sensitiveness to the relativity of things has brought him to a craving for something permanent, something constant. But already in the earlier *Essayes in Divinity* he had foreseen the end of scepticism and had felt that 'to be nothing is so deep a curse' that it is not even suffered by the prisoners of Hell.[2]

We are fortunate in having preserved for us, in one of the finest passages in *The Second Anniversary*, a record of the change in Donne's feeling towards inconstancy. His first experience of constancy, we feel, was in the love of Anne More; can it be that even in that love he discovered his despair at the great inconstancy of life? In any case, here is the telltale passage:

> And what essentiall joy can'st thou expect
> Here upon earth? what permanent effect
> Of transitory causes? Dost thou love
> Beauty? (And beauty worthy'st is to move)
> Poore cousened cousenor, that she, and that thou,
> Which did begin to love, are neither now;
> You are both fluid, chang'd since yesterday;
> Next day repaires, (but ill) last dayes decay.
> Nor are, (although the river keepe the name)
> Yesterdaies waters, and to daies the same.

[1] Alford, III. 472.   [2] Ed. cit., p. 61.

The Libertine Donne

So flowes her face, and thine eyes, neither now
That Saint, nor Pilgrime, which your loving vow
Concern'd, remaines; but whil'st you thinke you bee
Constant, you'are hourely in inconstancie.[1]

Whereas yesterday he delighted in the inconstancy of his feelings, today he laments that even though one hold fast to constancy, one cannot keep it, for nothing is permanent. Is it then to be doubted that one who creates a philosophy of naturalism upon the inconstancy of nature may, when he has plumbed the emotional depth of that inconstancy, erect in its place a philosophy of consolation for this impermanence? or that he who does so may not violate his own integrity? or that these philosophies may rest upon the same basis of experience? In other words, we may declare that Donne's progress is from the inconstancy of nature to scepticism to naturalism; then, following a profound emotional change, it is from despair at the inconstancy of life to scepticism to religious faith. The first two steps make the third step possible in each phase of his progress.

What Donne had gone through he reveals at the moment of ordination in the most intimate and exact piece of self-revelation that he ever wrote:

'Thou hast delivered me, O God, from the Egypt of confidence and presumption, by interrupting my fortunes, and intercepting my hopes; And from the Egypt of despair by contemplation of thine abundant treasures, and my portion therein; from the Egypt of lust, by confining my affections; and from the monstrous and unnaturall Egypt of painfull and wearisome idleness, by the necessities of domestick and familiar cares and duties. Yet as an Eagle, though she enjoy her wing and beak, is wholly prisoner, if she be held by but one talon; so are we, though we could be delivered of all habit of sin, in bondage still, if Vanity hold us but by a silken thred.'[2]

Though this lends itself to the 'division' to which Lancelot Andrewes submitted a text, we may remark briefly that the

---

[1] Ed. cit., p. 225.   [2] *Essayes in Divinity*, London, 1651, pp. 166-7.

personal letters of Donne bear constant testimony to the intimate precision of this diagnosis. With the consciousness that the silken thread of vanity is his most dangerous bond, he pens in the beginning of the *Essayes in Divinity* these significant words, 'It is then humility to study God.'[1] It had been his study in those middle years, and it was 'not such a groveling, frozen, and stupid Humility, as should quench the activity of our understanding'. It is simple fact to say that the cream of his *Verse Letters* may be found in his *Anniversaries*, and the cream of his *Anniversaries* in his *Sermons*, so much is one year the preparation for the next. *Biathanatos* was not only his profoundest indulgence in, but also his deliverance from, 'the Egypt of despair'. In the *First Anniversary* came the devastating vision of his and his age's world, when the 'new Philosophy calls all in doubt', and leaves it with

all cohaerence gone;
All just supply, and all Relation.

And his *Second Anniversary* revealed his soul's most passionate contemplation of life in relation to God during those middle years; the 'sickely inclination' of *Biathanatos* was there transmuted into the desire of dying into the religious life, but a desire that had not yet become a way.[2]

Thus we may conclude that *Biathanatos* is crucial in Donne's thought because it illuminates the intermediate ground between his earlier scepticism and naturalism and his later scepticism and mysticism. Apparently Donne was so constituted that he could not rest in reason as the Law of Nature; he must either go below or go above, always searching for that which 'elemented' the ecstasy of the flesh or the exaltation of the spirit. In youth he plumbed life on the naturalistic level, finally to reach the dead-end of 'queasie paine' and to rationalize its last despair—suicide. In maturity

[1] Ibid., p. 3.
[2] Donne himself remarks 'how quickly naturally man snatch'd and embraced a new way of profusing his life by martyrdome', after Christianity had quenched the ancient propensity to suicide (*Biathanatos*, ed. cit., pp. 57 ff. Cf. his 'Preface', p. 17).

he sought to reach to faith and grace, to 'die a death more mystical and high', doomed, as he was, always to draw his faith in pain. Is it then too simple to say that the ladder between these two states was scepticism grounded upon the inconstancy of things? that even a relativistic philosophy must at last be futile with 'all Relation' gone? If not, then *Biathanatos* may help to explain his progress from one state to the other, may surrender the secret of his affection for it, and may still justify its reception at the close of the century. Truly, it is the paradox of paradoxes; it is Donne putting off the old life that he may put on the new, but not so completely as to deceive the libertine eyes of the Restoration. Adams did not so much correct the portrait left by Walton as cut a new silhouette of Donne to hang in another wing of the gallery beside Hobbes and Montaigne.

III

The Convention of *The Extasie*

★

S ince Pierre Legouis challenged Grierson's interpretation
of 'The Extasie' and argued that it should be read as a
poem of seduction, it has attracted more attention than any
other poem by Donne. Merritt Y. Hughes, in reply, has
tried to establish its Platonic lineage by means of Castiglione's *Courtier*.[1] But the problem raised by Legouis has a
framework that has not been examined in subsequent discussion.

Long ago Morris W. Croll suggested this when he pointed
to the original pattern for Fulke Greville's *Caelica* 75 in
Sidney's Eighth Song of *Astrophel and Stella*:
'The two poems have in common the description of a
May landscape, the walk of two lovers through "an
enamel'd meade" (in Greville), in "a grove most rich of
shade" (in Sidney), the long silence of both, with nice
analysis of their emotions, finally a long casuistic dialogue
on love, in which the ardor of the lover is restrained by the
prudence of his mistress, or, in Greville's case, by her anger.'[2]
For this pattern Janet G. Scott, in *Les Sonnets Elisabéthains*,
found no precise antedecent, but a relation that lends support
to Legouis:
'La chanson VIII a quelque ressemblance avec ces Chants

[1] *Modern Language Review*, Vol. 27, No. 1.
[2] *The Works of Fulke Greville*, Philadelphia, 1903, p. 9.

de Mai ou "Reverdies" composés par les Trouvères et les Troubadours lorsqu'un souffle d'amour venait les troubler au printemps. L'oeuvre de la Pléiade est remplie de similaires invitations à l'amour, mais le dialogue du poète anglais avec Stella introduit quelques différences non sans originalité.[1]

Yet what Croll calls the 'casuistic dialogue on love' is a crucial difference in Sidney's invitation to love, and removes it equally from Marlowe's *Passionate Shepherd to his Love* or its successors.

In 1903 Croll outlined the 'convention' begun by Sidney in a footnote to his comparison of the imitation by Fulke Greville:

'Poems following this convention are numerous in later poets. Compare Donne's *The Ecstacy*, Lord Herbert's *Ode on a Question moved whether Love should continue forever*, Wither's *Fair-Virtue, The Mistress of Phil'arete*, Sonnet 3. In Donne's poem by a characteristic subtlety the dialogue is reduced to a monologue spoken by the undistinguished soul of the two lovers. There may be an original in some foreign literature, or Sidney's Song may have suggested the rest. Sedley shows the abuse of the form in various poems and Cartwright protests against the Platonism which found expression in it in his *No Platonic Love*.'

Various signs point to Sidney as the exemplar for the English poets, but his verse form undergoes some modification in the later poets. The popularization of Platonic theories, Miss Scott reminds us, was 'due à des ouvrages comme les *Asolani* de Bembo, et le *Cortegiano* de Castiglione'. Obviously Platonism is not the only love casuistry that finds expression in this convention. The variety of poets who employ this convention is in itself enough to challenge our interest, and more than enough to destroy some of our preconceptions. The probable chronological order of their poems is Sidney, Greville, Donne, Wither, and Lord Herbert. However, we shall examine their use of this convention not in chronological order but rather in

[1] Paris, 1929, p. 47.

that of complication: Sidney, Greville, Wither, Herbert, Donne. Various new elements or alterations of the old will enter into this complication.

Sidney's Song begins with a pastoral setting:

> *In a Grove most rich of shade,*
> *Where Birds wanton musique made,*
> *May, then young, his pyed weedes showing,*
> *New perfum'd, with flowers fresh growing,*
> Astrophell *with* Stella *sweete,*
> *Did for mutuall comfort meete . . .*

Theirs is an unhappy, forbidden love: 'Him great harmes had taught much care,/ Her faire necke a foul yoake bare.' Now they find solace for their grief in each other's company,

> *While their eyes by Love directed,*
> *Enterchangeably reflected . . .*
> *But their tongues restrain'd from walking,*
> *Till their harts had ended talking.*

Finally, 'Love it selfe did silence breake,' and Astrophell began a 'blazon' of her beauties leading to a request, which is suggested by the lines, '*Stella*, in whose body is/Writ each Character of blisse.' Fearing to put his request directly, he asks on his knees, 'That not I, but since I love you,/Time and place for me may move you.' Then all the elements of place and season conspire to preach love, 'And if dumbe things be so wittie,/Shall a heavenly grace want pittie?' Finally his hands 'Would have made tongues language plaine,' but her hands 'Gave repulse, all grace excelling.' His argument has been based on the analogies of nature suggested by the pastoral setting.

Then Stella's argument begins, 'While such wise she love denied,/As yet love she signified.' Asking him to 'Cease in these effects to prove' her love, she answers in terms of her situation, her 'foule yoake'. Thus she finds her only comfort in him, and swears her faith by the eyes he praised; in short, she gives all her love and faith, but not her body. For she is restrained by honour and would remain free of shame.

E

The Convention of The Extasie

There-with-all, away she went,
Leaving him to passion rent:
With what she had done and spoken,
That there-with my Song is broken.

She can say 'Tirant honour dooth thus use thee' because of the foul yoke which she wears, not because Stella herself would refuse him. Thus she does not argue in terms of the pastoral setting, but in terms of their social condition. These restraints lend vehemence to her vows.

In Greville's imitation of Sidney the brief setting is made more suggestive:

> *In the time when herbs and flowers,*
> *Springing out of melting powers,*
> *Teach the earth that heate and raine*
> *Doe make* Cupid *live againe:*
> *Late when* Sol, *like great hearts, showes*
> *Largest as he lowest goes,*
> Caelica *with* Philocell
> *In fellowship together fell.*

Her hair, however, is made suggestive of mourning, 'Of hopes death which to her eyes,/Offers thoughts for sacrifice.' The love of Philocell and the scorn of Caelica are then analysed as 'Through enamel'd Meades they went,/Quiet she, he passion rent.' Here the echo of Sidney leads into a reversal of roles in which Philocell protests his love when at length 'His despaire taught feare thus speake':

> *You, to whom all Passions pray,*
> *Like poore Flies that to the fire,*
> *Where they burne themselves, aspire . . .*

These resemblances to Donne's 'Canonization' begin a long appeal of the forlorn lover to the cruel mistress. Her cold answers show, says Greville, 'How self-pitties have reflexion,/Backe into their owne infection.' For she replies that her love is dead and advises him to 'let Reason guide affection,/From despaire to new election.' Now Philocell begs for pity, but implies doubt of Caelica; whereupon

66

The Convention of The Extasie

'His eyes great with child with teares/Spies in her eyes many feares.' In fury she tells him to be gone, that men are full of contradictions, that he has imposed on her enough, and finally, 'I will never rumour move,/At least for one I doe not love.'

Then Greville takes up the defence of Philocell against Caelica:

> Shepheardesses, if it prove,
> Philocell she once did love,
> Can kind doubt of true affection
> Merit such a sharpe correction?

Thus Greville begins to elaborate the love casuistry as he spells out the argument, which involves Philocell's jealousy and Caelica's wrong. He argues that the nature of love excuses and explains its abuses, and that Philocell will remain faithful to his martyrdom. Greville concludes, 'Here my silly Song is ended,' but hastens to assure the nymphs that they can find faith in men if they will be constant.

In Greville the seductive element is almost lost in the extension and complication of the love casuistry. Sidney's descriptive praise of the lady is greatly reduced, and the pastoral setting finds no place in the love casuistry. While a more hopeless Petrarchan atmosphere is developed, the poem ends with a real problem in love casuistry and thus justifies the argumentative resolution. Sidney's Song was broken by an action which also completed its argument.

Wither's Sonnet 3 of *Fair Virtue* begins with the familiar setting:

> When Philomela with her strains
> The spring had welcomed in,
> And Flora to bestrow the plains
> With daisies did begin,
> My love and I, on whom suspicious eyes
> Had set a thousand spies,
> To cozen Argus strove;
> And seen of none
> We got alone
> Into a shady grove.

67

The Convention of The Extasie

Here 'The earth, the air, and all things did conspire/To raise contentment higher'; so that if the lovers had 'come to woo', nothing would have been lacking. Hand in hand they walked, and talked 'Of love and passions past.' Their 'souls infus'd into each other were' and shared each other's sorrow. But then their bodies begin to betray their souls:

> *Her dainty palm I gently prest,*
> *   And with her lips I play'd;*
> *My cheek upon her panting breast,*
> *   .And on her neck I laid.*
> *And yet we had no sense of wanton lust . . .*

Soon their passions overpower them:

> *But kissing and embracing we*
> *   So long together lay,*
> *Her touches all inflamed me,*
> *   And I began to stray.*
> *My hands presum'd so far, they were too*
> *   bold . . .*

As Wither makes this turn upon Sidney, his lover's virtue is 'put to flight', and his lady in tears begins to plead with him not to spot their 'true love', protesting 'Whilst thee I thus refuse/In hotter flames I fry.' Her Platonic lament increases in vehemence:

> *Are we the two that have so long*
> *   Each other's loves embraced?*
> *And never did affection wrong,*
> *   Nor think a thought unchaste?*

Her argument now involves a line used by Sidney: 'I should of all our passions grow ashamed,/And blush when thou art named.' But her reasons are quite different, for those 'who are to lust inclin'd,/Drive love out of the mind.' And she is no Stella:

> *No vulgar bliss I aimed at*
> *   When first I heard thee woo;*
> *I'll never prize a man for that*
> *   Which every groom can do.*

68

The Convention of The Extasie

While she speaks he regains control of himself because in her

Those virtues shine
Whose rays divine
First gave desire a law.

Thus the blush of shame returns to him, for his 'soul her light of reason had renew'd'. Then he preaches to 'wantons' contempt of the body, 'Since every beast/In pleasure equals you.' And because the conquest of evil brings 'peace without compare'. But lest the wantons still think his conquest slight, he puts it beyond the labours of Hercules and the chastity of Diana. Whether this persuaded the wantons of his higher love seems at best doubtful.

Wither has certainly made the Sidney convention a vehicle for a prurient Platonism. Nature conspires with the body, not the soul, but the argument turns against nature in the conclusion. When the rescued lover expresses the moral of Platonic love, he counts its dividends too much in the old currency to establish the new. Altogether the pastoral framework is at odds with the Platonism, and matters are not improved by mixing mythology into the realism of the poem.

Lord Herbert's 'Ode upon a Question moved, whether Love should continue for ever?' has the most elaborate pastoral setting of all. Nature in flower waits for the sun, 'the wish'd Bridegroom of the earth'. Birds, wind, brook, lovers, all 'An harmony of parts did bind.' The lovers walked 'towards a pleasant Grove' and reposed on the grass,

Long their fixt eyes to Heaven bent,
Unchanged, they did never move,
As if so great and pure a love
No Glass but it could represent.

Then Celinda raises the question of love's end at death, and does so in stanzas that are a temptation to quote, asking whether if love's fire is kindled with life, it will not go out with life. Since this also raises the problem of sense in love, Melander answers that their love is beyond but not above

69

sense, and that they must reach toward the invisible through the visible.

Rephrasing her question, he answers that since their 'virtuous habits' are born of the soul, they 'Must with it evermore endure.' In Herbert's *De Veritate* (ed. Carré, p. 123) this argument rests upon this proposition: 'It is then reasonable to believe that the faculties with which we are born do not perish at death.' If sin's guilt never dies, the joy of virtuous love is still more certain of survival. Otherwise Heaven's laws would be vain, 'When to an everlasting Cause/They gave a perishing Effect.' Where God admits the fair, he does not exclude love; nor does he exclude sense if bodies rise again:

> *For if no use of sense remain*
> *When bodies once this life forsake,*
> *Or they could no delight partake,*
> *Why should they ever rise again?*

The final postulate here alters the statement in *De Veritate* (p. 124): 'When that which is corruptible in us is separated from what is incorruptible, which I hold to be the great unceasing work of nature, it is not the faculties which fall into decay, but the sense-organs.' And if love is the end of knowledge here in imperfection, how much more perfect will it be in perfection. Then his argument takes its final turn: 'Were not our souls immortal made,/Our equal loves can make them such.' Although this suggests the end of Donne's 'Good morrow', it turns toward propagation as a final answer to the question moved:

> *So when one wing can make no way,*
> *Two joyned can themselves dilate,*
> *So can two persons propagate,*
> *When singly either would decay.*

In this persuasive figure their relation to heaven is not forsaken as 'Each shall be both, yet both but one.' Indeed, her eyes 'Look up again to find their place':

The Convention of The Extasie

While such a moveless silent peace
Did seize on their becalmed sense,
One would have thought some influence
Their ravish'd spirits did possess.

Thus Herbert exhibits no such dislocation of the Platonic mode as we find in Wither. But it is not quite so simple as saying that since their love is of the soul and the soul is immortal, therefore their love is immortal. For body is involved in this awareness, and so it becomes the last resort in persuasion and fulfilment, because God is best known and loved in his creatures.

Herbert's argument, however, needs to be understood not simply as Platonism but in terms of his *De Veritate*. It may be judged by this summary of his remarks on love (pp. 196–8): 'Consequently, though our mind can become immersed in physical feelings while it concerns itself with the common good, yet I place love among the intellectual and spiritual faculties, because lust and similar cravings can be found in a plethoric body apart from love. . . . As for the objects of the intellectual and spiritual faculties, there are two kinds, namely, particular and general. In this respect they are also distinguished from the physical faculties, which seem only to have particular objects. The particular objects of the internal intellectual faculties are the divine attributes, while the common objects are physical objects. . . . Love was the first of the inner emotions. This faculty is above all sensitive to the divine beauty and goodness and afterwards to all the divine attributes. . . . The common object of this faculty is physical love. For this reason the feeling which relates to the perpetuation of the species, so long as it is not infected with unlawful lust or concupiscence, is humane and may spring from the faculty which seeks the general good.'

While the final statement in this summary gives another dimension to the conclusion of his *Ode*, the relation between the physical and intellectual in love explains the form which his answer takes in arguing 'that the faculties with which we are born do not perish at death'. Once this has been said, however, one must return to the poetic cogency of the *Ode* which may be illuminated but cannot be replaced by the structure of *De Veritate*. The ambiguity of the conclusion to the *Ode* appears more clearly by virtue of our comparison, but we have to take care not to lose the meaning of the physical because of its intellectual implication, or else we will transform the primary impact of the poem and blunt the surprise of its ending. For the conclusion seems both to consummate their love and to compromise his answer. But even the beauty of stanzas like

> *This said, in her up-lifted face,*
> *Her eyes which did that beauty crown,*
> *Were like two starrs, that having faln down,*
> *Look up again to find their place:*

may owe something to the idea in Plato's *Timaeus* that souls, before their human birth, were in the stars. And Herbert's final turn gives a rarefied air to the conclusion of 'The Extasie'.

Donne, like Herbert, is interested less in the moral casuistry of love than in the philosophical questions provoked by it. Hence the debate in 'The Extasie' may involve body and soul rather more than two lovers. Croll has said that 'In *Astrophel and Stella* and the *Arcadia* the prevailing idea is the contrast between the abstract spiritual ideals which appeal to the soul alone and the concrete forms on which ordinary human desire is fixed.' But he adds that the Platonic mode of thought is used by Sidney rather as a literary convention than as a serious philosophy. Obviously it is not a part of the convention of physical love introduced by Sidney's Eighth Song, which is more properly described as an invitation to love.

This convention may be restated for 'The Extasie' as follows: description of the burgeoning of nature; description of lovers and their emotions; their absorption in the rapture of love; their relationship to some problem arising from

The Convention of The Extasie

this state of rapture; its investigation and solution; relation of the solution to their initial rapture.

The pastoral setting of 'The Extasie' is reduced to the shortest and most carnally suggestive form yet found in this convention:

> *Where, like a pillow on a bed,*
> *A Pregnant banke swel'd up, to rest*
> *The violets reclining head,*
> *Sat we two, one anothers best.*

Hands and eyes as yet were 'all the meanes to make us one',

> *And pictures in our eyes to get*
> *Was all our propagation.*

In Sidney, it may be remembered, their eyes 'Enterchangeably reflected'. The last line sounds as if Donne were beginning where Herbert concluded, but it simply introduces the consummation of physical union toward which they seem bent. This consummation, however, remains uncertain because it must be decided by the souls, 'which to advance their state' had left the bodies, their prisons. Now they 'hung 'twixt her, and mee', preventing consummation until they have negotiated an agreement; meanwhile the bodies lie inanimate, like statues. Now this negotiation involves a discovery about the nature of their love, but it can be understood only by one refined enough by love to understand the language of the soul. Hence the character of the invoked witness and yet his inability to distinguish voices in a union of minds. For they discover that it was not sex but a mingling of souls that moved them to love. At this point it seems as if their original physical means to union have been completely invalidated. But a violet from the pastoral setting provides an analogy to show how transplanted souls also redouble in the abler soul of love.

> *Wee then, who are this new soule, know,*
> *Of what we are compos'd, and made,*
> *For, th' Atomies of which we grow,*
> *Are soules, whom no change can invade.*

73

And so their love acquires the superior powers that belong to the soul, and the negotiations would seem to have gone against the bodies, if it were not for the fact that the violet helped to elucidate the mystery of their love. Even so the shift to the voice of feeling takes us by surprise:

> *But O alas, so long, so farre*
> *Our bodies why doe wee forbeare?*

We might suppose that isolated superiority is too much for them, or that some 'defects of lonelinesse' are not controlled by their souls. But of course their ecstasy had a physical origin, and their negotiation requires some solution for the problem of the bodies.

In this argument the apology for body now begins. The bodies are not the souls, but their senses first brought the souls together. As sphere to intelligence, or as air to heaven, the body is the agent or medium of the soul. As blood ascends to spirits to unite body and soul, so even pure lovers' souls must descend to affections and faculties which sense may reach, or else the living soul is locked in a bodily prison, except in ecstasy.

> *To' our bodies turne wee then, that so*
> *Weake men on love reveal'd may looke;*
> *Loves mysteries in soules doe grow,*
> *But yet the body is his booke.*

Weak men require physical revelation, but initiates in love's mysteries, who do not, will see small change when their spiritual unity is manifested in the physical. Thus their original physical union may be consummated without spiritual adulteration, for the bodies are not 'drosse to us, but allay'. Thus the problem of the physical in love posed by the original situation has been solved by inclusion, not by rejection. Again the hypothetical listener—for the souls are still speaking—is called to witness the final turn of the argument.

Only the rejection of the physical would have saved 'The Extasie' from any suggestion of an invitation to love, but even its inclusion probably did not assure its success for Dryden because it still 'perplexes the minds of the fair sex with nice speculations of philosophy'. And this philosophical turn is given form by Croll's observation: 'In Donne's poem by a characteristic subtlety the dialogue is reduced to a monologue spoken by the undistinguished soul of the two lovers.' And the reason for this form is that there is no contrariety between the lovers but only in the subject of their discourse. Hence the monologue is instrumental to the philosophy, and Donne uses the ecstasy for this mingling of souls or rise to the Platonic level. He does not, like Bembo in Castiglione's *Courtier*, make a kiss the cause of this mingling of souls, though 'one alone so framed of them both ruleth (in a manner) two bodies' in his poem. But he did use the ecstasy as an expressive device in *Ignatius his Conclave*:

I was in an *Extasie*, and

My little wandring sportful Soule,
Ghest, and Companion of my body

had liberty to wander through all places . . .

Here of course it is a satiric device, not a Platonic device. In Donne's poem it becomes a means arising from the rapture of love by which to analyse that rapture in terms of the nature of man. In a subtler form this poem is a debate between the soul and body or an analysis of love in these terms without the sharp oppositions found in 'A Valediction: of the booke' or 'A Valediction: forbidding mourning'.

Thus into a convention of physical love Donne introduces the Platonic convention as a means to investigate the nature of love. Up to a point the steps in both conventions coincide, but the conclusion denies and harmonizes the extremes of both. The physical convention is clear from the beginning; the Platonic is introduced by the ecstasy. The former includes the latter and is modified by it. The sensual, idyllic convention, united with the Platonic, issues in a mediate or combined position; but while posing the carnal versus spiritual contention, the poem never surrenders the primacy of the spiritual, nor ever rejects or condemns the carnal like Wither.

Donne's poetry runs the gamut of love described by Bembo on the basis of his analysis of man in Castiglione's *Courtier*:

'And because in our soule there be three manner waies to know, namely, by sense, reason, and understanding: of sense there ariseth appetite or longing, which is common to us with brute beastes: of reason ariseth election or choice, which is proper to man: of understanding, by the which man may be partner with Angels, ariseth will.'

Donne is more likely to base his analysis on the three souls mentioned in 'A Valediction: of my name, in the window':

> *Then, as all my soules bee,*
> *Emparadis'd in you, (in whom alone*
> *I understand, and grow and see,) . . .*

Here the three souls are named by their major faculties in this order: rational, vegetable, animal or sensitive. But whichever scale is used, Donne treats the various kinds of love and lovers described by Bembo. On the sensual level it is bound by the limitations of the senses; on the Platonic level it is a relation of souls or mind, unaffected by the physical and its limitations of time and space. The problem of absence is usually solved on this level. But Donne is seldom a pure Platonist; he usually inhabits the region of 'The Extasie', occasionally ascending higher on the scale or descending lower. He even has moments of scorn for 'That loving wretch that sweares,/'Tis not the bodies marry, but the mindes,' but it never reaches the mockery of Cartwright's 'Tell me no more of minds embracing minds.' Nevertheless, Bembo's discussion in the *Courtier* is the best introduction to Donne's treatment of love.

The study of this convention gives us a concrete lesson in the kind of literary continuity and change that took place between Elizabethan and Jacobean times. It also provides us with some insight into the relations between tradition and

The Convention of The Extasie

the individual talent in these poets. Of course the poems are not equally representative of their poets; but since the broad form is dictated by the convention, their own formal powers, both poetic and metrical, can be measured comparatively within a limited area. If such a comparison is thought to be altogether unfair, perhaps we could agree that this convention does not provide easy examples by which to illustrate the decline of poetry in Jacobean times. And possibly also that the usual course of such conventions is towards decline rather than the reverse. I do not think Donne and Herbert need to fear the verdict, and I find Greville worthy of more serious interest than either Sidney or Wither.

IV

Textual Difficulties in Donne's Poetry

✭

Conceite: fetch me a couple of torches, sirha.
I may see the conceite: quickly! its very darke!
        —*Every Man in his Humour*, quarto 1601

Of the many great services which Sir Herbert Grierson has rendered the poetry of Donne, none is more important than his vindication of the 1633 text.[1] His labours with the manuscripts have given that text an authority which was not apparent to the earlier editors of Donne.[2] Where so much has been accomplished, little can be added; but where our understanding of Donne is mainly the work of Sir Herbert, any addition will bear its tribute. If I have anything to add, it is only in the direction of further vindi-

[1] *The Poems of John Donne*, ed. Herbert J. C. Grierson (2 vols.; Oxford, 1912). Hereafter referred to by volume and page. The later edition without commentary (1929, 1933) reproduces the 1912 text with a few corrections but none of the changes suggested here.

[2] More recent editions of Donne's poetry are the 'Nonesuch' and the 'Everyman': *Complete Poetry and Selected Prose*, ed. John Hayward (London, 1929); *The Poems of John Donne*, ed. Hugh I'A. Fausset (London, 1931). These editions differ from the Grierson text occasionally, but seldom by a return to 1633. The text which returns most completely to 1633 or 1635 is that found in *Poetry of the English Renaissance* 1509–1660, ed. J. W. Hebel and H. H. Hudson (New York, 1929). This is, of course, a selection.

cating the 1633 text, or occasionally the 1635 text, when the manuscripts disagree, and once or twice when they do not. Sometimes it amounts to no more than siding with Sir Herbert's better judgment against a seductive reading. My other concern in this essay will be to suggest the kinds of textual difficulty which confront the reader of Donne. These will be illustrated in the different ways in which Sir Herbert and I read the same passage in Donne; they will be involved in the defence of one text against another. Since none of the texts presumes to bear the warrant of Donne's authority, the validity of the readings themselves must be tested by internal evidence, and will have to await the suffrage of other readers who find Donne worth the trouble.

I

Sir Herbert Grierson resorts very infrequently to emendation, and then, I think, with not too happy results. We may begin with the most striking examples of outright emendation. Although 'outright' is hardly the word for Sir Herbert's practice, and can scarcely be reserved for the present instances, it may describe the extreme degree of textual liberty which he allows himself. This is to modify the grammatical function, or to change the part of speech, of a word or phrase, and so to alter the syntax of the poem.

His now famous emendation, 'bearing-like Asses', appears slight but introduces no slight shift in the meaning, and arises from what seem to him the syntactic requirements of the verse. He prints the passage in *Satyre II* thus;

> *Now like an owlelike watchman, hee must walke*
> *His hand still at a bill, now he must talke*
> *Idly, like prisoners, which whole months will sweare*
> *That onely suretiship hath brought them there,*
> *And to every suitor lye in every thing,*
> *Like a Kings favourite, yea like a King;*
> *Like a wedge in a blocke, wring to the barre,*
> *Bearing-like Asses; and more shamelesse farre*

Then carted whores, lye, to the grave Judge; for
Bastardy abounds not in Kings titles, nor
Symonie and Sodomy in Churchmens lives,
As these things do in him; by these he thrives

[ll. 65–76: I, 152].[1]

He departs from *1633* by raising the comma after 'Asses' to a semicolon and by putting a hyphen between 'Bearing' and 'like'; he considers 'asses' to be the object of 'wring'. Lastly, he offers this comment:

'The subject of the long sentence is "He" (l. 65), and the infinitives throughout are complements to "must": "He must walk . . . he must talk . . . [he must] lie . . . [he must] wring to the bar bearing-like asses; [he must], more shameless than carted whores, lie to the grave judge, &c." This is the only method in which I can construe the passage, and it carries with it the assumption that "bearing like" should be connected by a hyphen to form an adjective similar to "Relique-like", which is the MS. form of "Relique-ly" at l. 84 [II, 112].'

Except for the wholly unjustifiable assumption and the damage which it does, this statement is self-evident; and being self-evident, it disposes of the assumption. His paraphrase, like *1633*, sets up the presumption that 'wring' is like its parallel predications and therefore intransitive; the exception must be justified in face of both the paraphrase and the 1633 text. If 'bearing-like asses' are the 'patient Catholics', as Sir Herbert asserts, 'bearing-like' is still not 'an adjective similar to "Relique-like",' for 'bearing' *qua* 'patient' is already an adjective needing no 'owlelike' alteration. Now 'wring' had in Donne's time, according to the *OED*, the intransitive use of 'writhe' or 'labour', and 'bear' had the equally good intransitive use of 'press', to move with effort or persistence. Hence the emended passage can simply mean '[he must], like a wedge in a block, labour to the bar, pressing like asses', etc. Coscus, the lawyer, certainly has become a slave to his profession: like a wedge in

---

[1] Ll. 69–70 were censored and represented by dashes in 1633.

the block, he labours to the bar—an ambiguity instrumental both to his profession and to the driven wedge; perhaps he even 'rings' to the bar, for he 'wooes in language of the Pleas and Bench'. Pressing like asses (stupidly), he becomes the more deeply wedged, like the ass in its yoke; and far more shameless than carted whores, he must lie to the grave judge. Thus the earlier comparison to 'prisoners' is extended, and Coscus becomes shameless enough to lie like a lawyer. It should be apparent that Sir Herbert has introduced, without justification, a transitive 'wring' in a series of intransitives, thus perverting the meaning of what otherwise makes consistent sense in coherent structure. Not only the 1633 text but even Donne's syntax is against him.

Sir Herbert again resorts to emendation in order to solve a difficulty in *Farewell to love*. Here the text derives from *1635*, and again no manuscript offers an alternative reading. He prints the difficult stanza as follows:

> *Ah cannot wee,*
> *As well as Cocks and Lyons jocund be,*
> *After such pleasures? Unlesse wise*
> *Nature decreed (since each such Act, they say,*
> *Diminisheth the length of life a day)*
> *This, as shee would man should despise*
> *The sport;*
> *Because that other curse of being short,*
> *And onely for a minute made to be,*
> *(Eagers desire) to raise posterity* [I, 71].

The extent of his alteration may be discovered by a comparison with the crucial part of the stanza as it appeared in *1635*:

> *This; as shee would man should despise*
> *The sport,*
> *Because that other curse of being short,*
> *And onely for a minute made to be*
> *Eager, desires to raise posteritie.*

Sir Herbert justifies his emendation in the following manner:

Textual Difficulties in Donne's Poetry

'What has happened is, I believe, this: Donne here, as elsewhere, used an obsolescent word, viz. "eagers", the verb, meaning "sharpens". The copyist did not recognize the form, took "desire" for the verb, and made "eager" the adjectival complément to "be", changing "desire" to "desires" as predicate to "curse" [II, 52–3].'

Why both manuscript sources should also edit the poem in the same uniform way is a little puzzling, especially when Sir Herbert is as much put out by the alteration as the copyist was by 'eagers'. I suggest that the copyist took what he saw, that his so-called changes give the meaning which Donne intended. 'What Donne had in mind,' continues Sir Herbert, 'was the Aristotelian doctrine that the desire to beget children is an expression of man's craving for immortality'; and he concludes:

'Donne's argument then is this: "Why of all animals have we alone this feeling of depression and remorse after the act of love? Is it a device of nature to restrain us from an act which shortens the life of the individual (he refers here to a prevalent belief as to the deleterious effect of the act of love), needed because that other curse which Adam brought upon man, the curse of mortality,

> of being short,
> And only for a minute made to be,
> Eagers [i.e. whets or provokes] desire to raise
> posterity" [II, 53].'

Presumably, if the poem is any guide, what Donne had in mind is the act of love with the two limitations discovered in the second stanza. Experience has revealed two facts about the act of love: that desire is short, and that it 'leaves behinde a kind of sorrowing dulnesse'. It is the latter fact that separates man from the animals and calls for an explanation. The only answer seems to be that nature decreed it to restrain man from an act which is said to shorten life; but it is necessary (and here we desert Sir Herbert for the copyist) because of the other limitation of love, i.e., brevity:

Textual Difficulties in Donne's Poetry

> Because that other curse of being short,
> And onely for a minute made to be
> Eager, desires to raise posteritie [i.e., to increase
> and multiply].

For only by multiplying itself, only by repetition, can the curse of shortness and momentary ardour escape its limitation. Nature decreed the dulness, as if she would that man should despise the sport (in consequence of its ensuing dulness); but she decreed it because brevity was an insufficient check, proved to be anything but a restraint. By cutting off the complement to 'be', Sir Herbert impairs not only the syntactic movement but also the rhythmical flow of the lines, and merely to avoid regarding ' "desires" as predicate to "curse" '. Even as emended, if the curse is referred to its proper object, brevity still 'eagers' desire to multiply its moments. Aristotelian doctrine and Adam's curse are fetched into the poem to account for 'posterity'; but it is to be feared that 'the desire to beget children', especially as 'an expression of man's craving for immortality', has little to do withDonne's cynical farewell to love. Nature has arranged an argument of its futility that is more convincing than Aristotle.[1]

Our last example has illustrated incidentally the alteration of thought by the revision of punctuation. To this we may add the change which Sir Herbert effects by the insertion of an apparently innocent comma. It may be observed in general that Sir Herbert is on safer ground when he raises the power of punctuation than when he lowers it; when he raises a comma to a semicolon than when he lowers a semicolon to a comma. By the former practice he may clarify seventeenth-century punctuation for the modern reader, but by the latter he may seriously distort the relations of thought, and structure, in the verse. The insertion of punctuation where none was before is a wholly different matter; sometimes helpful, sometimes harmful. The last stanza of *The Primrose* offers a case in point:

[1] For a fuller discussion see 'Donne's "Farewell to love" ', *Modern Philology*, XXXVI (1939), 301–3.

Live Primrose then, and thrive
With thy true number five;
And women, whom this flower doth represent,
With this mysterious number be content;
Ten is the farthest number; if halfe ten
   Belonge unto each woman, then
   Each woman may take halfe us men;
Or if this will not serve their turne, Since all
Numbers are odde, or even, and they fall
First into this, five, women may take us all [I, 61-2].

In the last line the comma after 'this' is Sir Herbert's addition to *1633*—an addition which he explains in this note:

'I have introduced a comma after "this" to show what, I think, must be the relation of the words. The later editions drop "this", and it seems to me probable that an original reading and a correction have survived side by side. Donne may have written "this" alone, referring back to "five", and then, thinking the reference too remote, he may have substituted "five" in the margin, whence it crept into the text without completely displacing "this". The support which the MSS. lend to *1633* make it dangerous to remove either word now, but I have thought it well to show that "this" *is* "five" ' [II, 49].

The stanza itself suggests a much simpler explanation why we find 'this five' in *1633*, and why Donne should have written it. Donne's mathematical analogy becomes a little shaky when he comes to make his final point: neither 'this' nor 'five' alone will make sure that 'odde' and 'even' fall first into woman's five and not into man's, since Donne's equation has already allotted five to each. When he decides to make the last devastating point that even a mere woman may turn out to be more than a woman, and so become too 'inclusive' in her relation to man, he sees that his final turn on five can be used against man as well as against woman, and so he covers the analogical weakness by specifying 'this five', woman's true number. While Sir Herbert may think 'it well to show that "this" *is* "five" ', Donne, if I am not

84

mistaken, thought it well to show that this is the five he has attributed to woman. Even if no question of sense were involved, this comma introduces a hobble into the verse quite unworthy of Sir Herbert's ear for the 'rhetorically effective position of the stresses' in Donne; and no one knows better how rhetoric and rhythm in Donne depend upon right pointing. But Sir Herbert inclines to rather too much punctuation.

   Still another kind of perversion of meaning is that of misinterpretation provoked by the difficulty of the original text; this is a kind of emendation by interpretation. An example is Sir Herbert's classification of *Aire and Angels* as a love poem 'touched with cynical humour at the close'.[1] In a seminar at the University of Chicago he expanded this view in his interpretation of the poem. For the sake of contrast, we may observe that in this same classification of Donne's 'songs and sonets' *The Primrose* appears as 'Petrarchian'. Let us look at the stanza which is touched with cynical humour:

> *Whilst thus to ballast love, I thought,*
> *And so more steddily to have gone,*
> *With wares which would sinke admiration,*
> *I saw, I had loves pinnace overfraught,*
> *   Ev'ry thy haire for love to worke upon*
> *Is much too much, some fitter must be sought;*
> *   For, nor in nothing, nor in things*
> *Extreme, and scatt'ring bright, can love inhere;*
> *   Then as an Angell, face, and wings*
> *Of aire, not pure as it, yet pure doth weare,*
> *   So thy love may be my loves spheare;*
> *   Just such disparitie*
> *   As is twixt Aire and Angells puritie,*
> *'Twixt womens love, and mens will ever bee* [I, 22].

The so-called 'cynical humour' is, of course, in the last three lines and depends upon equating man with the angel in the preceding comparison. But is such an equation correct? Most readers feel that some violence is done to the poem by

[1] II, 9.

such a conclusion, but usually explain it by saying that such twists are characteristic of Donne. Before buckling down to the crucial passage, let us recall some necessary facts from the first stanza. The title and first line of the poem give us two relationships: one between angels and man; the other between man and woman. Sir Herbert gives us the relevant information about air—'the nature of the body assumed by Angels when they appear to men'.[1] Observe that 'air' is significant when angels *appear* to men, and hence the relationship suggested by the title. Now it is obvious that, since man is the common term in these two relationships, Donne has two opportunities or alternatives: he can show that angel and woman are alike in their relation to man, or that they are unlike. Thus in the beginning of the poem the lady is like a disembodied angel in her effect on the lover. Accordingly the man's love is Platonic, the child of his soul; but, like its parent, must have a body if it is to act. Therefore, his love 'assumes' the body of the lady ('assume' is Donne's word). This is the situation at the opening of the stanza which I have quoted.

Now the embodiment of his love has not ballasted it, but rather overweighted it, although with wonderful wares; even a single hair proves too much for love to work upon; hence some fitter embodiment must be sought. Observe that Donne manages to flatter the lady and at the same time convey the impression that even her body is too material for his love. This is done with wonderful skill by attenuating her physical aspects, so that when he states his dilemma the alternatives approach one another in their brilliant diffusion:

> *For, nor in nothing, nor in things*
> *Extreme, and scatt'ring bright, can love inhere;*

the 'nothing' being the 'lovely glorious nothing' of the lady before embodiment. There may be a way out of this dilemma if he can find something in which love can 'inhere' rather than something it may 'assume' temporarily; obviously, this fitter object must be neither pure spirit nor pure

[1] II, 21.

body. Whether by chance or not, the rhymes to 'inhere' carry us to the answer: love can inhere in love. But this is the crux of the poem. The difficulty arises because the same line, 'So thy love may be my loves spheare,' gives the conclusion both to the problem of the proper embodiment of love and to the way in which the lady may become that embodiment. Otherwise the analogy to the angel is a straight proportion: as an angel is to a body of air so thy love is to the body of my love; in becoming corporeal each remains pure, but not so pure as its essence. Or the analogy may be put in this fashion: as an angel may become a body of air so thy love may become the body of my love; what is true of the angel is true of thy love. Both 'bodies' are significant in relation to man; each body is necessary if an angel or her love is to 'appear' to man. Thus the cynical humour at the close disappears, for Donne merely generalizes the disparity between air and angel's purity into the difference between the love of man and the love of woman; it is a difference in corporeality, but it does not favour man. Thus women and angels are alike in having to put on corporeality in their relations with men. It is a Platonic love poem with the same essential philosophy that is found in *The Extasie*.

II

After these examples of difficulties which may defeat the best intentions, let us look at the *Songs and Sonets* in Sir Herbert's text for other departures from *1633* that materially affect the meaning.

The third stanza of *The Canonization* presents a difficulty which begins with the punctuation:

> *Call us what you will, wee are made such by love;*
> *Call her one, mee another flye,*
> *We'are Tapers too, and at our owne cost die,*
> *And wee in us finde the'Eagle and the Dove.*
> *The Phœnix ridle hath more wit*
> *By us, we two being one, are it.*
> *So to one neutrall thing both sexes fit,*

Wee dye and rise the same, and prove
Mysterious by this love [I, 15].

In *1633* 'Dove' has a comma instead of a period; 'So' is followed by a comma, and 'fit' by a period. For his punctuation of the latter line Sir Herbert cites manuscripts, but declares that he 'adopted it independently as required by the sense'.[1] Here is his justification: 'To me it seems the line *must* go with what follows, and that "so" (which should have no comma) is not an illative conjunction but a subordinate conjunction of effect. "Both sexes fit *so* entirely into one neutral thing that we die and rise the same," &c.' He is arguing against editors who connect the line with what has gone before, but he is equally unable to permit the line to stand alone as in *1633*. The structure of the stanza is suggested in the first line: for every word against the lovers, love provides an answer. 'So call us flies, we are tapers too; if you say that we will get burnt, we answer that we are self-consumed.' In the association of ideas, by way of response, the fly becomes the eagle, dove, and phoenix; the taper dying at its own cost unites with the phoenix; both fly and taper reach an apotheosis in the phoenix. Even this apotheosis acquires more wit by association with the lovers, and that addition to the phoenix riddle is the crux of the stanza. But Sir Herbert's way of construing the lines does not release the wit; the old punctuation is a better guide:

> *So, to one neutrall thing both sexes fit.*
> *Wee dye and rise the same, and prove*
> *Mysterious by this love.*

The first line is parallel to, 'Call us what you will'; the others to 'wee are made such by love', for they constitute the response. 'So, fit both sexes to one neutral thing (the phoenix); yet we are still like the Phoenix.' They die and rise the same, and prove mysterious by this love because they add both sexes to the riddle of the phoenix. Thus the

---

[1] II, 15.

implications of 'two being one' are developed into a wit which surpasses that of the phoenix: the neutrality of the lovers is undisturbed by duality of sex, and hence the mystery of their love. If 'both sexes fit *so* entirely into one neutral thing', it is because they must if two lovers are to repeat the phoenix riddle. Although Sir Herbert forces the sense less than the syntax of Donne, the 1633 text provides a surer guide to both. The full stop after 'fit' suggests, in the general structure of the stanza, a new challenge, which may upset the latest boast of love; but the separated answer sustains the boast. Sir Herbert's comma confuses this structure and relates the challenge so closely to its response that he fails to perceive the real syntax of the verse.

The third stanza of *A Valediction: of the booke* presents a similar problem. Sir Herbert prints it as follows:

> *This Booke, as long-liv'd as the elements,*
> *Or as the worlds forme, this all-graved tome*
> *In cypher writ, or new made Idiome,*
> *Wee for loves clergie only'are instruments:*
> *When this booke is made thus,*
> *Should againe the ravenous*
> *Vandals and Goths inundate us,*
> *Learning were safe; in this our Universe*
> *Schooles might learne Sciences, Spheares Musick,*
> *Angels Verse* [I, 30].

In *1633* 'Idiome' has a semicolon, and 'instruments' a comma. Sir Herbert justifies his alteration in this note:

'I take the first three lines of the stanza to form an absolute clause: "This book once written, in cipher or new-made idiom, we are thereby (in these letters) the only instruments for Loves clergy—their Missal and Breviary." I presume this is how it is understood by Chambers and the Grolier Club editor, who place a semicolon at the end of each line' [II, 27].

But the Grolier Club editor follows *1633* by placing a comma at the end of the preceding stanza, where Sir Herbert places a period. The last two lines of that stanza,

> *That sees, how Love this grace to us affords,*
> *To make, to keep, to use, to be these his Records,*

show clearly that the first three lines of this stanza are another complement to 'be' or an appositional development of 'these his Records'. *Loves exchange* exhibits a similar relation between stanzas 4 and 5, even though separated by a full stop. If Sir Herbert had not changed the punctuation of *1633*, he would have been obliged to avoid the crabbed construction that he discovers and defends. In *1633* line 4 of this stanza not only sums up the thought begun in stanza 2 but prepares the way for the ensuing development. If we compare the punctuation of Sir Herbert and the Grolier Club editor in the crucial third and fourth lines, we may well believe that it is more dangerous to lower than to raise the power of punctuation in Donne.

This stanza as printed by Sir Herbert shows still another variant from 1633. In that text line 7 reads,

> *Vandals and the Goths invade us,*

but Sir Herbert prefers the line which he draws from the manuscripts. He believes the 1633 editor mistook a contracted 'inundate' for 'invade'; he cites the sermons, 'The Torrents, and Inundations, which invasive Armies pour upon Nations', as support for the metaphor of inundation.[1] But this citation also gives us 'invade'. No doubt Donne liked his 'inundations', but which metaphor best fits the context?

> *When this booke is made thus,*
> *Should againe the ravenous*
> *Vandals and the Goths invade us,*
> *Learning were safe;*

but why? Surely not because it was contained in one volume, but because 'this booke is made thus'—'in cypher writ, or new made Idiome'. Can this line be pointless here? Only pointed when we come to, 'Here Statesmen, (or of them,

[1] II, 28.

they which can reade)'? No, learning is safe because, even if
the plundering Vandals and Goths should 'invade' us, they
would not be able to read us. To say 'inundate' (overflow)
us is surely to spoil the point: this book is for the initiate.
Sir Herbert's line has the advantage in metrical regularity,
but it is inferior to *1633* not only in sense but in the rhetorically effective distribution of stresses. It seems to me that the
1633 editor did not mistake what he saw.

Nor is this all that concerns us in this poem. In the sixth
stanza Sir Herbert has preferred another reading from the
manuscripts and the editions *1635–54*. It may be sufficient
to quote merely the lines directly involved:

> *In this thy booke, such will their nothing see,*
> *As in the Bible some can finde out Alchimy.*

1633 and *1669* read 'such will there something see'; but Sir
Herbert defends his adoption of the 1635 reading:
'I do so because (1) the MSS. support it. Their uncertainty as to "their" and "there" is of no importance; (2)
"there" is a weak repetition of "in this thy book", an em-
phatic enough indication of place; (3) "their nothing" is
both the more difficult reading and the more characteristic
of Donne. The art of a statesman is a "nothing" ' [II, 29].
It is apparent that the manuscripts also display the weak
repetition 'there'. Sir Herbert's third reason, however,
seems to me most odd. Surely statesmen, whose art (he reminds us) is the art of 'bluffing', will not 'their nothing see
as in the Bible some can find out alchemy'. Statesmen who,
having lost their 'bluff', could see their 'nothing' would be
well-nigh saved. I am afraid that statesmen, if they remain
in character, 'will there something see, as in the Bible some
can find out alchemy' (which is not there). This book, we
may recall, is for the initiate; and no one who could find
'alchemy' in the Bible would admit that he found 'nothing'.
I agree with Sir Herbert that 'their nothing' is the more
difficult reading, but not that it is the subtler; it is more
difficult because it is supported by a simile which, in that
context, is nonsense. Beyond this, it is the 'lie direct' rather

than the 'lie with circumstance', and it is not characteristic of Donne to prefer the obtuse way.

In *A nocturnall upon S. Lucies day* the 1633 text offered Sir Herbert an opportunity which he denied himself, only to join all modern editors in blurring the development of the second stanza. This is how he prints it:

> *Study me then, you who shall lovers bee*
> *At the next world, that is, at the next Spring:*
> > *For I am every dead thing,*
> > *In whom love wrought new Alchimie.*
> > > *For his art did expresse*
> *A quintessence even from nothingnesse,*
> *From dull privations, and leane emptinesse:*
> *He ruin'd mee, and I am re-begot*
> *Of absence, darknesse, death; things which are not* [I, 44].

1633 gives no punctuation after 'emptinesse'; but let us hear Sir Herbert:

'I have after considerable hesitation adopted the punctuation of *1719*, which is followed by all the modern editors. This makes "dull privations" and "lean emptinesse" expansions of "nothingnesse". This is the simpler construction. I am not sure, however, that the punctuation of the earlier editions and of the MSS. may not be correct. In that case "From dull privations" goes with "he ruined me" [II, 38].'

Here we want to interrupt Sir Herbert to ask why he of all people should prefer *1719* before both *1633* and the manuscripts. His explanation is interesting:

'Milton speaks of "ruining from Heaven". "From me, who was nothing," says Donne, "Love extracted the very quintessence of nothingness—made me more nothing than I already was. My state was already one of 'dull privation' and 'lean emptiness', and Love reduced it still further, making me once more the non-entity I was before I was created." Only Donne could be guilty of such refined and extravagant subtlety. But probably this is to refine too much. There is no example of "ruining" as an active verb used in this fashion.'

Here is the real rub for Sir Herbert, and what an awkward reason! Perhaps he means there is no example of 'ruin' as an intransitive verb used in this fashion, for his example from Milton is unusual because intransitive. But Donne's use of ruin is transitive: 'from one state he reduced me to another (ruins)'. The 'new Alchimie' by which Love extracted a quintessence even from nothingness is described in the last three lines: 'From a state of deprivation and want in love he reduced me to ruins (the remains of a less negative state), and I am re-begot of the very essentials of negation or nothingness.' He is made a quintessence of his former state, for negation is the essence of want.

As for the subtlety, Sir Herbert has the last ounce in 'a quintessence even from nothingnesse', whether he chooses to let the verse reveal the process of its extraction or not. The 1633 punctuation simply makes clear the passage from nothingness to its quintessence, which *1719* obscures. That Sir Herbert keeps all the subtlety, though not the syntax, is clear from the way in which he continues his note:

'In the next verse Donne pushes the annihilation further. Made nothing by Love, by the death of her he loves he is made the elixir (i.e. the quintessence) not now of ordinary nothing, but of "the first nothing", the nothing which preceded God's first act of creation. The poem turns upon the thought of degrees in nothingness.'

This is the heart of the matter, but it would be more helpful if Sir Herbert did not blur one degree that he cannot ignore: the 'reduction' to a quintessence of 'ordinary nothing'. To ignore the development of the alchemical figure in this stanza is to neglect its recapitulation in the next:

> *I, by loves limbecke, am the grave*
> *Of all, that's nothing.*

If, in this instance, we side with Sir Herbert's better judgment, we may save an admirable poem from an undeserved inconsequence.

The Prohibition both in *1633* and in *1635*, reflects the chaotic state of this poem in the manuscripts. For his own

text Sir Herbert has combined *1633* and *1635* with one
variant from the manuscripts. Until the final stanza there is
only one important difference, which I will give:

> *By being to mee then that which thou wast; 1633*
> *By being to thee then what to me thou wast, 1635*
> *By being to mee then what to me thou wast, MSS.* B, P [I, 67].

To which may be added the fact that this line is omitted in
the two important groups of manuscripts. Even more
singular is the fact that any one of these variants makes the
same sense in the first stanza: 'by being thrifty as you were
thrifty'. No doubt the sharper antithesis of *1635* makes it
the preferred reading.

But in the last stanza the difficulties mount, and Sir
Herbert becomes more eclectic.

> *Yet, love and hate mee too,*
> *So, these extreames shall neithers office doe;*
> *Love mee, that I may die the gentler way;*
> *Hate mee, because thy love is too great for mee;*
> *Or let these two, themselves, not me decay;*
> *So shall I, live, thy Stage, not triumph bee;*
> *Lest thou thy love and hate and mee undoe,*
> To let mee live, O love and hate mee too [I, 67–8].

This pointed conclusion is supplied only by *1633* and MS
B. But Sir Herbert argues that 'the *1633* editor was somewhat at sea about this poem' because of the variant in the
first stanza and because in the last stanza some copies have
'my' instead of 'thy' in line 4, and 'of' instead of 'Oh' in the
last line. Certainly it is just as easy to argue that the latter
instances are 'corrections' and show the alertness of the
editor 'while the edition was printing'.[1] In line 2 'neithers'
comes from the manuscripts; *1633* has 'ne'r their'. Sir Herbert argues that 'neithers' is the original and more characteristic reading: 'These extremes shall by counteracting each
other prevent either from fulfilling his function.' But it
may be argued that 'ne'r their' is the more unusual and

[1] II, 51.

pointed reading, since these extremes, unlike most extremes, have the same function. Either love or hate alone
means death; but if combined they will prevent one another, and so 'ne'r their office doe'. While the meaning is
not changed, 'their' points the novelty of these extremes—
identical ends.

Where Sir Herbert may be said actually to err is in the
line,

So shall I live thy stay, not triumph bee;

as it appears in *1633*. Sir Herbert remarks: 'I have placed a
comma after I to make quite clear that "live" is the adjective,
not the verb.' Such indulgence is almost a weakness in Sir
Herbert, for he again confuses Donne's syntax. Donne's
comma points the antithesis; his syntax cannot be mistaken
if the reader will pause after 'live' or put a comma between
the two predicates. It is perversion to turn 'live' into an
adjective. 'Stage' comes from *1635* and a majority of the
manuscripts. Sir Herbert admits that 'stay' is defensible, but
concludes: 'All the MSS. I have consulted support "stage";
and this gives the best meaning: "Alive, I shall continue to
be the stage on which your victories are daily set forth;
dead, I shall be but your triumph, a thing achieved once,
never to be repeated" ' (II, 51). Now the prohibition of her
love in the first stanza is for this reason: 'least thy love, by
my death, frustrate bee'; and the prohibition of her hate in
the second for this: 'least my being nothing lessen thee'. In
other words, his death by her love will mean frustration for
her love, and his death by her hate will lessen her (deprive
her of 'the stile of conquerour'). The effect of his death will
be either frustration or diminishment for her; as the cause of
his death, she will be entitled to the triumph. But if she is
willing to forego the triumph, he will be the 'stay' or support of both her love and her prestige. She can forego the
momentary triumph either of love or of hate, and he can
become her stay in both, if she will both love and hate him.
To lose her triumph is to have her cake and eat it too. Thus
'stay' seems to me not only defensible but actually more

convincing in the argument of the poem. Altogether *1633* offers a text of *The Prohibition* in some respects superior to that printed by Sir Herbert.

III

We may now concern ourselves with instances in the *Songs and Sonets* of departures from *1633* which have smaller, though not inconsiderable, effects. Here my defence of *1633* may seem more debatable or less consequential.

The first example will appear most unhappy, for it concerns the substitution of 'groane' for 'grow' in *Twicknam garden*. The garden in its glory seems to mock the lover:

> *But that I may not this disgrace*
> *Indure, nor yet leave loving, Love let mee*
> *Some senslesse peece of this place bee;*
> *Make me a mandrake, so I may groane here,*
> *Or a stone fountaine weeping out my yeare* [I, 29].

1633 has 'grow', and the manuscripts are divided between the two readings. In justification of 'groane' Sir Herbert remarks: 'It is surely much more in Donne's style than the colourless and pointless "growe". It is, too, in closer touch with the next line' (II, 26). For Sir Herbert the chief difficulty is that mandrakes shriek or howl rather than groan. Now Donne himself teaches us to prefer colour and to have regard for point. And, no doubt, 'groane' is in closer touch with 'weeping'; but does it have no earlier obligation? What of becoming a 'senseless piece' so as not to be mocked by the garden? Moreover, 'senseless', 'mandrake', and 'grow' have almost inevitable associations: they represent the 'vegetal' soul, the soul of growth, which is below the 'sensible' soul and without sense or movement.[1] Hence an

---

[1] Though not 'a catch that will draw three souls out of one weaver', *A Valediction: of my name, in the window* has the three souls (which I italicize):

> 'Then, as all my soules bee,
> Emparadis'd in you, (in whom alone
> I *understand*, and *grow* and *see*,) . . .' (I, 26.)

admirable way of evading the mockery of the garden and yet of remaining faithful to love would be to become a mandrake (not quite insensible) so that he might 'grow' but not be 'sensitive' in her garden. Just such a 'vegetal' soul is found in stanza 16 of Donne's satirical *Progresse of the Soule*: 'this living buried man, this quiet mandrake'. Sir Herbert's own reference to the *Elegie upon . . . Prince Henry* presents the mandrake as symbolic not so much of 'a life of groans' as of a life of misery that would sink into the grave:

> *Therefore we live; though such a life wee have,*
> *As but so many mandrakes on his grave.*

It is at this very low ebb that the lover must live if he is to solve his problem. To become a stone fountain is to pass from the animate to the inanimate, or to complete immunity to 'sense'; by 'weeping' the stone fountain remains faithful to love. In *A nocturnall* (stanza 4) a similar descent in the scale of being terminates in the passage from plant, which has the lowest (vegetal) soul, to stone, which has no soul; yet both 'detest and love', repel and attract. It should be clear that 'grow' is far from pointless, that it is only superficially colourless, and that its relation to its context is much richer than 'groane', which is more obviously included in 'mandrake'.

Loves growth contains a passage in which Donne lies somewhat at the mercy of Sir Herbert, assisted by punctuation. It is found in the opening of the last stanza (next the last in the later edition):

> *And yet no greater, but more eminent,*
> > *Love by the spring is growne;*
> > *As, in the firmament,*
> *Starres by the Sunne are not inlarg'd, but showne.*
> *Gentle love deeds, as blossomes on a bough,*
> *From loves awakened root do bud out now* [I, 33–4].

The period after 'showne' derives from Sir Herbert; *1633* has a comma. He quotes the passage (except the first two lines) in his note, and then comments:

'P reads here:

> *As in the firmament*
> *Starres by the sunne are not enlarg'd but showne*
> *Greater; Loves deeds, &c.*

This certainly makes the verse clearer. As it stands l. 18 is rather an enigma. The stars are not revealed by the sun, but hidden. . . . But *P's* emendation shows what Donne meant. By "showne" he does not mean "revealed"—an adjectival predicate "larger" or "greater" must be supplied from the verb "enlarg'd". "The stars at sunrise are not really made larger, but they are made to seem larger." It is a characteristically elliptical and careless wording of a characteristically acute and vivid image' [II, 31].

Having altered Donne's poetic syntax, Sir Herbert tries to save his powers of observation. Actually he spoils one of Donne's prettiest efforts. If the 1633 comma after 'showne' is retained, the so-called enigmatic line is caught up in Donne's comparison: 'As, in the firmament, Starres . . . (so) Gentle love deeds', etc. And we find that not only stars but gentle love deeds and buds 'are not inlarg'd, but showne' by the spring sun. For 'showne' nothing need be supplied, even with Sir Herbert's punctuation, but one of the preceding lines which he omits in his note: 'And yet no greater, but more eminent.' If one feels inclined to quibble that buds are enlarged rather than shown as blossoms, one must admit that it is very pretty, particularly when 'gentle love deeds' carry the 'stars' over to the 'bough'.

Loves Alchymie offers an interesting study in the nuances of punctuation. This is the conclusion and point of the poem:

> *Hope not for minde in women; at their best*
> *Sweetnesse and wit, they'are but* Mummy, *possest* [I, 40].

This punctuation Sir Herbert draws from the manuscripts because he finds (II, 36) the punctuation of *1633* ambiguous. Here is *1633*:

> *Hope not for minde in women; at their best,*
> *Sweetnesse, and wit they'are, but, Mummy, possest.*

Textual Difficulties in Donne's Poetry

The ambiguity I fail to see, since 'they are' controls both members, and it is normal to make the second member rather than the first elliptical. Observe the nice distribution of parts: 'at their best, sweetness and wit they are, but they are mummy, (when) possest.' The punctuation of *1633* seems to be concerned with phrasing; it makes a suave, even undulant, approach to a quick, sharp point. Sir Herbert's punctuation throws more weight on the 'mummy', making the sweetness and wit a grudging admission; the surprise of antithesis is obscured. In *1633* 'but' is adversative, marking a turn; in Sir Herbert's text it is a blunt 'only'. The fact which favours Sir Herbert's disposition of the line is not ambiguity but the elision or speeding-up in 'they'are', which makes it harder for the caesura to fall after 'they'are'. But the change does alter the rhythm.

Among the alterations which Sir Herbert makes in the 1633 text of *The Extasie*, the most important occur in this passage:

> *But O alas, so long, so farre*
>   *Our bodies why doe wee forbeare?*
> *They are ours, though they are not wee, Wee are*
>   *The intelligences, they the spheare.*
> *We owe them thankes, because they thus,*
>   *Did us, to us, at first convay,*
> *Yeelded their forces, sense, to us,*
>   *Nor are drosse to us, but allay.*
> *On man heavens influence workes not so,*
>   *But that it first imprints the ayre,*
> *Soe soule into the soule may flow,*
>   *Though it to body first repaire* [I, 53].

1633 reads in the third line, 'though not wee'; in the fourth, 'spheares'; in the seventh, 'senses force'; and in the eleventh, 'For' instead of 'Soe'. The manuscripts appear to be massed solidly against the first three readings. In this passage Sir Edmund Chambers follows *1633*; subsequent editors have generally followed Sir Herbert except for 'spheare'. The first variant is primarily metrical, and my preference is

1633; the second is a question of rhyme versus sense. Sir Herbert admits that Donne is capable of making a singular rhyme with a plural, but defends 'spheare' on the ground of sense: 'The bodies made one are the Sphere in which the two Intelligences meet and command.'[1] But the poem has been engaged in discovering that the two Intelligences are made one in love. While 'spheare' may suit all that follows in Sir Herbert's eyes, it has not done so for most later editors. Obviously, the poem proceeds to justify bodies as the instruments of souls; otherwise, the soul must lie in prison, except when released by 'ecstasy' or death. Only at the end of the poem is 'this dialogue of one' to be seen on a lower level, 'when we'are to bodies gone'; and *one*, moreover, 'because both meant, both spake the same'.

For the last two readings Sir Herbert feels that he has introduced 'two rather vital emendations'. The 'forces, sense', he thinks, is the original reading, which was emended in *1633*. It is 'right' in the poem for this reason: 'It is more characteristic of Donne's thought. He is, with his usual scholastic precision, distinguishing the functions of soul and body' (II, 43). Perception is the function of soul, and 'sense' of body. 'The bodies must yield their forces or faculties ("sense" in all its forms, especially sight and touch—hands and eyes) to us before our souls can become one. The collective term "sense" recurs.' Precisely, and because the collective term 'sense' recurs, it may well epitomize 'body' here as elsewhere in Donne—'paining soule, or sense'—and, as Sir Herbert suggests, the body enabled the soul to act, being no less essential because 'Love sometimes would contemplate, sometimes do.'[2] Now in the poem and in the reading 'their senses force' it is this enabling power of the bodies that is stressed. Sir Herbert distinguishes without establishing any real difference; the bodies may contribute 'their senses force' or 'their forces, sense', without impairing Donne's scholastic precision as to their function. Sir Herbert, rather than Donne, seems to have a weakness for appositives, since he has sometimes placed them where Donne did not. 'Senses force' is

---

[1] II, 43.   [2] *Loves growth*, I. 33.

not only more characteristic of Donne's syntax, but it distributes the emphasis a little more sharply on the important element in the context. There is even more manuscript support for 'spheare' than for 'forces, sense'.

In the last reading Sir Herbert is anxious to acquit Donne of unorthodoxy. Where the older view did not distinguish between body and soul in the influence of the heavenly bodies upon man, the later Thomistic view did. Aquinas distinguishes: as bodies, the stars affect man only indirectly and mediately; as intelligences, the stars operate on man directly and immediately. And Sir Herbert concludes:

'Now if "Soe" be the right reading here then Donne is thinking of the heavenly bodies without distinguishing in them between soul or intelligence and body. "As these high bodies or beings operate on man's soul through the comparatively low intermediary of air, so lovers' souls must interact through the medium of body" ' [II, 45].

Here we may interrupt to observe that the insertion of 'must' on one side of the equation and not on the other may save Donne's orthodoxy, but ought, one would presume, to weaken his argument. Sir Herbert continues:

'If "For" be the right reading, then Donne is giving as an example of soul operating on soul through the medium of body the influence of the heavenly intelligences on our souls. But this is not the orthodox view of their interaction. I feel sure that "Soe" is the right reading.'

One may answer that it is a most useful view for the purposes of the poet, who is not always so scrupulous as to sacrifice argument to orthodoxy. But what is the argument of the poem in this passage?

> *On man heavens influence works not so,*
> *But that it first imprints the ayre,*
> *For soule into the soule may flow,*
> *Though it to body first repaire.*

Donne has argued that the souls were first conveyed to one another by the power of the senses which the bodies provided; because of the bodies they are in communication.

Now he says that on man heaven's influence does not work thus, except that (only) it first imprints the air, makes use of physical conveyance. If he means 'without that it first imprints the air', he still makes 'air' the basis of analogy between them; there is no reciprocal use of 'sense'. But air itself had a part in the lovers' communication. When Burton discusses the 'sensible soul' (here 'sense'), he makes clear that the senses require three things: 'the *object*, the *organ*, and the *medium*'.[1] For the senses of 'commodity'—hearing, sight, and smell—the medium is air. Hence, when Donne distinguishes the operation of the heavens on man from the operation of their souls on one another, his exception provides a real analogy between them. And the exception allows him to relate things which are really in higher and lower orders. Now he can assert a genuinely argumentative 'for': 'For (as the heavens show) soul may flow into soul, even though it first resort to a physical medium.' This restores the emphasis on soul but retains the physical medium, associating it with air, the angelic body.

At the beginning of the poem sight and touch are the means to make the lovers one. Now the medium of sight has been employed in the argument from 'air'. But the 'medium' of touch is most closely associated with body; as Burton puts it, 'This sense is exquisite in men, and by his nerves dispersed all over the body, perceives any tactile quality.'[2] In arguing for a return from 'extasie', the poem advances by degrees of increasing corporeality: from 'air' to 'animall spirits' to 'sense' to 'body'. By distinguishing the heavens' influence from the lovers' influence, Donne is able to find a likeness in difference which seems to universalize his argument for body. By saying 'for' Donne assures the lady that body does not, or need not, interrupt the communion of souls. Sir Herbert believes that Donne meant to say, 'so lovers' souls must interact through the medium of the body'; but he bolsters 'soe' by altering 'may' to 'must'.

The Funerall concludes with the request of love's martyr

[1] *Anatomy of Melancholy*, I, i, 2, 6.
[2] Ibid., I, i, 2, 6.

that the wreath of hair be buried with him, lest it prove a relic. He points his request with this turn:

> *As'twas humility*
> *To afford to it all that a Soule can doe,*
> *So, 'tis some bravery,*
> *That since you would save none of mee, I bury*
> *some of you* [I. 59].

Over the last line Sir Herbert hesitated a good deal before substituting the manuscript 'save' for the 1633 'have'. The grounds for adoption are these:

'(1) It seems difficult to understand how it could have arisen if "have none" was the original. (2) It gives a sharper antithesis, "You would not save me, keep me alive. Therefore I will bury, not you indeed, but a part of you." (3) To be saved is the lover's usual prayer; and the idea of the poem is that his death is due to the lady's cruelty' [II, 47].

The validity of the last reason is established, no doubt, by the assumption that this is a Petrarchian poem addressed to Mrs. Herbert. As for the 'sharper antithesis', I am afraid Sir Herbert forgets the major antithesis, which is between 'humility' and 'bravery'. More than that, it is between 'humility' and 'some bravery'. Humility gave or offered all, but she would have none; equal bravery would take all, but some bravery will bury part. His advantage is as 'some' is to 'none'. What irks this 'Petrarchian' lover is that she would 'have' none of him; but he has some of her which he may bury in revenge, and so prevent idolatry. If 'save' sharpens the minor antithesis, it blunts the major antithesis.

In *The Blossome*, another so-called Petrarchian poem, the lover's heart speaks thus to him:

> *Here lyes my businesse, and here I will stay:*
> *You goe to friends, whose love and meanes present*
> *Various content*
> *To your eyes, eares, and tongue, and every part.*
> *If then your body goe, what need you a heart?* [I, 60]

1633 reads 'tast' for 'tongue' and 'need your heart' for

'need you a heart'. Here are Sir Herbert's reasons for the changes:

'I have adopted the MS. readings "tongue" and "what need you a heart?" because they seem to me more certainly what Donne wrote. He may have altered them, but so may an editor. "Tongue" is more exactly parallel to eyes and ears, and the whole talk is of organs. "What need you a heart?" is more pointed' [II, 48].

But if ' "tongue" is more exactly parallel to eyes and ears', what shall we say of the parallel in the last line?

If then your body goe, what need your heart?

And if it is 'your eyes, eares, and tongue', as well as 'your body', may it not be 'your heart'? The next stanza plays on the theme 'how shall she know my heart when she doth not know a heart?' and there is no need to anticipate the distinction. But if the parallel is urged for 'heart', should it be disallowed for 'tongue'? To be sure, 'the whole talk is of organs', and yet the whole concern is the distinction between 'sense' and 'feeling'. The lover goes to various content for the senses; he has no use for emotion (heart). Moreover, 'tongue' is not as ready a substitute for 'taste' as eyes and ears are for sight and hearing; Burton could not, or did not, define the organ of taste without including the word: 'His *organ* is the *tongue* with his tasting nerves.'[1] Of course, organ or 'part' is necessary for the cynical contrast between sense and emotion; but the satisfaction of these organs, except the heart, is sensuous. Hence there is no real necessity that 'tast' must become 'tongue'; it may even be argued that 'tongue' is not so precise as 'tast'.

IV

It is only proper that we carry our investigation of the validity of *1633* into the other important section of Donne's poetry, his *Divine Poems*. In Sir Herbert's text we may consider, first, departures from *1633* that materially affect the

[1] Ibid., I, i, 2, 6.

meaning; and second, some instances of the change that results from smaller departures. In two cases the departures are from *1635*, where the poems first appeared; in nearly all cases the departures are in favour of manuscript readings. The *Songs and Sonets* and the *Divine Poems* ought to provide sufficient illustration of any value that may be attached to *1633* beyond its justification by Sir Herbert Grierson.

Our first example of the modification of meaning is found in *Holy Sonnet III*, which reveals a departure from *1635*.

> *O might those sighes and teares returne againe*
> *Into my breast and eyes, which I have spent,*
> *That I might in this holy discontent*
> *Mourne with some fruit, as I have mourn'd in vaine;*
> *In mine Idolatry what showres of raine*
> *Mine eyes did waste? what griefs my heart did rent?*
> *That sufferance was my sinne; now I repent;*
> *'Cause I did suffer I must suffer paine* [I, 323].

The alteration in the last line but one is made clear by Sir Herbert's note:

'I have followed the punctuation and order of *B*, *W*, because it shows a little more clearly what is (I think) the correct construction. As printed in *1635–69*,

> *That sufferance was my sinne I now repent,*

the clause "That sufferance was" &c. is a noun clause subject to "repent". But the two clauses are co-ordinates and "That" is a demonstrative pronoun. "*That* suffering" (of which he has spoken in the six preceding lines) "was my sin. Now I repent. Because I did suffer the pains of love, I must now suffer those of remorse" ' [II, 231–2].

But *1635* is right, as Sir Herbert would have seen if he had looked more closely at the 'six preceding lines' and at 'sufferance'. The poet wishes that his 'spent' sighs and tears might return so that he might mourn fruitfully as he once mourned in vain. Consequently, he now repents that 'sufferance' was his sin. As the poem suggests, 'sufferance' is an ambiguity, meaning both 'suffering' and 'indulgence';

Textual Difficulties in Donne's Poetry

likewise, 'suffer' means both 'tolerate' and 'endure'.[1] Thus he now repents that indulgence in suffering was his sin; because he tolerated pain he must endure pain. The punishment is like the sin; hence the advantage which the drunkard, thief, and lecher have over him; hence the conclusion,

> *for long, yet vehement griefe hath beene*
> *Th'effect and cause, the punishment and sinne.*

Sir Herbert's alteration disguises, if it does not destroy, the subtler relations between the effect and the cause. It may also be remarked that he puts a semicolon after 'sinne', where his manuscript sources have a comma.

Holy Sonnet XIII presents a 'picture of Christ crucified' which leads to the question, 'can that tongue adjudge thee unto hell'?

> *No, no; but as in my idolatrie*
> *I said to all my profane mistresses,*
> *Beauty, of pitty, foulnesse onely is*
> *A signe of rigour: so I say to thee,*
> *To wicked spirits are horrid shapes assign'd,*
> *This beauteous forme assures a piteous minde* [I, 328].

In the last line *1633* has 'assumes' instead of 'assures'; but Sir Herbert concludes: 'In this case the MSS. enable us to correct an obvious error of *all* the printed editions.'[2] But is 'assumes' an obvious error? It is the commoner word in Donne; elsewhere 'assure' appears, so far as I recall, only in 'inter-assured'. But what is the context for either word? For any answer to the question with which the sonnet opens, 'What if this present were the worlds last night?' the significance of Christ is paramount. Donne's 'picture of Christ crucified' represents a figure of mingled pity and rigour,

> *Teares in his eyes quench the amasing light,*
> *Blood fills his frownes, which from his pierc'd head fell.*

[1] Here, as elsewhere, I have verified my glosses in the *OED* (without denying the power of metaphor).
[2] II, 234.

The significance of this figure will become altogether clear when it can be determined 'whether that countenance can thee affright'. To this end the poet calls upon a proposition which he had applied to his 'profane mistresses':

> *Beauty, of pitty, foulnesse onely is*
> *A signe of rigour.*

The resolution is to be logical, and aesthetic criteria are to determine ethical significance, playing upon 'affright'.

It is clear, I think, that 'foulnesse' is the more positive criterion, for 'onely' is attached to it; and this criterion is strongly reasserted for spirits, 'To wicked spirits are horrid shapes assign'd.' Since 'foulnesse' or a 'horrid shape' is absent in the 'picture', the 'rigour' is excluded; for wicked or rigorous spirits must appear in horrid shapes. Thus he cannot be 'affrighted' either aesthetically or ethically. Of course, what remains is beauty and pity, and so the last line asserts, either with 'assures' or 'assumes'. But 'this beauteous forme' *assumes* the opposite which remains after the exclusion of the opposite to which a 'horrid shape' is *assigned*. The objection to 'assures' is that it makes 'beauteous' more important in the proof than it actually is; it makes a 'piteous minde' depend upon the less positive element in the proof. The sonnet seems to develop primarily by the exclusion of 'rigour' through the exclusion of 'foulnesse'; whereas 'assures' makes the resolution turn on the less emphasized and less supported factor. With 'assumes' the poet says by his logic that this beautiful form supposes or takes for granted a piteous mind, and by his religious symbolism (crucifixion) that this beautiful form takes upon itself the character of pity. In brief, 'assumes' carries the full weight of the sonnet, but 'assures' makes everything depend upon the assertion of this 'beauteous' form. If I am not mistaken, there is a case for 'assumes' that needs more refutation than a bare assertion of its error.

Perhaps the easiest way to show the change effected in *Holy Sonnet XVI* by alterations in the pronouns will be to quote it in full.

Father, part of his double interest
Unto thy kingdome, thy Sonne gives to mee,
His joynture in the knottie Trinitie
Hee keepes, and gives to me his deaths conquest.
This Lambe, whose death, with life the world hath blest,
Was from the worlds beginning slaine, and he
Hath made two Wills, which with the Legacie
Of his and thy kingdome, doe thy Sonnes invest.
Yet such are thy laws, that men argue yet
Whether a man those statutes can fulfill;
None doth; but all-healing grace and spirit
Revive againe what law and letter kill.
Thy lawes abridgement, and thy last command
Is all but love; Oh let this last Will stand! [I, 329].

In line 9, *1633* reads 'these laws'; and in line 11, 'thy all-healing'. Of his first departure Sir Herbert remarks:

'I have adopted the reading "thy" of the Westmoreland and some other MSS. because the sense seems to require it. "These" and "those" referring to the same antecedent make a harsh construction. "Thy laws necessarily transcend the limits of human capacity and therefore some doubt whether these conditions of our salvation can be fulfilled by men. They cannot, but grace and spirit revive what law and letter kill" ' [II, 234].

Does this statement take into account all the facts in the poem? Christ, whose death brings the legacy, was slain from the beginning; hence he has had, so to speak, two deaths, and has made two Wills. The Protestants made much of these two Wills: they were the Old Testament of Law, and the New Testament of Grace. Inheritance of the 'kingdom' under the old Will was regarded as virtually impossible; men could not fulfil the letter of the Law. Christ's own conflict with the laws and his interpretation of them gave support to this view. Having distinguished Father and Son, and having made the Son author of both Wills, Donne cannot say 'thy laws' without referring them back to the Father; 'his' is Christ's pronoun in the poem. And since this

is the impossible Will, it is best spoken of without a posses-
sive, as 'these laws', suggesting the multiplicity which
makes them impossible of fulfilment. But why does Sir
Herbert make 'all-healing grace and spirit' impersonal?
Here are his reasons:

'I have dropped the "thy" of the editions, following all
the MSS. I have no doubt that "thy" has been inserted: (1)
It spoils the rhyme: "spirit" has to rhyme with "yet", which
is impossible unless the accent may fall on the second syllable; (2) "thy" has been inserted, as "spirit" has been spelt
with a capital letter, under the impression that "spirit"
stands for the Divine Spirit, the Holy Ghost. But obviously
"spirit" is opposed to "letter" as "grace" is to "law". . . .
"Who also hath made us able ministers of the new testament; not of the letter, but of the spirit: for the letter killeth,
but the spirit giveth life." 2 Cor. iii. 6' [II, 234–5].

The text from St. Paul, however, has a relevance to the
two Wills that Sir Herbert ignores; for the letter of the old
Law killeth, but the spirit of the Gospel giveth life. Donne's
curt 'None doth' is eloquent; but for the second Will, this
fact would be fatal. Hence the following 'but' is of tremen-
dous significance, and what it introduces must be ascribed
gratefully to its giver, the Father:

> *but thy all-healing grace and spirit*
> *Revive againe what law and letter kill.*

God sent Christ to make a second Will, offering another
chance of inheritance; doomed under Law, man revives
under Grace. Now 'law' is referred to the Father, but as
'Thy lawes abridgement' in the great commandment of
love. 'Oh let this last Will stand!' In using Christ as the
agent of God's actions, Donne is orthodox; in separating
the Father from the fatal Laws, Donne is at least ingratiat-
ing. The 'lawes abridgement'—a common enough Protestant phrase—is sufficient to make quite certain the proper
context for the two Wills or 'testaments'.

In *The Crosse* Sir Herbert preserves an emendation to

which his better judgment apparently does not subscribe. It is the insertion of 'all' in the following line,

Make them indifferent all; call nothing best [I, 333].

The 'all' derives from *1635*, where it replaces 'call', and is unsupported by the manuscripts. 'I should withdraw it,' says Sir Herbert, 'but cannot find it in my heart to do so.'[1] Although 'all' does not change the meaning, it does modify the incisiveness of the line by introducing a chime with 'call'. But it is another matter with the succeeding lines:

> *But most the eye needs crossing, that can rome,*
> *And move; To th'other th'objects must come home.*
> *And crosse thy heart: for that in man alone*
> *Points downewards, and hath palpitation.*
> *Crosse those dejections, when it downeward tends,*
> *And when it to forbidden heights pretends.*

For 'points' *1633* reads 'pants', and the manuscripts are divided. Sir Herbert offers this justification:

'I think the MS. reading is probably right, because (1) "Pants" is the same as "hath palpitation"; (2) Donne alludes to the anatomy of the heart, in the same terms, in the *Essayes in Divinity*, p. 74 (ed. Jessop, 1855): "O Man, which art said to be the epilogue, and compendium of all this world . . . and hast thy head erected to heaven, and all others to the centre, that yet only thy heart of all others points downward, and only trembles"' [II, 237].

But neither this parallel nor his quotation from contemporary anatomy is quite relevant. Obviously, the third couplet is related to the second couplet; and that relationship makes nonsense of 'points downewards', if only because you cannot then say, 'when it downeward tends'. No, 'Pants' is right, and not precisely the same as 'hath palpitation'. Man's heart pants or beats downwards; other hearts do not. Man's heart pants in ebbing, palpitates in rising activity. Donne employs the ambiguity in both 'pants' and 'palpitation'. When the heart ebbs in its activity, it gasps for

[1] II, 237.

air but yearns for extinction; hence 'dejections' must be crossed. When the heart increases its activity ('hath palpitation') the cause may be either physical or emotional; hence emotional heights must also be opposed. The point is that only man's heart fluctuates emotionally; it must therefore be controlled, must be crossed in its extremes.

In the conclusion of this poem Sir Herbert adopts two questionable readings from the manuscripts.

> *Then doth the Crosse of Christ worke fruitfully*
> *Within our hearts, when wee love harmlessly*
> *That Crosses pictures much, and with more care*
> *That Crosses children, which our Crosses are.*

1633 reads 'faithfully' for 'fruitfully', and 'The' for 'That' in 'That Crosses pictures'. For 'fruitfully' Sir Herbert gives this argument:

'The improved sense, as well as the unanimity of the MSS., justifies the adoption of this reading. A preacher may deal "faithfully" with his people. The adverb refers to his action, not its results in them. The Cross of Christ, in Donne's view, must always deal faithfully; whether its action produces fruit depends on our hearts' [II, 237–8].

If this were all, there would be no disagreement. But has Sir Herbert forgotten his first remark about the poem? 'Donne has evidently in view the aversion of the Puritan to the sign of the cross used in baptism.' Must the Cross, in the Puritan view, always deal faithfully? That is the real problem, which Sir Herbert forgets. Obviously, the Cross does not work 'faithfully' for the Puritans in baptism, for it seemed 'unlawful'. Donne is justifying the Cross in faith rather than in works, and the adverb 'harmlessly' suggests as much. The Cross will work faithfully when we love innocently its images, and with more anxiety its children, our crosses. *1633* seems to me to have the advantage also in reading 'The Crosses pictures', for 'The' emphasizes less heavily than 'That', and so fits into the distribution of emphasis between 'The Crosses pictures' and 'That Crosses children'. This adjustment of emphasis helps to accommodate the poem to the more rigid Protestant view. It seems rather evident that 'faithfully' suits Donne's purpose, if not his view, in the poem.

Sir Herbert makes two departures from the 1633 text in *Good-friday, 1613. Riding Westward.* In the lines,

> *And as the other Spheares, by being growne*
> *Subject to forraigne motions, lose their owne* [I, 336],

he adopts 'motions' from the manuscripts where *1633* has 'motion', since he believes that the final *s* has been dropped in the latter. He supports his reading by this comment: 'The reference is to the doctrine of cycles and epicycles.'[1] But elsewhere Donne has used the eastward (natural) motion and westward (foreign) motion of the spheres in this fashion: 'As the motions of an upper sphere imprint a motion in the lower sphere other than naturally it would have; so the changes of this life work after death.'[2] Since the opposition of these two motions sets the problem of the poem, it is certainly more pointed to read, 'Subject to forraigne motion, lose their owne.'

The more considerable departure, however, comes in these lines:

> *Could I behold those hands which span the Poles,*
> *And turne all spheares at once, peirc'd with those holes?*
> [I, 336].

1633 reads 'tune' for 'turne', and the manuscripts are divided. For this reading Sir Herbert offers the following argument:

'The "tune all spheares" of the editions and some MSS. is tempting because of (as it is doubtless due to) the Platonic doctrine of the music of the spheres. But Donne was more of a Schoolman and Aristotelian than a Platonist, and I think there can be little doubt that he is describing Christ as the "first mover". On the other hand "tune" may include "turne" ' [II, 238].

[1] II, 238.
[2] *Fifty Sermons* (1649), Sermon 28; *Works*, ed. Alford, IV, 508. Cf. James Howell's use of these motions, *Familiar Letters*, VI, xxxii; and Dryden's, *Essays*, ed. Ker, I, 70.

Textual Difficulties in Donne's Poetry

The last remark is prompted by the translation of the Dutch poet Huyghens, to whom he always refers with respect, and who in this case either read 'tune' or derived it from 'turne'. But whatever Donne was, his use of the music of the spheres has been demonstrated sufficiently by Mr. Hayward in the 'Nonesuch' edition. Neither 'music' nor 'tune' is an uncommon term in Donne's religious poetry. *The Litanie* instances, 'A sinner is more musique, when he prayes, Then spheares'; *Vpon the translation of the Psalmes*, 'The Organist is hee Who hath tun'd God and Man, the Organ we'; and the *Hymne to God my God, in my sicknesse*, 'I shall be made thy Musique; As I come I tune the Instrument here at the dore.' To these examples we may add the opening of the *Obsequies to the Lord Harrington*:

> Faire soule, which wast, not onely, as all soules bee,
> Then when thou wast infused, harmony,
> But did'st continue so; and now dost beare
> A part in God's great organ, this whole Spheare: [I, 271]

and this passage from the *Sermons*:

'God made this whole world in such an uniformity, such a correspondency, such a concinnity of parts, as that it was an Instrument, perfectly in tune: we may say, the trebles, the highest strings were disordered first; the best understandings, Angels and Men, put this instrument out of tune. God rectified all again, by putting in a new string, *semen mulieris*, the seed of the woman, the *Messias*. . . . Gods hand tun'd it the second time. . . .'[1]

Thus the music of the spheres took on a peculiar significance for Donne in his imagery of tuning an instrument, even to a second tuning in Christ, and nowhere is it more striking than in his religious poetry. In the light of his work 'tune' would be a more likely choice than 'turne' wherever he might employ the imagery of spheres.

'Turne' is right for Sir Herbert because 'there can be little doubt that he is describing Christ as the "first mover" '. But there is a good deal of room for doubt. The 'first mover'

---

[1] *XXVI Sermons* (1660), Sermon 2; *Works*, ed. Alford, V, 384.

seems to be 'The intelligence that moves, devotion', which is supplanted by the foreign motion, 'Pleasure or businesse'. Sir Herbert himself reminds us of the nature of the 'intelligence': 'i.e. the angel. Each sphere has its angel or intelligence that moves and directs it'.[1] And since he names an angel for each sphere, I presume he feels that Donne was exceptional in making Christ an angel.

If 'tune' may include 'turne', there seems to be little argument for 'turne', except on the ground that 'tune' includes too much. But to 'turne all spheares at once', if 'at once' means 'together', could scarcely produce harmony, since 'the note of each is due to the rate at which it is spun'. In another place Sir Herbert asserts that 'the chief idea here is of God's power'.[2] Inasmuch as the hands are 'peirc'd', this statement is oversimplified; the chief idea seems to be, rather, the paradox of his power and his mercy: 'hands which span the Poles . . . peirc'd with those holes'. Donne, it may be remarked, here gives us one of his best examples of the telescoped image—one image superimposed on another:

> *Could I behold those hands which span the Poles,*
> *And tune all spheares at once, peirc'd with those holes?*

The crucified figure is superimposed on the figure spanning the poles. It is in this connection that I would argue the superior efficiency of 'tune'. For 'tune' suggests a purpose as 'turne' does not. And Donne's use of this imagery elsewhere reinforces the suggestion that here too he envisages the second tuning of the world by God—or through Christ the tuning of God and man ('Let mans Soule be a Spheare') which makes possible the resolution of the poem.

The next six lines develop the paradox of God and man in the crucifixion of Christ. 'Humbled below us' strikes the keynote for all, but Sir Herbert misreads the first two:

> *Could I behold that endlesse height which is*
> *Zenith to us, and our Antipodes,*
> *Humbled below us?*

[1] II, 238.   [2] *Metaphysical Lyrics & Poems* (Oxford, 1921), p. 229.

Textual Difficulties in Donne's Poetry

As paraphrased by Sir Herbert, the point of view in this paradox is shifted from man to God: 'height so infinite that for Him the difference between us and our antipodes is non-existent. He is zenith to both.'[1] But Donne's syntax is this: '. . . which is both our zenith and our antipodes'. By crucifixion the 'endlesse height' is levelled and, being 'humbled below us', ironically becomes our antipodes. With the cosmographical terms, however, Donne actually says: 'Could I behold that endless magnanimity which is our highest happiness, and our very opposite, humbled below us?' Herein lies the awfulness of the spectacle, in which he participates. As the poem continues, 'that blood . . . made durt of dust' provides a parallel but degraded image of this humbling below the state or dignity of man. And so the telescoped image of the earlier lines is developed by its connections with man.

Among two or three items in *The Litanie* the one most worthy of mention occurs in the seventh stanza.

> *And let thy Patriarches Desire*
> *(Those great Grandfathers of thy Church, which saw*
> *More in the cloud, then wee in fire,*
> *Whom Nature clear'd more, then us Grace and Law,*
> *And now in Heaven still pray, that wee*
> *May use our new helpes right,)*
> *Be satisfy'd, and fructifie in mee;*
> *Let not my minde be blinder by more light*
> *Nor Faith, by Reason added, lose her sight* [I, 340].

1635 and manuscripts support 'satisfy'd' against 'sanctified' in *1633*. Sir Herbert makes no comment on his adoption of 'satisfy'd', perhaps thinking that 'desire' ought to be 'satisfied'. As one of the earliest religious poems of Donne, this is most interesting for the light it throws on his state of mind. Hence the interest of this variant. As the text stands, Donne simply asks that 'thy Patriarches Desire . . . that wee May use our new helpes right, Be satisfy'd, and fructifie in mee'. But if 'sanctified' is the right word, the idea becomes

[1] Ibid.

115

sharper, and the point of the conclusion a little more incisive. Donne would then be asking that their desire 'be made conducive to holiness'—a more significant petition in the light of what follows. He does not want his mind to be made blinder by more light; nor his faith, by the addition of reason, to lose her sight. This final petition makes 'sanctified' the more pointed word because the patriarchs are those 'Whom Nature clear'd more, then us Grace and Law.' Apparently 'satisfy'd' is the more obvious and redundant, but less significant, term.

Finally we may regard two small departures from *1633* and *1635* in Sir Herbert's text of Donne's hymns. The first is in *A Hymne to Christ, at the Authors last going into Germany.*

> *I sacrifice this Iland unto thee,*
> *And all whom I lov'd there, and who lov'd mee;*
> *When I have put our seas twixt them and mee,*
> *Put thou thy sea betwixt my sinnes and thee* [I, 353].

In the last line *1633* has 'seas', which Sir Herbert cannot accept:

'I have adopted "sea" from the MSS. in place of "seas" *1633*. It was easy for the printer to take over "seas" from the preceding line, but "sea" is the more pointed word. The sea is the blood of Christ. The 1635–69 editions indeed read "blood", which is as though a gloss had crept in from the margin. More probably "blood" was a first version, changed by a bold metaphor to a more striking antithesis [II, 243].'

The trouble with this argument is that the first stanza has already anticipated the 'bold metaphor':

> *What sea soever swallow mee, that flood*
> *Shall be to mee an embleme of thy blood;*

and these lines could easily supply the variants of 1635, 'flood' and 'blood'. This fact may suggest that the second stanza develops, rather than repeats, the ideas of the first stanza, where the thought is of salvation by the 'Arke' and 'blood'. And therefore 'sea' may be too pointed a word in the second stanza, too repetitive of the first. In the second,

Textual Difficulties in Donne's Poetry

Donne speaks as one who has sacrificed all in order to follow Christ, but he speaks in the 'emblems' that he introduced in the first. As Sir Herbert has quoted a sermon associated with the same event as the *Hymne*, I may quote the *Devotions* on the emblems that are employed here. In 'XIX. Expostulation' Donne writes at some length on a 'metaphorical God', saying among other things:

'But wherefore, O my God, hast thou presented to us the afflictions and calamities of this life in the name of waters? so often in the name of waters, and deep waters, and seas of waters? Must we look to be drowned? are they bottomless, are they boundless? That is not the dialect of thy language; thou hast given a remedy against the deepest water by water; against the inundation of sin by baptism; and the first life that thou gavest to any creatures was in waters: therefore thou dost not threaten us with an irremediableness when our affliction is a sea. . . . All our waters shall run into Jordan, and thy servants passed Jordan dry foot; they shall run into the red sea (the sea of thy Son's blood), and the red sea, that red sea, drowns none of thine; but *they that sail on the sea tell of the danger thereof*. . . . Since thou art so, O my God, and affliction is a sea too deep for us, what is our refuge? Thine ark, thy ship.'

Here we have the imagery of the first part of the *Hymne*. When in a favourite 'dialect' Donne asks,

> *When I have put our seas twixt them and mee,*
> *Put thou thy seas betwixt my sinnes and thee,*

the remedial waters are just as great as the seas of affliction, the seas of his sacrifice. Furthermore, the swallowing sea, the 'embleme of thy blood', of the first stanza now becomes the 'seas betwixt my sinnes and thee', which are both the purifying and the redeeming waters. Thus it seems to me that the 'seas' of *1633* is the richer term—not merely a repetitive 'sea'—in a context which stresses the cost of following Christ and has therefore developed beyond that of the first stanza.

In the *Hymne to God my God, in my sicknesse* Sir Herbert

departs from *1635* in favour of the only manuscript source he could find.

> *Whilst my Physitians by their love are growne*
> *Cosmographers, and I their Mapp, who lie*
> *Flat on this bed, that by them may be showne*
> *That this is my South-west discoverie*
> Per fretum febris, *by these streights to die,*

> *I joy, that in these straits, I see my West;*
> *For, though theire currants yeeld returne to none,*
> *What shall my West hurt me?* [I, 368]

1635 reads 'those currants' and Sir Herbert gives no reason for his adoption. The reason which occurs to me is that he is much less tolerant of the collocation of 'these' and 'those' than is Donne. But here, as in *Holy Sonnet XVI*, he seems to obscure Donne's precision by the change in pronouns. Donne expresses the central ambiguity of 'straits' in this passage: (1), 'by these streights to die' (fever); (2), 'in these straits . . . my West'. The straits of death and the geographical straits are mingled in (1) and (2); but in (1), (2) is submerged; and in (2), (1) is submerged. Yet the nature of the 'currents' is not common to both, for both are not one-way passages; hence 'their' confuses them. 'Those', however, points to the former, the passage through death to another world, and is therefore more exact. Of course 'their' would be justifiable if Donne thought the Straits of Magellan so dangerous as to be identifiable with the straits of death. Otherwise 'their' hardly conforms with his usual precision; meanwhile 'those' requires more than silent rejection.

Further support for 'those' may be found in the 'here' and 'there' opposition of the poem. 'Here I joy that I see my West; once there, and return is impossible, what shall my West hurt me?' So 'these straits' go with joy in the prospect; 'those currents' with the possibility of danger beyond. The gentler image of tuning an instrument in the first stanza, which also has its 'strait' in 'dore', gives way to the strenuous voyage of discovery and the necessity of resolving any

fear. The poem proceeds by mingling contemplative joy
with active suffering, and culminates in the violence of
'Therefore that he may raise the Lord throws down'. If
'those currents' belong to the 'streights' of death, the spelling becomes significant when Donne thinks of his 'home'
in terms of eastern destinations:

All streights, and none but streights, are wayes to them.

Such otherwise unresolved details persuade me that Donne
meant 'those currents' to refer primarily to the straits from
which there is no returning.

In conclusion I need only repeat that these arguments in
favour of *1633*, and occasionally of *1635*, as opposed to the
manuscripts, must abide the suffrage of other readers. Nothing said here can diminish the imposing reality of Sir
Herbert Grierson's great work on Donne; his labours in
vindication of *1633* laid the foundation to which some few
bricks, perhaps, may be added. Any lessons in reading
Donne that may be drawn from this essay are left in illustration rather than in precept; thereby my own shortcom-
ings will remain palpable but not invidious. If I have anything to contribute to part of Donne's text, it is because Sir
Herbert Grierson taught me to respect the 1633 text and its
editor. Any contribution that may be found will be, at best,
only a restoration. It is my hope that the arguments will not
detract from the appreciation of Donne.[1]

---

[1] In checking Sir Herbert's collation against one of the 'better' copies of *1633*,
I find that l. 18 of *A Valediction: of the book* is closed by a period instead of a
comma. The collation is thus altered, but the argument for continuing the
sense remains.

V

Strong Lines

✶

The poetry of the first half of the seventeenth century is distinguished for the modern reader by 'conceits', but for the contemporary reader it was distinguished by 'strong lines'. Not only literary history but even the *New English Dictionary* has neglected this critical term. Jacobeans, however, used it to hall-mark the peculiar excellence of their literature, both verse and prose. For us it has the merit of describing Jacobean literary talent in Jacobean language and at the same time of marking a definite literary period. 'Strong lines' epitomized the literary qualities which were most prized in this period; but what did 'strong lines' mean? The answer to this question provides an interesting as well as illuminating footnote to literary history, but requires something like a chapter as the account of a fashion.

In apologizing for his style Burton tells us that the *Anatomy of Melancholy* was 'writ with as small deliberation as I do ordinarily speak, without all affectation of big words, fustian phrases, jingling terms, tropes, strong lines, that like *Acestes'* arrows caught fire as they flew, strains of wit, brave heats, elogies, hyperbolical exornations, elegancies, &c. which many so much affect.'[1]

'Strong lines, that like *Acestes'* arrows caught fire as they flew,' exacted at least that much description from Burton.

[1] Bohn ed., I, 30; cf. p. 25.

Strong Lines

In 1656 Francis Osborn exhorts his son to 'spend no time in reading, much less writing *strong-lines*; which like tough meat, aske more paines and time in chewing, then can be recompensed by all the nourishment they bring.'[1] This remark indicates their nature, but implies a passing fashion. In fact, between the independence of Burton and the distaste of Osborn we shall find the reign of strong lines.

The best approach to an understanding of strong lines is unfortunately too extensive for this paper; it involves knowledge of the cultivation of Silver Latin style in the later Renaissance. At best I can only suggest this approach and refer the reader to the various articles by Professor M. W. Croll. In 1580 Muretus defended Tacitus in a passage which sounds like a startling forecast of a fashionable taste in Jacobean prose and verse:

'For although a bare and clear style gives pleasure, still in certain special kinds of writing *obscurity* will win praise sometimes. By diverting discourse from common and vulgar modes of expression, it wins a dignity and majesty even out of strangeness (*peregrinitas*) and grips the reader's attention. It acts as a veil, to exclude the view of the vulgar. Thus those who enter the dark crypt of a temple feel a kind of awful solemnity sweep in upon their souls. *Asperity* of style, again, has almost the same property as bitterness in wine: which is thought to be a sign that the wine will bear its age well.'[2]

This Anti-Ciceronian doctrine reached England and touched Francis Bacon. In 1591 the first English translation of Tacitus was recommended to the reader by Anthony Bacon with the statement 'that hee hath writen the most matter with best conceyt in fewest wordes of anie Historiographer ancient or moderne. But he is harde. *Difficilia quae pulchra*'. In the second edition of 1598 Richard Grenewey declared in his dedication that there is in Tacitus 'no woord

[1] *Advice to a Son* (Oxford, 1656), p. 9.
[2] Cf. M. W. Croll, 'Muret and the History of "Attic" Prose', *PMLA*, XXXIX (1924), 300. See also his 'Attic Prose in the Seventeenth Century', *Studies in Philology*, XVIII (1921); and 'Attic Prose: Lipsius, Montaigne, Bacon', *Schelling Anniversary Papers*, New York, 1923.

121

not loaden with matter, and as himselfe speaketh of *Galba*, he useth *Imperatoria brevitate*: which although it breed difficultie, yet carrieth great gravitie'. Here we may recall Jonson's praise of Lord Bacon as 'one noble speaker who was full of gravity'. In 1595, however, the Tacitean qualities defended by Muretus had been suggested for poetry by Chapman's dedication of *Ovid's Banquet of Sense*:

'But that Poesy should be as pervial as oratory, and plainness her special ornament, were the plain way to barbarism. . . .

'That *Energia*, or clearness of representation, required in absolute poems, is not the perspicuous delivery of a low invention; but high and hearty invention expressed in most significant and unaffected phrase. . . .

'There is no confection made to last, but it is admitted more cost and skill than presently-to-be-used simples; and in my opinion, that which being with a little endeavour searched, adds a kind of majesty to Poesy, is better than that which every cobbler may sing to his patch.

'Obscurity in affection of words and indigested conceits, is pedantical and childish; but where it shroudeth itself in the heart of his subject, uttered with fitness of figure and expressive epithets, with that darkness will I still labour to be shadowed.'

Such qualification distinguishes the 'full and haightned stile of Maister Chapman' from 'Marlowe's mighty line'.[1] If we compare this passage which defends the doctrine of 'significant darkness', with what Muretus said of Tacitus, we shall see that Chapman is here reconsecrating to poetry the poetic qualities which contaminated Silver Latin prose. Muretus, Grenewey, and Chapman all conclude that obscurity or difficulty produces gravity or majesty of style, and Jacobean writers were not slow in putting this doctrine into practice. In satire Joseph Hall felt, after the example of Persius, that poetry should be 'both hard of conceit and harsh of style', and he was obliged to defend himself (in the

[1] Cf. my *Donne Tradition* (Cambridge, 1930), chap. III: 'Chapman and Donne'. Reprinted by *The Noonday Press*, New York, 1958.

'Postscript' to *Virgidemiarum*, 1597) both against the learned
for being 'too perspicuous' and against the vulgar for being
'too obscure'.[1] He apologized for his 'too much stooping' by
declaring that 'men rather choose carelessly to lose the
sweet of the kernel, than to urge their teeth with breaking
the shell wherein it was wrapped'. And some thirty years
later Henry Reynolds (*Mythomystes*, 1633) attacked the
modern poets for lacking that 'closenesse' which 'was the
intent and studied purpose of the Auncient Poets all'—but
chiefly because they had no mysteries worth concealing.
The Jacobeans, however, found this closeness in the Silver
Latin writers, with whom they felt a special kinship, and
hence they cultivated the obscurity and asperity of style
that, with a wit of their own, produced strong lines. Briefly
as this doctrine has been put, it may suggest the literary
background from which the cult of strong lines emerged.

In essence strong lines belong to what we have come to
know as 'metaphysical poetry'. It was such lines that made
Jasper Mayne feel Donne's poetry so far above its readers
'that wee are thought wits, when 'tis understood'. The
'Elegies upon the Author' which were included in the
Poems, published in 1633, give a strong-lined character to
Donne. For instance, Carew's 'Elegie' describes the strong
line when it declares that Donne has:

> . . . *open'd Us a Mine*
> *Of rich and pregnant phansie, drawne a line*
> *Of masculine expression . . .*

For Carew the triumph of Donne over the ancients is the
greater,

> *Since to the awe of thy imperious wit*
> *Our stubborne language bends, made only fit*
> *With her tough-thick-rib'd hoopes to gird about*
> *Thy Giant phansie, which had prov'd too stout*
> *For their soft melting Phrases.*

A stout fancy produced strong lines, with strenuous rather

---

[1] See also his 'Prologue' to Book III of *Virgidemiarum*.

than 'soft melting Phrases'; and such lines were 'rich and pregnant'. But in *Mythomystes* Reynolds, being engrossed in the mystical interpretation of poetry, warns his reader to expect no mention of the 'Accidents of Poesy', such as 'where the strong line (as they call it), where the gentle sortes best'. As a preacher this style put Donne into disfavour with the Puritans, for R. B.'s elegy tell us that 'they humm'd against him' and 'call'd him a strong lin'd man . . . but a bad edifier'.

Jonson, on the other hand, is praised for his laborious art by the contributors to *Jonsonus Virbius* (1638), but only James Howell speaks of his 'strenuous lines'. Owen Feltham, none the less, writes of 'solid Jonson',

> *from whose full strong quill,*
> *Each line did like a diamond drop distil,*
> *Though hard, yet clear.*

And in 1640 (in verses prefixed to Samuel Harding's *Sicily and Naples*) S. Hall uses the precise term:

> *Nor neede they other halter,* Catiline
> *Affords them* rope *enough, in each* strong line.

If not in the full sense of the term, Jonson belongs, nevertheless, to the strong-lined tradition by virtue of the close and strenuous style which he opposed to the soft, melting, and diffuse style of the Spenserians. Even the prefatory verses to Randolph's *Poems* (1638), though they say nothing of strong lines, show that some of Randolph's admirers were afraid lest his poetry be thought too facile.

Critical opinion turns definitely against strong lines in Thomas Hobbes's *Answer to Davenant* (1650), where he attacks the practice that 'with terms to charm the weak and pose the wise' brought the poet to write obscurely. Hobbes concludes:

'To this palpable darkness I may also add the ambitious obscurity of expressing more then is perfectly conceived, or perfect conception in fewer words then it requires. Which Expressions, though they have had the honor to be called strong lines, are indeed no better then Riddles, and, not onely to the Reader but also after a little time to the Writer himself, dark and troublesome.'[1]

It is apparent that to Hobbes 'ambitious obscurity' and undue pregnancy of expression are responsible for 'strong lines', which often prove no better than riddles. We can now sympathize with Endymion Porter when, in his verses, 'To My worthy Friend Mr. William Davenant' (prefixed to *Madagascar*, 1638), he offers this apologetic couplet:

> *As when I heare them read strong-lines, I cry*
> *Th'are rare, but cannot tell you rightly why.*

In the extraordinarily long group of commendatory elegies which introduce Cartwright's *Comedies, Tragi-Comedies, with Other Poems* (1651), we find enough material to test our knowledge of strong lines. The publisher, Humphrey Moseley, casually likens Cartwright to 'the highest Poet our Language can boast of (the late *Dean* of St. Paul's)', but Cartwright's eulogists are not agreed upon the likeness. The same Jasper Mayne who praised Donne praises Cartwright for exactly opposite qualities, because Cartwright's wit was:

> *No Oracle of Language, to amaze*
> *The Reader with a dark or Midnight phrase.*

But John Leigh, running over a catalogue of poets which includes 'rare Cartwright', implores Moseley to

> *Give us all* Cleveland, *all his gallant lines,*
> *Whose Phansie still in strong Expressions shines.*

John Berkenhead decries the swarm of small poets who have come up since Cartwright's death:

> *For thy Imperiall Muse at once defines*
> *Lawes to* arraign *and* brand *their weak* strong lines.

---

[1] Spingarn, *Critical Essays of the Seventeenth Century*, II, 63. The 'terms' were those of scholastic philosophy.

Strong Lines

Though 'Wit in Cartwright at her Zenith was', for Henry Vaughan,

> *. . . not a* line (*to the most* Critick he)
> *Offends with* flashes, *or obscurity*

For Ralph Bathurst his verse is both 'smooth' and 'deep':

> *No Myst'ry there blocks up the way, no sowre*
> *Nor rugged Verse that must be scann'd twice o'r;*
> *But his soft Numbers gently slide away,*
> *Like Chrystall waters, Smooth, and Deep, as they.*

For Thomas Philipott his design.

> *Is cloth'd with Sense so sinewy, so compact,*
> *Not witty loose Lines, or vitious Numbers slack'd.*

Thomas Cole indulges in a warning:

> *But O take heed ye worms of* Cartwright's *Wit,*
> *His Lines are strong, you may a surfeit get.*

But for B. C. neither is he short of substance,

> *Nor writes he in the clouds, and a dark Dress,*
> *That him you cannot understand, but ghesse.*

All of these verses have their reference to the obscurity or asperity of strong lines; but while the cult of strong lines is apparent enough in their criticism, the trend of critical opinion is toward the position of Hobbes. Although Cartwright must still be 'deep', he is not obscure, he offers no riddles. Depth or strength of wit and rugged verse are giving way to clear wit and smooth numbers as the desiderata of criticism.

In 1661 Izaak Walton, with a backward glance, relates how the milkmaid sang 'that smooth song which was made by Kit Marlow, now at least fifty years ago; and the milkmaid's mother sung an answer to it, which was made by Sir Walter Raleigh, in his younger days. They were old-fashioned poetry, but choicely good; I think much better than the strong lines that are now in fashion in this critical age.'[1]

And he makes Venator remark, apropos of Donne's variation on the same song:

'Yes, master, I will speak you a copy of verses that were made by Doctor Donne, and made to shew the world that he could make soft and smooth verses, when he thought smoothness worth his labour.'[2]

Besides informing us of the fashion of strong lines, Walton suggests that they were antithetic to smoothness, and this supports what we have already surmised. Another reminiscent remark comes from Meric Casaubon in 1655, when he says that Longinus has many words suggesting the divine inspiration of poets 'where no real *Enthusiasme* or supernaturall agitation' is intended:

'As when he saith, speaking of that kind of language, which when I was a Boy in the University, was called *strong lines*. . . . Many men, saith he, whilst they strain their wits to find somewhat that is very extraordinary, and may relish of some rapture, or Enthusiasme; they plainly rave, (or, play the fools) and not ravish.'[3]

Casaubon, who was at Oxford between 1614 and 1621, shows why strong lines came to be regarded as far-fetched and oracular in a bad sense; once the appropriate remark had been 'Th'are rare'. Both Walton and Casaubon help us to delimit the reign of strong lines as well as to determine their character.

The real strong-lined poet at this time was John Cleveland, and it will be interesting to see what contemporary criticism had to say of him. In 1662 Thomas Fuller gives him this character:

'A *general Artist*, pure *Latinist*, exquisite *Orator*, and (which was his *Master-piece*) eminent *Poet. His Epithetes* were pregnant with *Metaphors*, carrying in them a *difficult plainness,*

---

[1] *The Compleat Angler*, 'Temple Classics' ed., p. 74.
[2] Ibid., p. 166.
[3] *Treatise concerning Enthusiasme* (London, 1655), p. 142. For its full import see my 'Restoration Revolt against Enthusiasm'. in this volume.

difficult at the *hearing*, *plain* at the *considering* thereof. His lofty Fancy may seem to stride from the top of one mountain to the top of another, so making to itself a constant *Level* and *Champain* of *continued Elevations*.

'Such who have *Clevelandized*, indeavouring to imitate his Masculine Stile, could never go beyond the *Hermaphrodite*, still betraying the weaker Sex in their deficient conceits. Some distinguish between the *Veine* and *Strain* of Poetry, making the former to flow with facility, the latter press'd with pains, and forced with industry. Master *Cleveland's Poems* do partake of both, and are not to be the less valued by the Reader, because most studied by the Writer thereof.'[1]

One could find no better portrait of a strong-lined poet who, in reality, has sunk into the defects of his qualities. Strong lines were produced by the 'Strain of Poetry', and the difference between the 'Veine' and the 'Strain' allowed Ben Jonson a place in the strong-lined tradition. Of course this poetry could not succeed when it reminded the reader of any 'forced' quality.

The characteristic wit of strong lines was definitely outmoded by Thomas Sprat's *History of the Royal Society*, published in 1667. Sprat devotes an appendix[2] exclusively to the 'benefit of *Experiments*' to wits and writers, wherein he says:

'To this purpose I must premise, that it is requir'd in the best, and most delightful *Wit*; that it be founded on such images which are generally known, and are able to bring a strong, and a sensible impression on the *mind*.'

This premise leads him to discredit 'metaphysical' wit:

'The *Sciences* of mens Brains are none of the best Materials for this kind of *Wit*. Very few have happily succeeded in *Logical*, *Metaphysical*, *Grammatical*, nay even scarce in *Mathematical Comparisons*; and the reason is, because they are most of them conversant about things remov'd from the

---

[1] *The Worthies of England*, ed. John Nichols, I, 572. Dryden speaks of 'a catachresis or Clevelandism, wresting and torturing a word into another meaning'.
[2] See 1702 ed., pp. 413 ff.

Senses, and so cannot surprise the *fancy* with very obvious, or quick, or sensible delights.'

Being partial to the wit 'gather'd from the *Arts* of mens hands, and the *Works* of *Nature*', Sprat concludes that Bacon was 'one of the first and most artificial Managers of this way of *Wit*'. But in 1684 Gilbert Burnet, prefacing his translation of More's *Utopia* with some remarks on style, speaks of 'the trifling way of dark and unintelligible Wit' that preceded 'the coarse extravagance of Canting', and declares that even Bacon 'in some places has Figures so strong that they could not pass now before a severe Judg'. Strong figures bring us back to the wit of strong lines which Sprat had found wanting.

Dryden's attack upon Cleveland in the *Essay of Dramatic Poesy* (1668) will help to summarize our impressions of strong lines. Asserting that 'wit is best conveyed to us in the most easy language', Dryden comes down on Cleveland in these words:

'The not observing this rule is that which the world has blamed in our satyrist, Cleveland: to express a thing hard and unnaturally, is his new way of elocution . . . we cannot read a verse of Cleveland's without making a face at it, as if every word were a pill to swallow: he gives us many times a hard nut to break our teeth, without a kernel for our pains. So that there is this difference betwixt his *Satires* and doctor Donne's; that the one gives us deep thoughts in common language, though rough cadence; the other gives us common thoughts in abstruse words.'[1]

This, as we have seen, is a common analysis of strong lines; but in the *Original and Progress of Satire* (1693) Dryden does not let Donne off so easily:

'He affects the metaphysics, not only in his satires, but in his amorous verses, where nature only should reign; and perplexes the minds of the fair sex with nice speculations of philosophy, when he should engage their hearts, and entertain them with the softnesses of love.'[2]

---

[1] *Essays*, ed. W. P. Ker, I, 52. This recalls Hall on satire.
[2] Ibid., II, 19. Dryden continues: 'In this (if I may be pardoned for so bold a truth) Mr. Cowley has copied him to a fault. . . .'

Here Dryden adds an instance to Hobbes's criticism of the use of 'terms to charm the weak and pose the wise'; he likewise subscribes to Sprat. Altogether his reaction to Donne spells neo-classicism.

With respect to prose Richard Parr makes a remark in his *Life of Usher* (1686) which has led Mr. W. F. Mitchell to confuse the epithets 'florid' and 'strong-lined'. Parr thus describes Ussher's preaching during his stay at Oxford in 1642: '. . . notwithstanding the Learnedness of most of his Hearers, he rather chose a plain substantial way of Preaching, for the promoting of Piety and Vertue, than studied Eloquence, or a vain ostentation of Learning: so that he quite put out of countenance that windy, affected sort of Oratory, which was then much in use, called *floride* preaching, or strong lines.'[1]

But *floride* as applied to style belongs to the last half of the seventeenth century, as the *N.E.D.* shows; and where Taylor is 'floride' Donne is 'strong-lined'. Both terms were antithetic to a plain style, but nothing is to be gained by equating both to the 'purple patch'.

It may be regretted that the term 'metaphysical' has obscured the more inclusive epithet 'strong-lined'. For the early seventeenth-century poets no term but 'strong lines' seems to have abstracted the peculiar essence of their kind of poetry. If some of the Jacobean poets were pregnant with metaphors of a certain kind, this was their particular form of 'closeness'; if they often strained after the extraordinary, that also gave them strong lines. When Jonson criticized a 'metaphysical' poet, he said 'that Done himself, for not being understood, would perish'; 'a hard nut to break our teeth', or 'deep thoughts', were Dryden's words. While the 'metaphysical poets' affected intellectual 'conceits', they wrote 'strong lines'; and as such their poetry was praised by their contemporaries and condemned by their successors.

[1] Cf. W. F. Mitchell, *English Pulpit Oratory* (London, 1932), pp. 229-30. Burnet's objection, however, that Bacon's figures are too 'strong' recalls the words of Sir John Beaumont:

> *Strong figures drawne from deepe inventions springs,*
> *Consisting lesse in words, and more in things'* (1629).

But in a fateful passage Dryden spoke of 'metaphysics', and he never actually said 'strong lines'.

If Dryden had used the proper term, he might have saved Mr. John Drinkwater from this statement in his preface to the *Poems of Sidney Godolphin*: 'Apollo, says Suckling in a doggerel passage of the *Sessions of the Poets*, calling "little Cid" "out of the throng", advised him "not to write so strong". Unless the warning had some special allusion that now escapes us, Apollo could not well have talked greater nonsense.' Whatever we may think of Apollo's judgment, he was not talking nonsense; his warning had the special allusion which ought no longer to escape us.

VI

The Obsequies for Edward King

★

When Masson read the *Obsequies to the Memorie of Edward King* he pronounced them 'rubbish' or 'trash' except for the 'true poem' with which they concluded.[1] And so they have remained. Now and then somebody has cited Cleveland's elegy as an awful foil for the true poem. But the likenesses between *Lycidas* and the 'trash' are noteworthy and even instructive, for they help to define the difference. And the differences may also reveal the bias of Milton's thought in 1637. Miss Wallerstein did give serious attention to the *Obsequies*, but she was concerned with other questions in her *Seventeenth-Century Poetic*.

These elegists started with the same occasion and they brought to it similar resources of education. What they did may alter the questions and answers usually called forth by *Lycidas*. Most of the common elements come from the associations of drowning, the allusions which it stimulated, or the questions which it provoked in the minds of the elegists. Hardly any connection with water or the ocean is overlooked by the elegists, whether English or Latin.[2]

[1] My text is the *Justa Edovardo King* of The Facsimile Text Society, Columbia University Press, New York, 1939. Although some of the English elegists appear also as Latin or Greek elegists, Milton appears only as an English poet, and so is properly defined by the context of the separately paged and titled English group.

[2] In the Latin elegies the themes are commonly amplified by means of classical mythology. Few, if any, of the items used by Milton are omitted, local

Mythology is their storehouse here, especially with Milton, but some allusions come from the Bible. Only the two poems addressed to King's sister and the final *Lycidas* have any special title; otherwise they fall under the title repeated before the initial poem, 'Obsequies to the Memorie', etc. Except at the end *Lycidas* would have seemed quite out of place. No doubt we can describe *Lycidas* more exactly if we observe the common elements in Milton, then the uncommon, and finally the unique. Thus we may acquire some sense of the relative originality of the various themes and images, and of the skill with which the 'occasional' elements are developed in the elegiac mood.

This approach may even serve to correct another distortion of criticism. In our time Dr. Johnson's criticism of *Lycidas* has been misunderstood. It is not that he did not know how to read pastoral, but that he was distressed by the indecorum of Milton's vehicle: its fictions were improper to real grief, its equivocations 'indecent'. Some academic critics have found a new way to load every rift with ore. They extend the context of a poem back into the past until their lemon squeezer is squeezing a good deal more than the lemon. Perhaps some examination of the *Obsequies* may help to place *Lycidas* in a more candid perspective.

David Masson in *The Life of John Milton* (I. 514) has translated the Latin paragraph 'narrating the incident which occasioned the volume':

'Edward King . . . was on his voyage to Ireland . . . when, the ship in which he was having struck on a rock not far from the British shore, and being stove in by the shock, he, while the other passengers were fruitlessly busy about their mortal lives, having fallen forward upon his knees, and breathing a life which was immortal, in the act of prayer going down with the vessel, rendered up his soul to God, Aug. 10, 1637, aged 25.'

topography is also Latinized, and the 'numen' theme is common. Pastoral elements are involved, but the form of the pastoral elegy is not employed. And these elegies are certainly not less extravagant than the English ones.

The Obsequies for Edward King

It may be added that Edward King was a Fellow of Christ's, an occasional poet, and a prospective priest. Most of the elegists find the cause of wreck in a storm or rough seas. Milton and W. Hall blame the ship, but both make a more benign use of the sea. Only Beaumont includes the rock, and only Milton insists on a calm. Either the elegists were not equally acquainted with the facts of the shipwreck, or else they were unequally bound by them.

Thus death by water becomes a central concern of the elegists, who feel the necessity of making the nature of King's death an important motive in their elegies. In general they find in the drowning matter for praise or blame, praise of King, blame of the sea; or else of advantage and disadvantage, either no grave or a better grave; and finally, matter for the theme of resurrection, the ultimate consolation. Milton does not utilize the drowning in such rhetorical ways; rather he capitalizes on the conflict between it and his pastoral vehicle, with which it is fundamentally at odds.

Milton's 'remorseless deep' is amplified into a theme of blame by Henry King:

> Curst element, whose nature ever vies
> With fire in mischiefs, as in qualities!
> Thou sav'dst but little more in the whole ark,
> Then thou hast swallow'd now in this small bark;
> As if it strove the last fire to outrunne,
> And antedate the worlds destruction.
>   But we have sinn'd, and now must bear the curse,
>   Even that is our worst plague, which is our nurse.

Yet out of this blame he extracts hyperbolic praise of his brother and then justifies providence by deriving the curse from our sin. Cleveland gives another hyperbolic turn to these elements:

> What can we now expect? Water and Fire
> Both elements our ruine do conspire;
> And that dissolves us, which doth us compound:
> One Vatican was burnt, another drown'd.

134

The Obsequies for Edward King

Again Isaac Olivier begins his elegy on this theme:

> *What water now shall vertue have again*
> *(As once) to purge? The Ocean't self's a stain.*

But he too contrives to extract compliment out of blame, by means of allusion to John the Baptist and Christ:

> *Be this excuse; Since first the waters gave*
> *A blessing to him which the soul could save,*
> *They lov'd the holy body still too much,*
> *And would regain some vertue from a touch.*

The ultimate in blame is achieved when R. Brown extends it even to tears:

> *Weep forth your tears then, poure out all your tide:*
> *All waters are pernicious since King dy'd.*

But a new deluge raises a question for Samson Briggs:

> *How can my faith but startle now, that we*
> *Are yet reserv'd another floud to see,*
> *To drown this little World! Could God forget*
> *His covenant which in the clouds he set?*

And T. Norton finds the poets now deprived of a common-place which Milton used in his *Nativity Ode*:

> *Poets, then leave your wonted strain;*
> *For now you may no longer feigne*
> *Apollo, when he goes to bed,*
> *O'th' western billows layes his head:*
> *I'th' Irish sea, there set our Sun;*
> *And since he's set, the day's undone.*

How the drowning is turned into a theme of praise may be seen in the anonymous elegist:

> *Now the proud sea grown richer then the land,*
> *Doth strive for place, and claim the upper hand.*

Samson Briggs extends this theme until nature fully partici-pates in their grief:

135

The Obsequies for Edward King

each wave
Swell'd up, as coveting to be his grave;
The winds in sighs did languish; Phebus stood
Like a close-mourner, in a sable hood
Compos'd of darkest clouds: the pitying skies
Melted and dropt in funerall elegies.

Still greater consolation is found in the nature of the death by W. Hall:

Corruption there shall slowly seise its prize,
Which thus embalm'd in brinie casket lies.
The saucy worm which doth inhabit here
In earthy graves, and quickly domineer
In stateliest marbles, shall not there assail
The treasure hidden in that watry vale.
'Twas to secure thee from th'insulting power
Of these two hasty Tyrants, which devoure
Our common clay, that intomb'd thee there
(Dear friend) where these shall no dominion share.

If this rather than 'false surmise' is the comfort Hall finds in Milton's 'watry biere', he is no less concerned for the unrecovered body:

Scarce can the widow'd Sisters let thee have
An Epitaph, as thou dost want a Grave.
All fun'rall rite earth can afford thee, is
Not to attend, but weep: and even of this
The too officious seas the earth prevent,
And yeeld thee tears, as they a tombe have lent.

And for this 'occasional' problem Milton also must find an elegiac solution.

Milton's pastoral vehicle may be analyzed, at least roughly, into these topics: death must be mourned, association with the deceased, his loss to the Muse, the question of providence, cause of disaster, loss to learning, loss to church, pastoral consolation, the intrusion of reality, religious consolation, and pastoral resolution.

136

The Obsequies for Edward King

The other elegists share Milton's themes of lamentation. These arise from a sense of threefold loss as poet, scholar, priest. King's loss to the Muses is mourned by various elegists. For his brother Henry King,

> He drest the Muses in the brav'st attire
> That e're they wore, and taught them a strain higher,
> And farre beyond their winged horses flight.

For the anonymous elegist this theme becomes excuse:

> Till thou ly'dst down upon thy western bed,
> Not one Poetick starre durst shew his head;
> Athenian owls fear'd to come forth in verse,
> Untill thy fall darkned the Universe.

It is turned still another way by Cleveland:

> The Muses are not Mayr-maids; though upon
> His death the Ocean might turn Helicon.

Samson Briggs is more elaborate:

> One whom the Muses courted: rigg'd and fraught
> With Arts and Tongues too fully, when he sought
> To crosse the seas, was overwhelm'd. . . .

And R. Brown is more simply elegiac:

> Weep then, ye sonnes of Phebus, ye that know
> The burden of this losse, let your tears flow.

It is obvious that Milton was not alone in lamenting King's loss as a poet.

As Milton was provoked, after this loss of a poet, to exclaim, 'Alas! what boots it. . . ?' so Henry King begins with the impulse to question Providence:

> No Death! I'le not examine Gods decree,
> Nor question providence, in chiding thee:
> Discreet Religion binds us to admire
> The wayes of providence, and not enquire.

137

The Obsequies for Edward King

J. Beaumont finds that all his questions culminate in these:

> O why was justice made so blind?
> O why was heaven it self so kind,
> And rocks so fierce? O why were we
> Thus partly blest? O why was he?

Samson Briggs concludes by rejecting the temptation to question providence:

> But back, my Muse, from hence;
> 'Tis not for thee to question Providence;
> Rather live sober still: such hot disputes
> Riddle us into atheisme. . . .

It is a commonplace of elegy that premature deaths provoke such questions and require some reconciliation to the order of things.

In our earlier treatment of the use of water by the elegists we found that water was commonly blamed as the cause of disaster. For Milton, however, 'It was that fatall and perfidious bark.' And likewise for W. Hall:

> Heav'n would (it seems) no common grave intrust,
> Nor bury such a Jewel in the dust.
> The fatall barks dark cabbin must inshrine
> That precious dust, which fate would not confine
> To vulgar coffins. . . .

In the inquest into this death Henry King gives a novel turn to the fate motive:

> But oh! his fatall love did prove too kind,
> To trust the treacherous waves and carelesse wind,
> Which did conspire to intercept this prize
> Aiming t' undo the land by Piracies.

But while Hall turns the fatal bark to eulogistic advantage, Milton makes it take the blame off his pastoral mythology.

It is on the loss to learning that the other elegists are most prolix, although they often combine human and divine learning. For Milton *Chamus* is, at best, a man of few words:

The Obsequies for Edward King

Ah! who hath reft (quoth he) my dearest pledge?

But for Henry King, torn by grief, his brother

> *made divine and human learning friends;*
> *Of which he was the best edition,*
> *Not stuft with doubts, but all decision.*

Among the questions provoked by his death, J. Beaumont
asks:

> *Why strove he both the worlds to know,*
> *Yet always scorn'd the world below?*
> *Why would his brain a centre be*
> *To learnings circularitie,*
> *Which though the vastest arts did fill*
> *Would like a point seem little still!*

King's learning is a main theme for J. Cleveland:

> *Whose learning if we sound, we must confesse*
> *The sea but shallow, and him bottomlesse . . .*
> *The famous Stagirite, who in his life*
> *Had Nature as familiar as his wife,*
> *Bequeath'd his widow to survive with thee*
> *Queen Dowager of all Philosophie . . .*
> *Some have affirm'd, that what on earth we find,*
> *The sea can parallel for shape and kind:*
> *Books, arts, and tongues were wanting; but in thee*
> *Neptune hath got an Universitie*

While Samson Briggs shares the final conceit, W. More
makes a turn on the first one:

> *Nor do I like their pietie, who to sound*
> *His depth of learning, where they feel no ground,*
> *Strain till they lose their own. . . .*

Obviously the loss to learning is a natural theme for the
university world.

King's loss to the church helps to lessen his brother's
personal grief:

So I me thinks do feel my grief abate,
When I consider that both Church and State
Joyn in this losse. . . .

On this topic Milton is most extensive; the others at best, like Beaumont, involve it in the loss to learning. Milton's clerical spokesman is not only more voluble than his academic speaker, but 'He shook his mitred locks, and stern bespake.' Obviously he spoke as a bishop, and hence was not laying the axe of reformation to the Anglican edifice itself. Either Milton was not yet in the 'root and branch' mood or else he forgot that 'decorum is the grand master-piece to observe'. Of course he did ignore the decorum of style for the pastoral. In the heading which Milton added to the poem in 1645 he says, 'and by occasion foretells the ruin of our corrupted clergy, then in their height'. But this is hindsight and expressive of the more extreme position that Milton had reached in 1645 when he changed 'little said' to 'nothing sed'. The 'grim wolf' of 1638 was Roman, not Anglican. In the *Obsequies*, however, St. Peter's speech is countered when J.H. says, 'To the deceased's vertuous sister':

> *For our Cathedralls to a beamlesse eye*
> *Are quires of angels in epitomie,*
> *Maugre the blatant beast, who cries them down*
> *As savouring of superstition.*
> *Misguided people! But for your sweet self,*
> *Madame, you never dash'd against that shelf*
> *Of stubbornnesse against the Church; but you*
> *(Pauls virgin and saint Peters matrone too)*
> *Though I confesse you did most rarely paint,*
> *Yet were no hypocrite, but a true saint.*

If Milton was of the same mind in 1637 and 1645, then his bishop must have felt awkward in this cathedral and must have confused his readers.

For these topics of lamentation Milton introduces an embracing form: that of the pastoral elegy. This he sets in an

The Obsequies for Edward King

occasional framework; that is, a beginning and end which
assume and drop a mask of his college youth. Thereby he
assumes and drops the pastoral disguise, but the pastoral
form itself integrates all the elements into an effective form
of lamentation in which Milton treats his topics in terms of
myth.

Milton adjusts the décor of the pastoral convention to the
English scene and the requirements of the occasion. King's
drowning is not forgotten in the pastoral machinery, but
submerged in the water imagery. There it is a latent discord,
not an open contradiction. It will not do to say the pisca-
tory eclogue bridges the gap. By his use of the pastoral convention Milton dramatizes his mourning; the other elegists
reflected on the death and its meaning; they employed no
dramatic vehicle.

But Milton warns us that he is going to strain the pastoral
mode as Virgil strained it in his 'messianic' eclogue (IV).
Twice thereafter in his 'somewhat ampler strain' (*paulo
maiora*) the Sisters too 'loudly sweep the string', and each
time he calls attention to it by reinvoking the pastoral Muse.
In both cases he seeks higher consolation than he can find in
strictly pastoral terms.

After his pastoral introduction Milton begins his lament
on the theme of King's loss to the Muse of poetry. This he
speaks in his own person. But King's loss to learning is
spoken, appropriately, by Chamus; and his loss to the
Church, again appropriately if unexpectedly, by St. Peter.
Milton parcels out the various aspects of King's loss to
amplify his pastoral machinery. But it is significant that he
speaks to the first theme in his own person, and this he does
because he comes as a poet to mourn King's death, and
because it is this aspect of King with which he is now most
closely associated. This is why the theme of association ends
with the line,

And old Dametas lov'd to heare our song.

And why the theme of loss is pointed by the line,

Such, Lycidas, thy losse to shepherds eare.

141

Whether 'old Dametas' was Chappell or not, he had been the common tutor of Milton and King. Milton's *Elegia Prima* and the postscript to the *Elegies* offer the best background for this part of *Lycidas*.

'Where were ye Nimphs' begins the fate theme—and the pastoral illusion or fiction begins to break down, 'Ah me, I fondly dream!' The futility is amplified by the supreme example of Orpheus, whose lyre was the gift of Apollo and whose fate became a parallel to King's death. And this loss leads Milton, like the other elegists, to question providence: What's the use when Fate is indifferent? In terms of Milton's role this is properly a common question, and it is only proper that he should be deeply concerned in the answer. But 'Phebus repli'd' in terms beyond the range of pastoral thought and feeling, and the pastoral disguise grows very thin when the son Apollo lifts the question of reward to 'all-judging Jove'. Obviously Phoebus, who speaks the higher strain, has been baptized.

Having rejected Amaryllis, he turns to Arethusa in re-invoking the pastoral Muse. Arethusa had been changed by Diana into the 'fountain' which continues the 'sacred well' of the original invocation. But the addition of 'Mincius' generalizes the suggestion of pastoral waters. Then the pastoral procession takes up other questions. The fate theme is continued by an inquiry into the cause of the disaster. Wind and water are exonerated: 'It was that fatall and perfidious bark.' Thus the fate theme comes to rest on the ship.

Chamus speaks for King's loss to learning, the theme least suited to pastoral development. Here the allusion to 'that sanguine flower inscrib'd with wo' reminds us of one both favoured and slain by Apollo, and prepares us for the later development by 'every flower that sad embroidery wears'.

In the lament for King's loss to the Church, which is a proper theme of Christian pastoral, the higher voice again breaks the mood of pagan pastoral. Yet this loss is registered in the most detailed pastoralism of the entire poem. Of course the water symbolism is continued by seeing

The Obsequies for Edward King

Peter as 'The Pilot of the Galilean lake', that is, in an aspect propitious to King. St. Peter's credentials would seem to be adequate without the 'mitred locks', especially if his speech is regarded as a tirade against the bishops' edifice. It is reasonable to suppose that Milton is not confused, but that his idea of reformation does not yet extend to the Root and Branch Bill. St. Peter's lament concludes with a religious assurance like Apollo's before, promising the 'axe of God's reformation' as Milton later called it. St. Matthew seems to be on Milton's mind, for the keys come from Matthew (16. 19) and the axe from Matthew (3. 10), though he rejects Peter's fear of water in Matthew (14. 29).

This time the reinvocation of the pastoral Muse returns to the Arethusa myth by addressing Alpheus, the river god who continued to pursue her under the sea. It is interesting that Isaac Olivier, who has most pastoral myth in common with Milton, uses this myth in the dual capacity of lover and conqueror of the sea, although he conflates Alpheus and Achelous:

> *So should he, so have cut the Irish strand,*
> *And like a lustie bridegroom leapt to land;*
> *Or else (like Peter) trode the waves: but he*
> *Then stood most upright, when he bent his knee.*

Thus his ultimate consolation combines both pagan and Christian elements as it comes to rest on King's final posture. Here Milton's 'dread voice . . . that shrunk thy streams' incorporates the sense both of shrinking and of intimidating the pastoral flow. Now the Sicilian Muse is to water the vales into profusion for Lycidas. But even this floral offering modulates to 'sad embroidery' as 'our frail thoughts' take refuge in illusion. With the 'Ay me !' pastoral fiction again gives way to reality—that King still floats upon his 'watry biere' at the mercy of wind and wave. Isaac Olivier avoided this fiction but employed another motive:

> *Why did not some officious dolphine hie*
> *To be his ship and pilot through the frie*
> *Of wondring Nymphs. . . ?*

143

The Obsequies for Edward King

And then he too alluded to Christ,

> *Since first the waters gave*
> *A blessing to him which the soul could save . . .*

Before proceeding to Milton's resolution, let us observe some themes of consolation employed by the other elegists. The anonymous elegist opened with a sun figure and also closed with one:

> *As night, close-mourner for the setting sunne,*
> *Bedews her cheeks with tears when he is gone*
> *To th' other world: so we lament and weep*
> *Thy sad untimely fall, who by the deep*
> *Didst climbe to th' highest heav'ns. . . .*

This natural parallel is developed more fully by W. Hall:

> *Thus doth the setting sunne his evening light*
> *Hide in the Ocean, when he makes it night;*
> *The world benighted knows not where he lies,*
> *Till with new beams from seas he seems to rise:*
> *So did thy light, fair soul, it self withdraw*
> *To no dark tombe by natures common law,*
> *But set in waves, when yet we thought it noon,*
> *And thence shall rise more glorious then the sunne.*

This is close to Milton but more carefully adapted to the occasion. Instead of the natural parallel W. More turns to the supernatural:

> *Canst thou tell*
> *Who 'twas, that when the waves began to swell,*
> *The ship to sink, sad passengers to call,*
> Master we perish, *slept secure of all?*
> *Remember this, and him that waking kept*
> *A mind as constant, as he did that slept.*

With this allusion to Christ's stilling of the tempest (Mark 4. 37–8) More begins the most detailed parallel to the report of King's last moments. He continues with an allusion to Elijah:

The Obsequies for Edward King

Canst thou give credit to his zeal and love,
That went to heav'n and to those fires above
Rapt in a fierie chariot?

This prepares his final turn on King's going down in the attitude of prayer:

Pardon me, Reader, if I say he's gone
The self-same journey in a watry one.

Unless there is a latent sun figure in More's 'fierie chariot', only Isaac Olivier managed, like Milton, to combine pagan and Christian myth in his resolution. Of course More does have 'fires above'.

It must be remembered that Milton's pastoral mode betrayed him into his 'false surmise'. Though he capitalized on the contrast between reality and illusion, he did so here by destroying his illusion or by moving from a theme of comfort to a theme of grief. This procedure also induces a feeling of abruptness in shifting to the real consolation theme, 'Weep no more.' But now we perceive the cunning in his ordering of themes, for once more he is preparing to find consolation outside the strict pastoral convention. For a third time we are about to hear a 'somewhat ampler strain'.

Then the real consolation parallels the Alpheus myth, for he too sank 'beneath the watry floore' before he rose in the fountain of Arethusa. And the resurrection theme passes through the natural level in the figure of the setting and rising sun to the supernatural level through the figure of Christ walking on the water. This passage is explicitly marked from the natural parallel, 'So sinks the day-starre,' to the supernatural parallel, 'So Lycidas sunk low.'

But once again the elegy returns to the pastoral level with 'Now, Lycidas, the shepherds weep no more,' and Lycidas finds his recompense in becoming 'the Genius of the shore', his ultimate 'meed' within the pastoral convention. Thus Milton combines his pagan and Christian consolation in an appropriate pastoral figure which resolves the discords exploited in the poem. As 'the Genius of the shore' Lycidas

K   145

can return to men the protection that has been extended to him. Thus the consolation is again, and finally, rested in his pastoral fiction.

It is clear that the form of the pastoral elegy enabled Milton to organize and unify common topics in a far more effective way than his rival elegists. Only W. More is less inclined to blame the sea, but no one is less inclined to make it a motive of praise. Otherwise Milton shares the common motives of the elegists and most of the uncommon ones, but the rarest only with Isaac Olivier. Although the pastoral disguise gave Milton's elegy more objectivity, none except King's brother emphasizes the personal relation more than Milton. And Milton's dramatic method enables him to develop more emotional conflict than the more lyric elegists are able to produce.

But Milton's greatest source of power is the emotional tension generated by discords within his pastoral unity. We have seen these discords in the development of the poem, and they have taught us something about Milton's use of his convention. By his time, of course, the pastoral convention had assimilated Christian elements—at least since Petrarch. But in employing the pastoral elegy Milton exploited the basic conflict between pagan and Christian pastoralism, and so developed a new intensity in his use of the convention. In the more explicit form of dialogue, Marvell developed a similar opposition between these elements of the pastoral in his 'Clorinda and Damon'. For Milton it was an early conflict of the classical and Christian elements that were to divide his sensibility. Now the Christian interruptions show emotion breaking through the pastoral convention or display tension between Christian and pagan elements then combined in the pastoral convention. Thus they provide alternations of feeling, and give truer resolutions of problems for Milton, until the two strains are harmonized at the end.

Some discords of style in Milton's elegy unfortunately do not remove it sufficiently from the so-called 'rubbish' of his rivals. It may seem ungracious to cite the early lines:

The Obsequies for Edward King

> *He must not flote upon his watry biere*
> *Unwept, and welter to the parching wind*
> *Without the meed of some melodious tear.*

But the purity of Milton's style is not exemplary here, for, with the best will in the world, we cannot hold 'melodious tear' at the metaphorical level so long as it is recompense both for a drying wind and a watery bier. For the moment Milton, unexpectedly, slips from a Virgilian idiom to that of his second poem 'On the University Carrier'. Likewise we may boggle at a late passage:

> *So sinks the day-starre in the Ocean bed,*
> *And yet anon repairs his drooping head,*
> *And tricks his beams, and with new spangled ore*
> *Flames in the forehead of the morning skie.*

This again is not a style inspired by the pastoral classics, but rather by Sylvester or some minor Spenserian. It belongs with the 'Sun in bed' passage of the *Nativity Ode*. It is a style which ended in Benlowes and Butler's 'Character of a Small Poet'. The classical vein of Milton is restored in the later lines,

> *And now the sunne had stretch'd out all the hills,*
> *And now was dropt into the western bay.*

This, Dryden would have agreed, is more in the Virgilian vein.

VII

Milton and the Mortalist Heresy

★

The question of Milton's philosophical background still obliges us to look through a glass darkly. In asserting that 'we come closest of all to Milton's most personal ideas in a group of his immediate contemporaries, the Mortalists', Professor Saurat[1] appears not to have been fully aware either of the company or of the controversy into which he plumped Milton. As a matter of fact, when we examine the mortalist heresy, we discover that mortalism partly projects Milton from the spirit world of More into the more substantial world of Hobbes.[2] But is it true that Richard Overton's pamphlet, *Mans Mortallitie* (1643), inspired the controversy which produced so many books on immortality in the 1640's and 50's? Not that Professor Saurat actually says this, but it is a pertinent question. We can answer that a far more popular book than Overton's had raised this ancient Arabian heresy in 1642, and that when *Mans Mortallitie* appeared this book was in its third edition.

And that book was Sir Thomas Browne's *Religio Medici*. In Section VII Browne confesses the heresies with which his 'greener studies have been polluted':

[1] *Milton: Man and Thinker* (New York, 1925), p. 310; see chap. on 'The Mortalists, 1643-1655'.

[2] Cf. Marjorie H. Nicolson, 'The Spirit World of Milton and More', *Studies in Philology*, XXII (1925), 433-52.

Milton and the Mortalist Heresy

'Now, the first of mine was that of the Arabians; that the souls of men perished with their bodies, but should yet be raised again at the last day: not that I did absolutely conceive a mortality of the soul, but, if that were (which faith, not philosophy hath yet thoroughly disproved), and that both entered the grave together, yet I held the same conceit thereof that we all do of the body, that it should rise again. Surely it is but the merits of our unworthy natures, if we sleep in darkness until the last alarm. A serious reflex upon my own unworthiness did make me backward from challenging this prerogative of my soul: so that I might enjoy my Saviour at the last, I could with patience be nothing almost unto eternity.'[1]

But the numerous defences of the immortality of the soul which follow the *Religio Medici* attempt to show that philosophy as well as faith can disprove the mortality of the soul;[2] this is Digby's point in his observation on this section.[3] In 1645 Alexander Ross animadverted upon both the *Religio Medici* and Digby's *Observations* (1643): 'this may be indeed *religio Medici*, the religion of the House of *Medicis*, not of the Church of England'.[4] And on the heresy which I have just quoted, Ross remarks:

'First . . . your vessell retaines yet the sent of that liquor,

[1] *Works*, ed. S. Wilkin (Bohn ed., London, 1852), II, 329–30. 'By 1646,' remarks G. Keynes, 'eight editions of the *Religio Medici* in English and Latin had been sold, and its author was a famous man.'

[2] In matters of religion Browne raised his imagination above his reason; he declared (ibid., p. 333): 'I am now content to understand a mystery, without a rigid definition, in an easy and Platonic description. That allegorical description of Hermes pleaseth me beyond all the metaphysical definitions of divines. Where I cannot satisfy my reason, I love to humour my fancy.' Bacon encouraged this attitude (but he did not applaud it) in his *Advancement of Learning*, where he wrote: 'For we see that in matters of Faith and Religion we raise our Imagination above our Reason; which is the cause why Religion sought ever access to the mind by similitudes, types, parables, visions, dreams' (*Philosophical Works*, ed. J. M. Robertson, pp. 110–11). Cf. A. C. Howell, 'Sir Thomas Browne and Seventeenth-Century Scientific Thought', *Studies in Philology*, XXII (1925), 61–80. For the contemporary criteria of truth and reality, see my 'Restoration Revolt against Enthusiasm', in this volume.

[3] See Browne, *Works*, ed. cit., II, 455 ff.

[4] *Medicus Medicatus* (London, 1645), p. 2. The stiff orthodoxy of Ross makes him a useful detector of heresies.

with which at first it was seasoned. Secondly, if you have forgot, reade over againe *Plato*, and you shall find, that *Philosophy* can throughly prove the soules immortality: reade also Aristotle.'[1]

Ross finds another point of attack in Browne with which, it is safe to say, no discussion of immortality or atheism in this time was unconnected. This is his apology for the atheism of Epicurus, which is condemned by Ross in these terms:

'But, I say, hee is no lesse an *Atheist* that denies Gods providence, or any other of his Attributes, then hee that denies his Essence. Though *Epicurus* and *Democritus* babbled something of a Deity, yet in holding the world to be casually and rashly agglomerated of small *atomes*, they were very *Atheists*.'[2]

How Epicurus has been 'traduced', adds Browne in the *Vulgar Errors*, 'the learned pen of Gassendus hath discovered'. But in religious minds the hypothesis of atoms, to which the science of the time (for example, Boyle) was especially congenial, made disconcerting religious connections with Epicurean physics and libertine ethics (to which even Boyle objected); and to thinkers like Cudworth, these involved the materialist Hobbes.

In the same year, 1645, but in another work, Ross attacked both Digby and Overton on the question of immortality, under this comprehensive title:

'The Philosophicall Touch-stone: or Observations upon Sir *Kenelm Digbie's* Discourses of the nature of Bodies, and of the reasonable Soule. In which his erroneous Paradoxes are refuted, the Truth, and *Aristotelian Philosophy* vindicated, the *immortality* of mans *Soule* briefly, but sufficiently proved.

[1] Ibid., p. 10. In view of Ross's Aristotelian conservatism, this use of Plato is significant, as other items will prove.

[2] Ibid., p. 33; see *Religio Medici*, Sect. XX. Epicurus is again defended by Browne in *Vulgar Errors* (1646), and Browne is again reprobated on this score by Ross in *Arcana Microcosmi* (1652): see Browne's *Works*, ed. cit., II, 275–6 and footnote. Browne's reference in *Vulgar Errors* to Gassendi's *De Vita & Moribus Epicuri* must have been added to the second edition (1650), for Gassendi's book was not published until 1647.

And the weak Fortifications of a late Amsterdam Ingeneer,
patronizing *The Soules mortality*, briefly slighted.'
Much of the argument is directed against the hypothesis
of atoms: 'You have been too much conversant in the
schools of *Democritus*, who held the world to be made of
Atomes'; 'and to flye upon every occasion to *Democritus* his
Atomes, is a poore *asylum*.'[1] Ross considers 'what hath of old
been, or can of late be objected against this knowne and
generally acknowledged truth [of immortality], by the im-
pugners thereof'.[2] And he lets us see how *Mans Mortallitie*
struck one contemporary when he says:

'Here I had ended, but that I have now lighted on a
Pamphlet by chance, the *Scribler* of which was ashamed to
put to his name, his cause is so bad. He undertakes to prove
the soules mortalitie, but so weakly, that I should lose too
much time, and spend too much paper to answer him
according to his *folly*: For there is nothing in it but the *froth*
of a luxurious wit, wantonly abusing *Scripture*, and obtrud-
ing a *cloud* instead of *Juno*, *shadowes* of reason in stead of
solid arguments.'[3]

It is plain that for the contentious Ross, Overton was not
an opponent worthy of more than passing attention. This
much is clear, or will become so, that the controversy was
much larger than Overton's group, that it made strange
alliances, and that anything less than orthodoxy tended to
place one among the Epicurean atheists.

Some points about Overton's pamphlet which Professor
Saurat neglects ought to be noticed. On the title-page of the
first edition found in the Thomason Tracts (British
Museum), Thomason has crossed out 'Amsterdam' and
written 'London'; to the date 1643 he has added 'Jan: 19'. It
was, of course, not uncommon to print books in London
and label them Amsterdam as a matter of caution. In the

---

[1] *The Philosophicall Touch-stone* (London, 1645), pp. 16 and 57. On the
revival of 'Atomism' see an article which came to my attention after this essay
was written: C. T. Harrison, 'Bacon, Hobbes, Boyle, and the Ancient Atomists',
Harvard Studies and Notes in Philology and Literature, XV (1933), 191–218.

[2] Ibid., p. 117.

[3] Ibid., pp. 123–4.

second edition of 1655, as it is called on the title-page (neglecting the re-arranged issue of 1644), the title is changed to *Man wholly mortal,* and the contents are 'by the Author corrected and enlarged'. Professor Saurat's contention that Milton assisted in this correction and enlargement seems to me to rest upon rather tenuous grounds. As Browne suggests, it was the part of this heresy, and not merely of Milton, to insist on the resurrection; but in this Overton has but little belief according to Professor Saurat.[1] And yet even in Overton's very first issue that 'little belief' (in 'an infallible object, the Resurrection') is vital to man as 'a Compound wholly mortall':

'Therefore nothing of Man can be immortall, but what first hath seen corruption. So that, if that which is made the better and most excellent part of Man, without which he is NO MAN (as is held) titled the *Soul,* shall not see corruption, it shall not participate of the immortallity purchased by Christ, but must needs perish, except there be *Ens extra Deum,* as that strang invented *Entitie* must needs be: And so consequently, NO MAN shalbe saved: And as before it incur'd this Absurditie that the *Soules* of the Damned shall not perish, but stand as well as the *Stative Angels*: So by this, the *Soules* both of the *righteous* and *wicked* shall for ever cease, and never be immortallized at the *Resurrection*: And thence the denyall both of *Resurrection, Condemnation,* and *Salvation, Heaven* and *Hell, God* and *Christ* is in avoydable: After rusheth in the *Epicurean* Blasphemie, *Let us eat, and drinke, for to morrow we dye*: And so, *so many bellyes, so many Gods,* and no other.'[2]

[1] Op. cit., p. 319.
[2] *Mans Mortallitie* (Amsterdam, 1643), p. 47. Hobbes helps us to understand this argument in his mortalist reading of Scripture (*Leviathan,* Everyman ed., p. 337): 'yet the Doctrine is now, and hath been a long time far otherwise; namely, that every man hath Eternity of Life by Nature, in as much as his Soul is Immortall: So that the flaming Sword at the entrance of Paradise, though it hinder a man from coming to the Tree of Life, hinders him not from the Immortality which God took from him for his Sin; nor makes him to need the sacrificing of Christ, for the recovering of the same; and consequently, not onely the faithfull and righteous, but also the wicked, and the Heathen, shall enjoy Eternall Life, without any death at all; much lesse a Second. and Ever-

Milton and the Mortalist Heresy

This is arguing by negatives how much really depends upon man's mortality, and one cannot suppose that Overton was merely stacking the scales against immortality, in his ardour to make heretics. Finally, resting in the conviction of mortality, Overton concludes that man must 'cast him-selfe wholy on *Jesus Christ* with whome in God *our lives are hid*, that when he *who is our life* shall appeare, he might also with him appeare in glory, to whome be the honour of our immortality for ever, and for ever. *Amen.*'

These are the last words of the first version, and it is hard to see how Milton, with more logic, could make immortality any more necessary.[1] Overton makes the resurrection depend upon the mortality of the soul; to deny this (for he anticipates his opponents) is to let in the 'Epicurean Blasphemie' of unadulterated naturalism.

It is not that the ideas of Milton and Overton do not run very close to one another at times, but rather that these ideas are not always confined to them, which makes one hesitate to believe that they were quite so closely related as Professor Saurat makes out. The passage quoted on pages 320–1 of his *Milton: Man and Thinker*, to show the mark left by 'Milton's knowledge and intelligence' on the 1655 edition of *Mans Mortallitie*, is not really superior in these respects to the passage quoted on page 315 from the earlier edition.[2] Both

lasting Death. To salve this, it is said, that by *Second*, and *Everlasting Death*, is meant a Second, and Everlasting Life, but in Torments; a Figure never used, but in this very Case.' Cf. *Paradise Lost*, X. 782 ff., where Adam wonders whether God can make death that is not death, and 'extend His sentence beyond dust and Natures Law', which means here, 'That dust I am, and shall to dust returne,' rather than the Law of Nature which would make annihilation a contradiction in God.

[1] See D. Saurat, op. cit., p. 320.

[2] Not even the discovery (cf. *T. L. S.*, 14th June 1934, p. 424) that this passage derives from Peter du Moulin the Elder (*Anatomy of Arminianism*) convinces Professor Saurat that Milton is not responsible for it.

One can only take humorously his suggestion (ibid., pp. 321–2) that Milton may have added to the 1655 edition the idea that 'King Druis (hence the name druids) to encourage his subjects to fight, invented immortality of the soul'. For Overton had only to turn to Burton on immortality (cf. *Anatomy*, Part I. Sect. I. Mem. II. Subs. IX) to find 'those *British Druids* of old' and to be directed to Caesar 6. *Com.* (cap. 14), where he could read: 'Imprimis hoc volunt per-

quotations are from the same, though differently num-
bered, chapter in each edition. As for the similar doctrine,
and 'one of Milton's "noblest" ideas', that 'the soul goes
from father to son at generation because the soul is one with
the body',[1] was this really exclusive doctrine at that time?
Certainly, Browne also pondered the mystery of creation,
and was haunted by an objection to the orthodox opinion
which denied 'traduction' of the soul. This objection, he
says, was 'not wrung from speculations and subtleties, but
from common sense and observation; not pick'd from the
leaves of any author, but bred amongst the weeds and tares
of my own brain':

'And this is a conclusion from the equivocal and monstrous productions in the copulation of a man with a beast:
for if the soul of man be not transmitted and transfused in
the seed of the parents, why are not those productions
merely beasts, but have also an impression and tincture of
reason in as high a measure, as it can evidence itself in those
improper organs?'[2]

While this is neither 'noble' nor quite Miltonic, it has
greater pretensions to originality and even to pseudo-science
than has Milton's notion, which is common enough in the
Church Fathers; but 'traduction' was promptly denied by

suadere, non interire animas, sed ab aliis post mortem transire ad alios, atque
hoc maxime ad virtutem excitari putant metu mortis neglecto.' If Milton was
reading this 'ancient chronicle' for his *History*, so were the schoolboys; but
Milton did not think enough of the idea to record it in his *History*, although he
refers to Caesar on the Druids. Cf. also G. Hakewill's *Apologie* (London, 1635),
p. 21.

[1] Saurat, op. cit., pp. 318 and 321. The authorities cited by Overton and
Milton were common to this controversy; for, as Charles Blount points out,
'many good Moral men, and some of the Fathers, as *Tertullian, Lactantius*, etc.
held the Soul to be *ex Traduce* from Father to Son, and that for these reasons':
etc. (cf. *Miscellaneous Works*, 1695, 'Anima Mundi', p. 37). Peter du Moulin
(*Anatomy of Arminianism*) attacks 'traduction' as a part of Arminian doctrine.

[2] Op. cit., II, 377; cf. *Vulgar Errors*, ibid., p. 104. In Aristotelian thought the
body of a beast could not be the proper organ of the soul of man, and in
Cartesian thought a brute was an automaton. Overton also considers un-
natural progeny and 'why in some measure as far as by those improper *Organs*
can be expressed, may they not be *rationall*'.

Milton and the Mortalist Heresy

Digby.[1] 'Nor truly,' continues Browne, 'can I peremptorily deny that the soul, in this her sublunary estate, is wholly, and in all acceptions, inorganical'; but he did not leave the question untouched by an air of scepticism, particularly in the first edition. And this came from one who confessed the taint of mortalism in a book which attained extraordinary popularity, and from one whose intellectual impact on his own time we are liable to underestimate, for we forget how 'Dr. *Brown* (so justly admired as well by Foreigners as his own Country men, upon the Account of his Knowledge in all Gentile sorts of Literature) does both in his *Religio Medici & Vulgar Errors*, betray his many Doubts and Scruples', as Charles Blount remarked so late as 1693.[2] Browne was not then merely the stylist.

Milton's 'absorbing thirst for justice', insomuch as it prompted him to add 'the (to be) Kantian argument of practical.reason'[3] to his insistence on the resurrection, was hardly more hydroptic than Browne's desire for 'the day that must make good that great attribute of God, his justice', without which 'all religion is a fallacy'.[4] If Milton could say, 'God is neither willing, nor properly speaking, able to annihilate anything altogether',[5] it was not necessarily because Browne had said in the 1642 edition of *Religio*

[1] Ibid., p. 466. The reasons which Blount gives (op. cit., 'Anima Mundi', pp. 37 ff.) for holding 'the Soul to be *ex Traduce* from Father to Son' make a fair summary of the controversial points involved in this question. For example, if the soul is not *ex traduce* from the parents, 'Man begets not whole Man, for he consists of Body and Soul joyntly.' Even Browne's point is suggested here. The problem of 'traduction' and other problems related to the immortality of the soul are sketched by Burton (*Anatomy*, Part. I. Sect. I. Mem. II. Subs. IX), who cites many of the names and works, ancient or modern, that were connected with the 'doubtful subject' of the rational soul in his time. 'This question of the immortality of the soul is diversely and wonderfully impugned and disputed, especially among the Italians of late, saith *Jab. Colerus, lib. de immort. animae, cap. I.*' And Burton asserts that ·Pomponatius 'decided out of *Aristotle* not long since' against immortality. If only for a bibliography of the state of the question in the Renaissance, Burton merits consideration.

[2] See Blount, op. cit., 'The Oracles of Reason', p. 3.
[3] See Saurat, op. cit., p. 147.
[4] Browne, op. cit., II, 393-4.
[5] See Saurat, op. cit., p. 147.

Medici, 'What is made to be immortal, nature cannot, nor will the voice of God, destroy.'[1] The difference is that, although initiated in the Cabbala, Browne did not believe in a Christian materialism, except in so far as *forms* were associated with *atoms*. And at the last day, says Browne, 'when those corrupted relicks shall be scattered in the wilderness of forms, and seem to have forgot their proper habits, God, by a powerful voice, shall command them back into their proper shapes, and call them out by their single individuals. Then shall appear the fertility of Adam, and the magick of that sperm that hath dilated into so many millions.'[2]

This is a resurrection by means of the indestructible forms; and to Milton, although matter seemed merely to receive embellishment from the accession of forms, still the soul was a *form* in a modified Aristotelian sense.[3] If we turn to the notion of hell, there is Browne's declaration: 'I feel sometimes a hell within myself; Lucifer keeps his court in my

---

[1] Browne, op. cit., II, 395, note 9. Milton held that God 'can do nothing which involves a contradiction', and annihilation involves contradiction (cf. Saurat, p. 116). On the same problem Digby remarks of Browne, 'He needeth not be so scrupulous, as he seemeth to be, in averring downrightly, that God cannot do contradictory things' (Browne, op. cit., II, 463). And Browne had been 'scrupulous' when he wrote: 'I hold that God can do all things ["cannot do all things but sin", as Digby read it in the 1642 ed.]: how he should work contradictions, I do not understand, yet dare not, therefore, deny . . . I will not say that God cannot, but he will not, perform many things, which we plainly affirm he cannot' (ibid., pp. 362–3). Nor did he believe that the world 'will ever perish upon the ruins of its own principles. As the work of creation was above nature, so is its adversary, annihilation' (ibid., p. 391). But Digby contradicts him and asserts 'that no annihilation can proceed from God'. Thus one of the ideas in the *Christian Doctrine* upon which Milton (as well as Saurat) lays great stress, was debated in popular antecedent works as a problem of the time.
[2] Ibid., p. 395.
[3] Cf. *Prose Works* (Bohn ed.), IV, 180 and 193. In his chapter 'Of the Creation' Milton explains the creation in more or less Aristotelian terms: using matter ('it is only a passive principle') and the four Aristotelian causes (which are comprehended in God), he arrives at the goodness of matter, the impossibility of annihilation, the nature of the soul as *form*, and its 'traduction' by generation (ibid., pp. 178–93). Although Milton seems to make form itself material, he approximates the Aristotelian notion that 'Form is that which gives completeness to Matter by realizing its potential capacities; it is the Energy or Entelechy of Matter' (cf. E. Zeller, *Aristotle and the Earlier Peripatetics* [London, 1897], I, 354–80).

breast . . . for every devil is an hell unto himself.'[1] And so Milton in *Paradise Lost*, IV. 20:

> *The Hell within him, for within him Hell*
> *He brings, and round about him, nor from Hell*
> *One step no more then from himself can fly*
> *By change of place.*

But it would be rash to conclude, on these grounds, that there was any particular community of ideas between Browne and Milton; and it is only a little less rash to discover that Milton was influenced by, or that he influenced, *Mans Mortallitie*. Both with respect to biography and with respect to parallels, Professor Saurat's case attains at best the stage of probability; at times he suggests as much, but his general implication is more positive.

Mans Mortallitie did, however, receive more attention than it was given by either Ross or Thomas Edwards in his *Gangraena* (1645). In 1645 Guy Holland (J. Sergeant), the Jesuit, replied to it under this title:

'The Prerogative of Man: or, His Soules Immortality, and high perfection defended, and explained against the rash and rude conceptions of a late Authour who hath inconsiderately adventured to impunge it.'
In 1653 this work was revised and enlarged by Holland with the title of *The Grand Prerogative of Humane Nature*.[2] The enlargement appears chiefly in the obvious impact of Epicurean thought, mainly through Gassendi, and in the influence of Thomas Carleton's *Philosophia Universa* (1649), which employs Descartes in its section 'Ex Physica'. In his preface Holland quotes 'Ede, bibe, lude, post mortem nulla voluptas', and then remarks:

---

[1] Op. cit., II, 402.

[2] London: Printed by Roger Daniel, 1653 (Daniel was the English publisher of Gassendi). Holland declares (p. 78) that his first edition had been censured: 'In the first Edition of this small Tract, this argument of Apparitions brought up the rear; but it pleased the Censurer of it in Oxford to dash it quite out, though for what reason I do not know.' Cf. Browne (op. cit., I, 84) on the relation of the belief in spirits to the belief in immortality. The argument of apparitions was also adopted by More and Glanvill.

'Doubtlesse these later perswaders seem to be more
ruinous and corrupt then the former [Epicureans], and of
more dangerous consequence. And thus we see that on
either side there want not suspicions, namely, as well for
concluding of mortality as of immortality, if we will be
guided by them.'[1]
And these were the two kinds of mortalists that occupied
the contemporary mind, but of this we have already become
aware.

In setting about the proof of immortality Holland refers
to 'the learned Authour of *Religio Medici*' and his notion
'that the entity of the form remains still unperished after
corruption':

'This same doctrine of *Religio Medici*, and that also which
we deliver here touching the originations of forms, was
the doctrine of old *Democritus*, expressed by him in his constitution of Atomes, or *minima naturalia*, as we find it largely
expressed and illustrated by *Joan. Magnenus 1. de Philosophia
Democriti Disp. 2. c. 2. & seqq.* as also by *Petrus Gassendus* in
his voluminous work *de Philosophia Epicuri tomo 1.*'[2]
How this form passed from man to man Holland could
also find in Browne, but in his second edition he brings
Carleton to bear upon the problem, which he explains
thus:

'Neither again do we with *Epicurus* and some other old
Philosophers, maintain any casual meeting or accidental
confluence of them [atoms]; but contrariwise, an assembling
of them in generation by the force of seminall or spermatick
virtue, descending from the forms into the sperme or seeds,

---

[1] Preface to the 1653 edition of *The Grand Prerogative*. Another English
Catholic writer whose work must not be forgotten in connection with this
controversy is Thomas White, the friend of Digby, who earnestly recom-
mended the 'knowing Master White's' *De Mundo* to the author of *Religio
Medici*. In 1666 Parliament coupled White's book *Of the Middle State of Souls*
with Hobbes's *Leviathan* as atheistic, 'apparently on the ground of their common denial of a natural immortality'. On White see Charles de Rémusat's
Histoire de la Philosophie en Angleterre (Paris, 1875), I, 308. Cf. C. T. Harrison,
'The Ancient Atomists and English Literature of the Seventeenth Century',
Harvard Studies in Classical Philology, XLV (1934), 20 ff.
[2] *The Grand Prerogative of Humane Nature* (London, 1653), pp. 6 and 7.

and by the creatour infused at the first creation into the forms.'[1]

This idea, which Browne calls 'traduction', is also part of Milton's thought; but it is possible in Milton 'because the soul is one with the body', says Professor Saurat; or because 'every *form*, to which the human soul must be considered as belonging, is produced by the power of matter', says Milton, invoking the consent of almost all philosophers.[2] Holland will not, of course, allow the adverse judgment of Epicurus on immortality, for although Gassendi has washed and perfumed him, he still smells of the hogsty; 'but the errour it self, and the reasons brought for it by *Lucretius*, are exactly refuted by the same *Gassendus*, as also his other impious doctrines'.[3] Nor can the Stoic notion of virtue as its own reward be allowed:

'The Stoicks invented for man this harsh and miserable felicity, for supplying the defect of their doctrine touching providence and humane felicity, which they could not patch up otherwise then with such rotten stuff as this, which will not hold the examination, nor indeed can be without the Christian doctrine of the resurrection.'[4]

Here Browne, Holland, and Milton could all agree. Holland's condemnation of the idea that 'Virtue is rich, and

---

[1] Ibid., pp. 7–8.

[2] *Prose Works* (Bohn ed.), IV, 193. Though Milton is by no means clear, he certainly distinguishes at times body, soul, and spirit, or matter and form; yet he insists that man is 'not compound or separable', but 'a body, or substance individual, animated, sensitive, and rational' (ibid., 187 ff.). Hobbes, on the other hand, asserts that 'the *Soule* in Scripture, signifieth alwaies, either the Life, or the Living Creature; and the Body and Soule jointly, the *Body alive*' (*Leviathan*, ed. cit., p. 337). Milton's 'living soul' and Hobbes's 'living creature' ought to be defined in the light of Aristotle's view of the soul: 'The only right view is that the soul is the form of its body, since the form cannot exist without the matter to which it belongs, and yet it is not itself material. . . . Life is not a combination of soul and body, and the living being is not something joined together of these two parts; but the soul is the active force that operates in the body, or, if you will, the body is the natural organ of the soul' (cf. Zeller, op. cit., II, 6–9). In making form itself material Milton (op. cit., IV, 180) interprets Aristotle by approaching Hobbes, but not to the point of making the soul simply 'motion'.

[3] Holland, op. cit., p. 25.

[4] Ibid., p. 71.

is a reward unto her selfe', echoes Browne's disposal of Stoic virtue with respect to the resurrection: '*Ipsa sui pretium virtus sibi*, that virtue is her own reward, is but a cold principle.'[1] For all of these men the resurrection was necessary to give real force and meaning to virtue, no less than to the providence of God.

And finally Holland brings us to one of the most interesting connections between mortalism and the thought of the time, which is the discovery that Hobbes also was a mortalist:

'*Pomponatius* and *Sennertus* will not grant it [i.e. the soul's immortality] to be naturall; and now lately one Mr. *Hobbes*, in a prodigious volume of his, called by him as prodigiously *Leviathan*, is of opinion that no other immortality of the soul can be proved out of Scripture, if any at all can, besides that one of the lowest classe, which is of grace and favour merely.'[2]

But we need not take Holland's word for it: we can read Chapters XXXVIII, XLIV, and XLVI of the *Leviathan* (1651); or we can turn to Ross again, in *Leviathan Drawn out with A Hook* (1653): 'But he would fain prove out of *Job* 14. 7. That life immortal beginneth not in man, till the resurrection.'[3] Here Ross attacks Hobbes as a mortalist, descending upon Chapter XXXVIII with hammer and tongs. There is a certain irony in the fact that for Hobbes also, mortalism and justice are related in a system of highest reward and punishment. Holland's mention of Pomponazzi should remind us that the mortalist heresy attracted many Renaissance minds and long attached itself to the name of Pomponazzi.[4] If we are disconcerted by the juxtaposition of

[1] See Browne, op. cit., II, 393.
[2] Holland, op. cit., pp. 119–20.
[3] *Leviathan Drawn out with A Hook* (London, 1653), p. 48.
[4] Cf. S. B. Liljegren, 'Die englischen Quellen der Philosophie Miltons und verwandtes Denken', *Beiblatt zur Anglia*, XXXIII (1922), 196–206. As late as 1679 a writer like Charles Blount (op. cit., 'Anima Mundi', p. 94) still remarked: '*Pomponatius* under pretence of defending the Soul's Immortality, hath fought against it; and professing himself a *Peripatetick*, hath in this particular, embraced the Sentiment of *Epicurus*. . . .'

Milton, the Christian materialist, and Hobbes, the atheistic materialist, we are ready to appreciate the intricacy of the controversy into which Professor Saurat has plunged us.

The early stages of the mortalist controversy may be traced in Charles de Rémusat's *Histoire de la Philosophie en Angleterre depuis Bacon jusqu'à Locke*. Its Epicurean inception may be found in Nicholas Hill's *Philosophia Epicurea, Demo-criticana, Theophrastica* (1601), which raised disturbing ques-· tions, or in Sir John Davies's *Nosce Teipsum* (1599), which was often reprinted in the seventeenth century, appearing as 'A Work for none but Angels & Men' in 1653, and being recommended in the 1697 edition 'to the *Wits* and *Vir-tuoso's*' as an antidote 'against the Poyson they have suck'd in from *Lucretius* or *Hobbs*'. Rémusat makes an observation which penetrates to the centre of this controversy in respect to the mortalist inference of materialism, whether Christian or pagan:

'Le poëme de Davies est au fond une réfutation, tout au moins une rectification, de la définition classique de l'âme suivant Aristote. Cette définition offrait bien une apparence de matérialisme qui n'avait pas effrayé l'Église, mais que ne pouvait souffrir le platonisme du seizième siècle. Nous voyons donc poindre ici une discussion sur la nature de l'âme qui se prolongera pendant plus de cent années encore.'[1]

In William Hill's *Infancie of the Soule or the Soule of an In-fant* (1605), a work which undertook a very controversial point, the sensitive soul is declared mortal; only the rational soul is immortal, and it is not 'traducted', but 'infused'. But the immortality of the soul depends upon the existence of God, and to prove his existence to atheists Martin Fotherby resorted to natural reason in his *Atheomastix* (1622). His work, which gives more room to philosophy than to theology, Rémusat calls one of the first Christian treatises of natural

---

[1] Op. cit., I, 120. See especially his discussion of Davies, Hill, Fotherby, Pemble, and also his 'Controverses sur l'âme' (Vol. II, ch. 7). Davies gives the soul Platonic attributes, opposes its 'traduction' by the parents, argues for its immortality from both nature and divinity, and finds his chief opponents in the Epicureans. In turn Overton remarks (op. cit., p. 11) that 'this invention' of immortality is 'reported to be Platoes'. And others support this attribution.

theology to be produced in England, although the words
'natural religion' did not appear in the title of a book until
John Wilkins's *Principles and Duties of Natural Religion*
(1678). The rectification of Aristotle begun by Davies was
carried on by William Pemble in the first quarter of the
century; the debate centred round the nature and origin of
the soul as *form*, and may have influenced Milton's view of
Aristotle. Questions which were provoked, if not always
answered, are whether the soul is essentially a spirit, a
separate substance, or only the form of the body; whether
the soul is 'traducted' by the parents or 'infused' by God;
and if the soul is only the form of the body, how can the
soul be immortal. The classic Aristotelian definition,
slightly modified, may be seen in Richard Crakanthorp's
definition of the soul: 'Est spiritus seu incorporea substantia
ita sociabilis corpori ut forma vere materiam informans et
compositum essentialiter constituens.'[1] But 'incorporeal
substance' or 'form', whether the soul is spirit or substance,
or may be both—these are alternatives which made Pemble
question the distinction between form and matter, and
which never ceased to trouble the seventeenth century in
its long controversy over the soul.

In this controversy mortalism presented one of the main
challenges to the providence of God, and offered itself under
two guises: as a limited mortality in the so-called Mortalists,
and as an absolute mortality in the Epicureans. For the more
orthodox minds both were atheistic, but the Epicureans
presented the more serious denial of divine providence, if
the Mortalists were the more culpable offenders. It is time
that we recognized in this controversy one of the chief intellectual and religious problems of the mid-seventeenth
century. As evidence of this, we may recall, besides the
books already mentioned, the following works on atheism
or the immortality of the soul: Digby's *Two Treatises* (1644),
in which, as in More, the soul is regarded as 'an immateriall
or spiritual substance'; Walter Charleton's *Darkness of*

[1] Ibid., I, 181. Nicholas Hill had written: 'Spiritus est corpus subtilissimum
sensum subterfugiens acutissimum.'

Milton and the Mortalist Heresy

Atheism (1652) and *Immortality of the Human Soul* (1657); Henry More's *Antidote against Atheisme* (1652) and *Immortality of the Soul* (1659), in which both Hobbes and Epicurus figure; and John Smith's *Select Discourses* (1660), in which atheism means Epicurus and Lucretius, but not Hobbes. This list is suggestive rather than exhaustive; but with the books already mentioned, these are significant works between 1642 and 1660; with the Bramhall-Hobbes debate on liberty and necessity, they represent one of the most important problems in this time. To 'assert Eternal Providence, and justifie the wayes of God to men' is to penetrate to the very core of this problem. It is only when we have seen Milton in this relationship that we can appreciate the intellectual significance of *Paradise Lost* or the real place of Milton among the assertors of divine providence before what was felt to be a rising tide of atheism.

Chief of the modern atheists was Hobbes, and of the ancient, Epicurus—a classification which received standard form in Cudworth's *True Intellectual System* (1678). The opposition of Milton to Hobbes has been overstressed by Professor Nicolson in her 'Milton and Hobbes';[1] and part of my purpose is to demur to some of the implications of her provocative article. To speak of 'the outpouring of criticism which arose with the publication of the *De Cive*' is to put the matter beyond the facts, for that outpouring came only with the publication of the *Leviathan* (1651).[2] Hobbes's chief opponent before 1651 was Bramhall, but his criticism was not published until 1655. Prior to 1651 Hobbes had touched mainly upon the political aspect of the religious question, but in the *Leviathan* he exposed himself much more dangerously to the *odium theologicum*; and a book like the *Leviathan* was necessary to bring the storm which broke about his head with its publication.[3] It was only with the

[1] See *Studies in Philology*, XXIII (1926), 405–33. For his contemporaries Hobbes was an Epicurean.
[2] Ibid., p. 407. All of the published attacks to which Dr. Nicolson refers in her footnote came after the *Leviathan*.
[3] Cf. G. C. Robertson, *Hobbes* (Blackwood's Philosophical Classics), pp. 61 and 160 ff.

Leviathan that the charge of mortalism was brought against Hobbes; only in this book did Bramhall find a denial of the immortality of the soul;[1] and only by his *Catching of Leviathan* (1658) did Bramhall provoke Hobbes to answer the anti-Hobbists, if merely by making an example of him.

The Bramhall-Hobbes controversy was almost a case of Arminian free-will against Calvinistic necessity, for Hobbes's philosophical conviction was most nearly allied to the Puritan tenet. In this light Milton, who agrees with Hobbes on mortalism, approaches the Arminians on free-will; both aspects of Milton relate to his assertion of divine providence, which both Hobbes and the Epicureans challenged.[2] To Hobbes's part in this challenge we must add the Epicurean; for with this school, atheism was commonly associated, even when Hobbes was not in question. Gassendi, the friend of Hobbes and apologist of Epicurus, revived the Epicurean philosophy in his famous works, *De Vita et Moribus Epicuri* and *Syntagma Philosophiae Epicureae*, which were published in 1647 and 1649. Although Gassendi exercised no special influence on Hobbes, he did exercise a considerable influence upon English thought, of which we have already had some evidence. It is, therefore, a mistake to limit to Hobbes the challenge to divine providence which agitated the contemporaries of Milton. If Browne's leaning to an ancient heresy did not provoke the mortalist debate in England, it is improbable that Hobbes, a later convert to this heresy, did provoke a religious controversy which may claim to antedate the Hobbist quarrel.[3] The point is that there were several reasons why divine providence was felt

---

[1] Cf. J. Bramhall, *Works* (Oxford, 1844), IV, 536.

[2] *Areopagitica* shows that Milton recognized the Epicurean challenge: 'Of other sects and opinions, though tending to voluptuousness, and the denying of Divine Providence, they took no heed. Therefore we do not read that either Epicurus, or that libertine school of Cyrene, or what the Cynic impudence uttered, was ever questioned by the laws' (*Prose Works*, Bohn ed., II, 56; cf. also p. 59).

[3] It is even possible that Browne exerted a perceptible influence upon Hobbes, for the first words of the 'Introduction' to the *Leviathan*, 'Nature (the Art whereby God hath made and governes the World),' echo Sect. XVI of the *Religio Medici*, which concludes that 'nature is the art of God'.

to need justifying just then, and why these justifications should take the form of defences of immortality as well as attacks upon atheism and determinism. It is not too much to say that, failing to recognize such facts, we shall fail to understand the environment to which *Paradise Lost* belongs; it is this recognition that precludes our entertaining the notion that Milton was replying solely, or even primarily, to Hobbes the mortalist.

John Evelyn may serve to introduce us to the effect of the Epicurean mortalists upon English thought. In 1656 he published *An Essay on the First Book of T. Lucretius Carus De Rerum Natura*, for which Jeremy Taylor wanted him to atone by employing 'the same pen in the glorifications of God, and the ministries of Eucharist and prayer'.[1] Evelyn himself hopes that his 'animadversions upon it will . . . provide against all the ill consequences'.[2] In his preface to the reader Evelyn declares that although the poet prevaricates in points of speculative theology like providence and immortality, he gives many excellent precepts that persuade to a life the most exact and moral. But in his 'Animadversions' he explains that some ' even in this pretending age of ours, talk so much of the *providence of God*, yet so live they, as if they denied it in their Actions; to convince whom, since it is the duty of the Preacher, I should here beg pardon for having said so much, did not the present Argument, and frequent objection against our Poet, sufficiently justifie me. The great Lipsius in his book *de Constantia*, hath spoken well on this subject; or to come neerer home, the learned Dr. *Hackwel*, in his excellent Apology, as this of our *Carus*,

[1] *Diary and Correspondence of John Evelyn*, ed. W. Bray (London, 1854), III, 72.

[2] Ibid., p. 73. Although Evelyn translated the five remaining books, he never published them (see ibid., p. 247). J. E. Sandys (*History of Classical Scholarship*, II, 355 ff.) notes that 'the second half of the seventeenth century is marked by an interest in Lucretius'. The interest in 'the foppish casuall dance of attoms' began in the 1640's, and enticed even a Puritan like Mrs. Lucy Hutchinson into translating Lucretius, although she denounced him as 'this Dog' for his impious and execrable doctrine. In France Lucretius was popular with the *libertins* and condemned by the clergy; the French *libertin*, La Mothe le Vayer, was also translated by Evelyn in *Liberty and Servitude*.

with all his eight reasons, refuted by the ingenious Dr. Charlton, to all whose discourses I suppose nothing can easily be added, besides trouble to the reader.'[1]

If Lucretius attacks the immortality of the soul, Evelyn assures his reader that 'to deliver this vast controversie over to the Divines, as touching the Immortality thereof, Christians are sufficiently instructed; and meer *Rationalists* as sollidly convinced in that learned and renowned Piece of the honorable Sir K. Digby.'[2]

The piece to convince 'mere rationalists' (a phrase which goes to the heart of the controversy) was the famous *Two Treatises* published in Paris in 1644 and in London in 1645. In his 'Animadversions' on Lucretius, Evelyn often refers to Gassendi and 'the ingenious Dr. Charlton', to whose defence of divine providence nothing can easily be added.

Dr. Walter Charleton was an early and enthusiastic follower of Descartes, but his most influential work was to spread the ideas of Epicurus and Gassendi. Charleton was a man of consequence in his day whom time has conspired to forget. He was physician (in title at least) to both the Charles's, an admirer and imitator of Sir Thomas Browne, a fellow of the College of Physicians, and one of the first fellows elected to the Royal Society. Although the chief English disseminator of Epicurean thought, he was as quick as Henry More to attack atheism and defend immortality; in fact, his books on these subjects are, if anything, earlier than More's. He was a friend of Hobbes, and his 'Discourse concerning the Different Wits of Men' is said to have been consulted by Locke. At Oxford he had been tutored by the famous Dr. Wilkins, and in London he gave an occasional lecture at the College of Physicians, which young Dr. Edward Browne communicated to his father,

[1] *An Essay on the First Book of T. Lucretius Carus de Rerum Natura* (London, 1656), p. 108. George Hakewill's *Apologie or Declaration of the Power and Providence of God* (1627) regarded the idea of the decay of the world as an affront to divine providence, and found Lucretius and the Epicureans especially guilty on these counts.
[2] Ibid., p. 117. Browne, in *Vulgar Errors* (1646), refers to 'Sir Kenelm Digby in his excellent treatise of bodies' (*Works*, ed. cit., I, 161).

old Sir Thomas Browne, at Norwich. His portrait still hangs in the Bodleian, but his books are no longer read, although *Epicurus's Morals* may be had in a modern reprint (1926). It was not thus in his own day. In 1663 Dryden wrote the poem, 'To my Honor'd Friend, Dr. Charleton, on his Learned and Useful Works', to introduce his *Chorea Gigantum*; at that date some of Charleton's most important works were *The Darkness of Atheism* (1652), *Physiologia Epicuro-Gassendo-Charltoniana* (1654), and *The Immortality of the Human Soul* (1657), all of which are concerned with Epicurean thought. In Dryden's poem the value of Charleton is suggested by these lines:

> *Whatever truths have been by art or chance*
> *Redeem'd from error, or from ignorance,*
> *Thin in their authors, like rich veins of ore,*
> *Your works unite, and still discover more.*

Because Charleton's 'works unite and still discover more' ideas of the time, they are useful to any examination of the heretical thought of the mid-seventeenth century.

Undertaking to dispel the darkness of atheism which followed 'our Fatall Civill Warre', Charleton declared his indebtedness to learned writers, and had the good grace to add:

'Moreover, every Brain is not constellated for new *Discoveries*; nor can every Age boast the production of a *Copernicus, Gilbert, Galileo, Mersennus, Cartesius*, or a *Harvey*: Providence introducing such, as Time doth *New Stars*, single and seldom.'[1]

To refute atheism Charleton believes, with the mere rationalist, that reason or the Light of Nature must prove the existence and providence of God, the immortality of the soul, and the freedom of the will, without which all religion and morality are subverted. In demonstrating the existence of God, and responding to several objections made by Mersenne and Hobbes, he is chiefly indebted to 'the incomparable *Metaphysicks* of that heroicall Wit, Renatus

[1] *The Darkness of Atheism* (London, 1652), sig. c2r.

De's Chartes'.[1] But in defending divine providence, he falls into the debt of Lactantius, Raymundus de Sabunde, Aquinas, Ludovicus Vives, Bradwardinus, Valesius, 'and chiefly of *Gassendus* (in Animadvers. in phys. Epicuri:) the leaves of whose most learned Works' he has sullied by frequent turning.[2] For 'to enter the lists with a *Lucian*, or *Lucretius*, and there contend with him concerning the extent of *Gods Providence*', with no. other proof 'but the bare *authority of Canonical Writ*', is the ready way to confirm an atheist.[3]

In *The Darkness of Atheism* Epicurus and the Epicurean thinkers are Charleton's chief opponents. He admits that 'the *Atoms* of *Epicurus*', subject to the form, motion, and laws deriving from God, supply the most probable and rational of physical theories.[4] In denying the providence of God, however, the Epicureans were moved by their own interests:

'For, *first*, their own writings bare record, that they made it the grand scope of their studies to promote Atheisme, by plotting how to undermine the received belief of an omnipotent *eternal Being*, to murder the *immortality of the Soul* (the basis of all religion) and to deride the *Compensation of good and evil actions after death*.'[5]

The central problem for Charleton, as for Milton, is that of fate and free-will; and to meet his opponents Charleton tries to steer 'a midle way betwixt the *Absolute Fatality* of the *Stoicks*, on one extreme; and the absolute *Fortune* of the

[1] Ibid., sig. b3r.
[2] Ibid., sig. b4v.
[3] Ibid., pp. 4–5.
[4] Ibid., p. 44.
[5] Ibid., pp. 96–7. Charles Blount, in his *Anima Mundi*, ranks the pagan philosophers as mortalists: 'Of those that held the mortality of the Soul, the *Epicureans* were the chief Sect, who notwithstanding their impious Doctrines, yet some of their Lives were vertuous. *Cardan* had so great a value for their Moral Actions, that he appear'd in Justification of them. . . . The next Sect to the *Epicureans* in point of incredulity concerning the Soul, I conceive to be the *Scepticks*, who were by some esteemed not only the modestest, but the most perspicacious of all Sects' (op. cit., 'Anima Mundi', pp. 96 and 100). Upon Epicurus Charleton bestows, in greater extremes, the mingled praise and blame of the Christian advocate.

Epicureans, on the other'.[1] His problem resolves itself into an ample inquiry into 'how that long Civil war betwixt these three different *Notions* of *Fate*, *Fortune*, and *Free-will*, may be conciliated and brought to a full Combination and Consistence with *Divine Providence*'. With Milton too, Charleton can assert that God's decrees cannot 'work any the least mutation at all in the natures of his Creatures, or by violence pervert their Virtues to the production of any Effects, to which, by their primitive Constitution and individuation, they were not precisely adapted and accommodated. Since, in so doing, he must take away from his Creatures those peculiar Faculties, which he at their creation freely conferred upon their severall natures; and innovate the fundamental laws of Nature.'[2]

Or against the Hobbesian view, he can insist, in his chapter 'Of the Liberty Elective of Mans Will', that the absolute fatality of the Stoics (and of the 'Christians of that irreligious perswasion') entails the 'total sublation of all *Virtue* and *Vice*'; 'in a word, the subversion of all *Religion* and *Morality*'.[3] For his notion of free-will carries him towards Milton:

'*This Liberty* of election some men have founded only in the *Will*, others in the *Rational Faculty*; to whose opinion reason adviseth us to adhaere. For doubtless the *Will*, considered *per se* is a blind and undiscerning *Faculty*, or *Power*, which can make no progress, nor find the way towards convenient objects without the manuduction of the *Intellect*, which as it were lights the torch unto, and as a knowing guide conducts the Will: so that since it is the proper office of the Intellect to informe and conduct the Will, and the proper office of the Will to follow the direction and guidance of the Intellect; it is not only manifest, that the Will cannot deflect from the right way, towards the amplectence and fruition of Good, unless by the mistaking Intellect

[1] Ibid., pp. 205-6.
[2] Ibid., p. 243. In that last clause lies the rub both for Charleton and for Milton.
[3] Ibid., pp. 257-58.

it be seduced into the devious paths of Evil; but also, that the *Liberty* of election is consistent in the *Intellect primarily*, and in the *Will* onely at the *second hand*, or by way of *dependence*.'[1]

In short, Charleton's answer to the denial of divine providence is very much like that of Milton in the *Areopagitica*: 'Many there be that complain of divine Providence in suffering Adam to transgress. Foolish tongues! When God gave him Reason, he gave him freedom to choose, for reason is but choosing.'[2] To the arguments of Fate and Fortune, Charleton opposed the doctrine of free-will founded upon reason; the Epicurean free-will, good so far as it went, was not related to the providence of God. There is a strong presumption that the connections which this problem had for Charleton were also those which it had for Milton.

In 1654 Charleton published his account of Epicurean physics, *Physiologia Epicuro-Gassendo-Charltoniana*, which he described further as 'a fabrick of science natural, upon the hypothesis of atoms, founded by Epicurus, repaired by Petrus Gassendus, augmented by Walter Charleton'. This was followed in 1656 by *Epicurus's Morals*, to which Charleton attached 'An Apologie for Epicurus, as to the three Capital Crimes whereof he is accused'. These three crimes of opinion are as follows:

'(1.) That the Souls of men are mortal, and so uncapable of all, either happiness or misery after death. (2.) That Man is not obliged to honour, revere, and worship God, in respect of his beneficence, or out of the hope of any Good or

---

[1] Ibid., p. 263. On the other hand, Hobbes, in the *Leviathan* (ed. cit., p. 111), takes this position: '*Liberty* and *Necessity* are consistent: As in the water, that hath not only *liberty*, but a *necessity* of descending by the Channel; so likewise in the Actions which men voluntarily doe: which, because they proceed from their will, proceed from *liberty*; and yet, because every act of mans will, and every desire, and inclination proceedeth from some cause, and that from another cause, in a continuall chaine (whose first link is in the hand of God the first of all causes), they proceed from *necessity*.' This necessity Charleton calls 'Theological Fate' as distinguished from the Stoic Fate, which does not make the Will of God the first link (op. cit., pp. 215–16).

[2] *Prose Works* (Bohn ed.), II, 74.

Fear of any evil at his hands, but merely in respect of the transcendent Excellencies of his Nature, Immortality, and Beatitude. (3.) That Self-homicide is an Act of Heroick Fortitude in case of intolerable or otherwise inevitable Calamity.'[1]

Granting that the Light of Nature is scarcely bright enough clearly to demonstrate the immortality of the soul, Charleton remarks to 'a Person of Honour',

'You have, Sir, I presume, attentively perused that so worthily commended Discourse of Plato, touching the immortality of Mans soul, and acquainted your self more-over with all those mighty Arguments, alleged by Saint *Thomas*, *Pomponatius* (who will hardly be out-done in subt-lety, touching the same Theam, by any that comes after him, and yet he was forced to conclude himself a Sceptick, and leave the Question to the decision of some other bolder Pen) *Des Cartes*, our noble friend Sir *Kenelm Digby*, and divers other great Clerks, to prove the Soul of Man to be a substance distinct from, and independent upon that of the body, and to have eternal existence *a parte post*. . . .'[2]

These passages, in connection with what we have seen, throw a good deal of light on the heresy with which we are concerned, particularly on its descent from antiquity. The notion of the soul as 'substance' provides common ground for the differences of Hobbes, More, and Milton; for the impulse of the time was toward the explanation of religious problems in terms of natural reason or philosophy. Harking back to those Ancients who denied immortality, Charleton declares that some believed 'the soul to be nothing else but a certain *Act*, or *Form*, or *Quality* inseparable (*i.e.*) a certain special *Modification* of *Matter*' which vanished 'immediately upon the immutation of that Mode by death'.

'Which *Origen*, *Justine*, *Theodoret*, and some other *Fathers*, understanding to have been the Tenent of *Aristotle*, have written sharp invectives against him, as an assertor of the souls mortality, and this so justly, that if his Zealous Dis-

[1] *Epicurus's Morals* (London, 1926), sig. c8r.
[2] Ibid., sig. c8v.

ciple, honest Mr. *Alexander Rosse*, were alive again, he would never be able to discredit that their charge.'[1]

The Ancients who denied immortality are divided into two sects: those who believed in 'annihilation', and those who believed in 'dispersion'; to this latter sect, continues Charleton, 'we are to refer all such, as held the soul to be *Corporeal*'.

'For, as they would have it to be composed of *material* principles, so would they also have it to be, by death, again resolved into the same material principles; so that in their sence, the extinction of the Soul is no other, but the dissipation thereof into those very corporeal particles, of which it was composed. And this seems to be the true meaning of *Demonax* in *Lucian*, when being interrogated whether he thought the Soul to be immortal, he answered, *mihi videtur, sed ut omnia*; it seems to me to be immortal, but no otherwise than all things are immortal, i.e. as to the matter only, or component Principles of it, which are incapable of Annihilation.'[2]

[1] Ibid., sig. d3v. The tenet of Aristotle (for which, we can be sure, the ardent Ross would have found an explanation) is thus set forth by Zeller (op. cit., II, 130-1): 'As he came to conceive of body and soul as essentially united, and to define the soul as the entelechy of the body, and as, further, he became convinced that every soul requires its own proper organ, and must remain wholly inoperative without it, he was necessarily led, not only to regard the pilgrimage of the soul in the other world as a myth, but also to question the doctrines of pre-existence and immortality as they were held by Plato. Inasmuch as the soul is dependent upon the body for its existence and activity, it must come into existence and perish with it. Only incorporeal spirit can precede and outlast the bodily life. But this, according to Aristotle, is to be found only in the reason and in that part of it which is without taint of the lower activities of the soul—namely, the Active Nous.'

[2] Ibid., sigs. d3v-d4r. In 1695 M. S., writing on 'the Nature of Rational and Irrational Souls', draws the argument together in this fashion: 'He [Cudworth] adds, That *Democritus*, *Epicurus*, and *Lucretius* abus'd this Theorem [i.e. *De nihilo nihil in nihilum nil passere verti*], and built their Atheistical Philosophy upon it: But if they abus'd it, why did not the others rescue it? which we no where find. The difference between the *Incorporealist* and *Corporealist* was not about the meaning of this Theorem, that was admitted in its literal sence on both sides; but their difference lay about the Principles of Worldly Beings, and the efficient Cause which put those Principles into that form as we now see in the World: the one held Matter the only Principle, and Chance the efficient Cause; the others asserted two Principles, Matter and Spirit, and God the

In this class Charleton puts Marcus Antoninus and Seneca; as also Democritus and Epicurus, who are always 'conjoined by the good Lactantius as confederates in the Doctrine of the Dissolution of Souls'. No one can regard these ideas without being struck by the Christian metamorphosis which Milton seems to have worked upon them; Milton is not Lucian, but he can make Lucian a Christian by saying, 'God is neither willing, nor properly speaking, able to annihilate anything altogether'. It would be absurd to press this connection, but it is not absurd to say that Milton and More nowhere betray their relation to contemporary thought more than in the 'materialistic' aspect of their 'spirit world'.[1] If whole man is by nature corporeal and nothing can be annihilated altogether, then mortalism and the dissolution of souls are consequent, but the resurrection becomes more significant, and Milton achieves something like a synthesis of the theology and philosophy of his time. In short, the mortalist heresy and Epicurean thought demand consideration whenever we attempt to relate Milton to his intellectual background; opposition to Hobbes will not suffice to explain the nexus of *Paradise Lost*, for opposition does not cover all the points at issue.

In defending Epicurus on self-homicide, Charleton falls

---

efficient Cause: but they no where say, that God made these Principles out of nothing.' (*A Philosophical Discourse of the Nature of Rational and Irrational Souls* [London, 1704], p. 1.)

[1] Cf. Marjorie H. Nicolson, 'The Spirit World of Milton and More', *Studies in Philology*, XXII (1925), 433–52. Hobbes's view of the spirit world is important in this connection (cf. *Leviathan*, ed. cit., pp. 216–17): From Scripture we cannot conclude, says Hobbes, that 'there is, or hath been created, any permanent thing (understood by the name of *Spirit* or *Angel*) that hath not quantity'. Though Scripture may 'prove the Permanence of Angelicall nature, it confirmeth also their Materiality'. And 'in the resurrection men shall be Permanent, and not Incorporeall; so therefore also are the Angels'; for 'Incorporeall Substance' is a contradiction. While Hobbes was inclined to believe 'that Angels were nothing but supernaturall apparitions of the Fancy', Scripture, he says, has extorted from his feeble reason 'an acknowledgement, and beleef, that there be also Angels substantiall, and permanent'. If Dr. Nicolson can unite Milton and More on 'the corporeity of spirits', perhaps Hobbes might have adopted Milton's philosophy as well as More's (as the story goes), if he had been forced to give up his own.

back upon a libertine interpretation of the Law of Nature[1] which may be found in Donne's *Biathanatos* and Hobbes's *Leviathan*, and which is later attacked, with special reference to Donne, by John Adams in *An Essay concerning Self-Murther* (1700).[2] In opposition to such an interpretation Adams cites Milton as making the first Man argue against self-murder from the Light of Nature.[3] One could 'place' many writers in the current of seventeenth-century thought simply by determining their view of the Law of Nature; and this, as Professor Nicolson has suggested, reveals the true opposition between Milton and Hobbes. It does not, however, discover the full complexity of Milton's relation either to Hobbes or to his time. In the account of libertine thought in the seventeenth century which must one day be written, Charleton's apology for Epicurus and his morals will have an important place as a work which tried to repair 'the injuries done to the memory of the *Temperate, Good,* and *Pious* EPICURUS', whose philosophy could lead a Cowley or Temple to retirement in his 'Garden', but whose 'foppish casuall dance of attoms' could excuse the mad capers of the Restoration rake; and Charleton himself will occupy a position between Gassendi in France and St. Évremond in England.

But Charleton was not through with the mortalist heresy and Epicurean thought when he had written *Epicurus's Morals.* In 1657 he brought out *The Immortality of the Human Soul, Demonstrated by the Light of Nature*, in which he undertakes, as Athanasius, to prove the immortality of the soul against Lucretius, the disciple of Epicurus. Though he is forced to admit that he cannot give a 'Demonstration, *More Geometrico*', he is awarded the decision over Lucretius by Isodicastes, Lord Dorchester. In the two dialogues which make up this book, Charleton regards the soul as 'somewhat Incorporeal': he belongs definitely to the school which

---

[1] See *Epicurus's Morals*, ed. cit., sigs. d6r–d6v.

[2] See my article, 'The Libertine Donne', in this volume.

[3] *An Essay concerning Self-Murther* (London, 1700), p. 313. Cf. *Paradise Lost*, X, 1020–9.

believes 'that the Soul is an Immortal substance'. But Lucretius is left obstinately maintaining 'that it is not possible to convince a meer Natural man, of the Souls Immortality, by the testimony of pure Reason'. And here we return to the challenge which Browne seems to have given when he confessed, 'not that I did absolutely conceive a mortality of the soul, but, if that were (which faith, not philosophy hath yet thoroughly disproved), and that both entered the grave together, yet I held the same conceit thereof that we all do of the body, that it should rise again'. Browne stands between Bacon, who suggested that reason or philosophy had nothing to do with religion, and the Cambridge Platonists, who insisted that reason and philosophy had much to do with religion. But in that insistence the Cambridge Platonists were only in accord with the general impulse of their time. Certainly, we have seen enough in the writers whom we have examined to conclude that Browne's scepticism[1] stimulated, if it did not provoke, philosophy or natural reason to attempt the proof of the immortality of the soul. Only thus could 'meer Natural man' be convinced and saved from atheism.

It will not do, in this connection, to ignore the growing appeal and claim of geometrical reason, especially as it was manifested in philosophy and science, to which the Royal Society is a monument. I do not think that the transition in thought and point of view, which is represented even in the mortalist heresy, can be made as clear and vivid by indulging in lengthy exposition or glittering generality as by merely citing two passages of prose. The first is from Browne's *Religio Medici*:

'Methinks there be not impossibilities enough in religion for an active faith: the deepest mysteries ours contains have not only been illustrated, but maintained, by syllogism and the rule of reason. I love to lose myself in a mystery; to

---

[1] And scepticism it was to some of his contemporaries. Since Browne found favour with a Jesuit like Holland, Tillotson may have feared such favour when he attacked Browne in a sermon on 'The Reasonableness of a Resurrection', for the Jesuits used scepticism in their attack upon the authority of the Scriptures.

pursue my reason to an O *altitudo*! 'Tis my solitary re-creation to pose my apprehension with those involved enigmas and riddles of the Trinity—incarnation and resur-rection. I can answer all the objections of Satan and my rebellious reason with that odd resolution I learned of Tertullian, *Certum est quia impossible est.*'

And the second is from Tillotson's sermon on 'The Reasonableness of a Resurrection', where he argues that 'if the thing be evidently impossible, then it is highly un-reasonable to propose it to the belief of mankind':

'I know not what some men may find in themselves; but I must freely acknowledge that I could never yet attain to that bold and hardy degree of faith as to believe anything for this reason, because it was impossible: for this would be to believe a thing to be because I am sure it can not be. So that I am very far from being of his mind, that wanted not only more difficulties, but even impossibilities in the Christian religion, to exercise his faith upon.'

Browne could pose his reason with the triumphs of faith; Tilloston fears that faith will not survive the unreasonable. Tillotson addresses the 'meer Natural man' and believes that atheism can be effectively answered only by reason. 'To recommend the Christian religion from the absurdity of the things to be believed' is to Tillotson 'a strange recommen-dation of any religion to the sober and reasonable part of mankind'. His belief is a product of the controversy which we have investigated; it grew out of the effort to prove 'that this article of the resurrection was not in itself the less credible because the heathen philosophers caviled at it as a thing impossible and contradictious'. But Browne would have found things in Tillotson's 'Reasonableness of a Resur-rection' which had stretched his *pia mater*, if not his faith; employing the same terms, these two men arrive at the same conclusion from diametrically opposite points of view. Where Charleton still had some 'scepticity' of the power of natural reason to prove immortality, Tillotson rests in the assurance denied to Charleton's Lucretius, that one can be convinced by the testimony of reason. Religious faith must now answer in the terms of natural reason, and it should be remembered that the proof offered by the Mortalists was from both Scripture and natural reason.

It is into this larger frame of ideas, which involves not only Hobbes but also the Christian and Epicurean mortalists, that we must place Milton and *Paradise Lost*. We have seen the relation of Milton to some of the momentous issues of his age in sufficient outline to conclude that neither Hobbes nor the Mortalists provided an adequate motive for 'the most magnificent of all replies to Hobbes' or for 'Milton's most personal ideas'. To the complex challenge which was centred but not contained in mortalism, and provoked in an age deeply agitated by the claims of reason, there were many who asserted eternal providence and justified the ways of God to man, but none so audacious as the Milton who incorporated the mortalist heresy into his justification. If we limit the opposition to Hobbes, ignore the Epicurean denial, or forget these minor answers, we shall miss part of the significance which *Paradise Lost* must have held for its time. If this bold and splendid reply to the mere rationalist seems a little late, it was not so late as Cudworth's; nor was the question dead when Bentley inaugurated the Boyle Lectures in 1692 by assailing '*Epicurus's* Deism'.

VIII

Richard Whitlock, Learning's Apologist

★

Very little is known of the life of Richard Whitlock, and most of that comes from Wood's *Athenae Oxonienses*. A few details have been added by Foster's *Alumni Oxonienses*. Apparently he was not of sufficient biographical interest to earn a place in the *D.N.B.* beside a less important John Whitlock, who gets one sentence from Wood. However, Wood did not know whether John Whitlock had gone to Oxford, and the *D.N.B.* is right about Richard so far as common memory goes. But when it comes to the work of the two men, John is forgotten, and Richard at least appears in Mr. Holbrook Jackson's *Anatomy of Bibliomania*, in which he is not inappropriately remembered.

Richard Whitlock was the son of Richard Whitlock, gentleman, of London, where the younger Richard was born about 1616. He became a commoner of Magdalen Hall in Michaelmas term of 1632, matriculating on November 23rd at the age of sixteen. He took his B.A. on 16th June 1635; was elected a fellow of All Souls College in 1638, and admitted B.C.L. on 19th May 1640. He was called Doctor of Physic in 1640 according to Foster, and Wood notes the title in *Zootomia*, but no record of this degree has been found. It may possibly be explained by John Birkenhead's reference to '*his* Education *in our own and forraign* Academies' in 'The Publisher to the Reader' of *Zootomia*. His life is completed by Wood with this statement: 'After Mr. Whitlock had run with the times of Usurpation, he wheel'd about at the Restoration of K. *Ch.* II, took Holy Orders, and had a small Parsonage in *Kent* conferr'd on him by Archbishop *Sheldon*, where he finished his Course about 1672 or after, as I have been informed by Mr. *Henry Birkhead* his Contemporary in *Alls.* Coll.' His 'running with the times' does not appear to have alienated men like Sir John Birkenhead. Foster adds the details that he became vicar of Stowe, Bucks, in 1661, and of Ashford, Kent, in 1662. The rest of his story is contained in his one book, *Zootomia*, where we may learn some thing of his intellectual biography.

The full title-page of *Zootomia*, which is a rather scarce book, carries the following information:

'*ZΩOTOMI'A*, or, Observations on the Present Manners of the English: *Briefly Anatomizing the Living by the Dead.* With an Useful Detection of the Mountebanks of both Sexes. By *Richard Whitlock*, M.D. Late Fellow of *All-Souls* Colledge in *Oxford*. London, Printed by *Tho. Roycroft*, and are to be sold by *Humphrey Moseley*, at the Princes Armes in St. *Pauls* Church-yard, 1654.'

This edition exists in two impressions, or issues. The second issue is represented by the Guildhall copy (Library of the Corporation of the City of London), and the first issue by the British Museum copy. The changes in the second issue are exactly three: the preface of 'The Publisher to the Reader' is added; 'The *Preface*, or an *Antidote* for Authors, *against the* Poyson *of* Aspes', is renamed 'The Author to the Reader', and its first paragraph is revised. Finally, it was reissued with a new title-page in 1664 and again in 1679.

The Guildhall copy of *Zootomia* has a special interest in that it contains manuscript notes in a seventeenth-century hand which may have been the author's. Unfortunately the Guildhall copy has been rebound and the end-papers lost, so that no signatures remain. These notes supply corrections which, in some cases, could hardly have come from anyone but the author; however, they are interrupted by a few notes in another hand. They should be of value to anyone contemplating a new edition because many of the difficulties of the text are explained by the errata which are there corrected.

Our present concern with the Guildhall copy is that it identifies the authors of two pieces of prefatory matter. The epistle of 'The Publisher to the Reader', which is signed by the initials *J.B.*, carries this note following the initials: 'M: Art alias Aulicus.' Now John Birkenhead was made M.A. in 1639, found favour with Laud, was elected probation-fellow of All Souls College in 1640, and assisted Laud's party as the writer of the *Mercurius Aulicus*. This note, there-fore, establishes the fact that Whitlock's book was spon-sored by Sir John Birkenhead. The Guildhall copy also identifies the writer of the verses 'To his Ingenious, know-ing Friend, *The Author*' as 'M: Lluellin: M.D.' Although confirmation is lacking, familiarity with the verse of Martin Lluelyn, the author of *Men-Miracles*, substantiates this attribution.

While prefatory eulogies are not to be confused with criticism, they have something to do with reputation, and so we may give our attention to the three which introduce *Zootomia*. That there are not more is in itself a criticism when we think of the contemporary edition of Cartwright, with whom Whitlock had friends in common. This character of Whitlock is offered by John Birkenhead:

'*The* Author *did not (as the Fashion is) first write Bookes, and then fall to study; but after many yeers search into all* Arts *and* Languages *(accompanied with a naturall Promptitude and Sharp-ness) shew rather that he can be an* Author, *then that he will. This Book therefore is to have both* Wit *and* Learning, *else tis nothing like the* Author; *and if thou seek here for both, and finde them not, I dare pronounce thee one of the new Seekers, but not the right. Those who know the* Author, *will frankly say, his* Education *in our own and forraign* Academies *was well bes-*

180

towed; and so will thy houres be, if thou read what hee writes. One thing more is worth thy notice, and that is, his liberall and impartiall discovering the now Raigning Vanities (or Ignorance in Fashion) which are better cut up by no hand then by his.'[1]

Martin Lluelyn opposes Whitlock to one reigning vanity:

> *Some maze their Thoughts in Labyrinths, and thus*
> *Invoke no Reader, but an Oedipus.*
> *But whil'st Revealed Sense we finde in you,*
> *You write to th'Understanding, not the Clew.*
> *So Theseus through the winding Tow'r was led*
> *By Ariadnes Beauty, more then Thread.*

And Jasper Mayne subscribes to these words of praise:

'*If your Book did depend wholly on my Judgement of it, I would say, that in Truth, for* Wit, Learning, *and* Variety *of matter, put into a* handsom Dresse, *you have exceeded any* Writer *in this kinde which I have yet met with. . . .*'[2]

Mayne's praise is limited, as you see, to this kind of work; Lluelyn separates Whitlock from the cult of obscurity; and Birkenhead raises the general testimony to his wit and learning. This reputation, small though it may have been, is supported for us by *Zootomia* alone, and most obviously with respect to the 'search into all Arts and Languages'.

II

Zootomia is first of all an anatomy, then a volume of essays, and finally something of a book of characters. It also contains religious meditations and moral observations like those of Bishop Hall. Whitlock declares that Plutarch is the model most to his liking, but he is fully aware of Seneca, Montaigne, Bacon, Cornwallis, and Donne. Practically

---

[1] Perhaps the 'right Seeker' meant to Birkenhead what it meant to Glanvill: 'Though I confess that in *Philosophy* I'm a *Seeker*; yet cannot believe, that a *Sceptick* in *Philosophy* must be one in *Divinity*.' (*Vanity of Dogmatizing* [1661], p. 186.)

[2] Mayne apologizes for not writing in verse by saying that his country congregation has abated much of his fancy and that his poetry has been 'objected to him as a piece of Lightnesse'.

every variety of the seventeenth-century essay has made its impression upon his book. Peculiar to Whitlock, however, is the fact that his 'characters' dissect chiefly the medical quacks, both male and female, and allow him to display his 'morall chirurgery' along with his medical interest. This scientific interest, which also appears in 'Medicinall Observations', apparently never drew Whitlock to the practice of medicine, and may therefore furnish an early instance of an interesting observation made by Dr. Walter Charleton in his dialogues on *The Immortality of the Human Soul* (1657). *Isodicastes* (Marquis of Dorchester), speaking of the Civil War, makes this remark: 'When I view the train of sad and heavy Calamities, that commonly attend the Sword; I should rather have expected the incroachment of Ignorance and Barbarism upon our Iland, than the encrease of Letters and growth of Knowledge there.' To which *Athanasius* (Charleton) responds:

'You have reason for your wonder, Sir, I must confesse; Yet when you have considered, that every Age hath its peculiar Genius, which inclines mens Minds to some one study or other, and gives it a dominion over their affections proportionate to its secret influence; and that the vicissitudes of things ordained by Providence, require a general predisposition in mens hearts, to co-operate with Fate, toward the Changes appointed to succeed in the fulnesse of their time: You will think it lesse strange, that *Britain*, which was but yesterday the Theater of War and desolation, should today be the School of Arts, and Court of all the Muses. . . . Besides our late Warrs and Schisms, having almost wholly discouraged men from the study of Theologie; and brought the Civil Law into contempt: The major part of young Schollers in our Universities addict themselves to Physic; and how much that conduceth to real and solid Knowledge, and what singular advantages it hath above other studies, in making men true Philosophers; I need not intimate to you, who have so long tasted of that benefit.'[1]

In his scientific interest Whitlock, who knew both theo-

[1] *The Immortality of the Human Soul* (London, 1657), pp. 49–50.

logy and civil law, may be regarded as a weathercock pointing the new prevailing wind, which has already modified the 'climate' of his book.

Zootomia is not unlike a compound of Burton, Browne, Donne, Hall, and the character-books. It has the flavour of Burton's learning, something of Browne's scepticism, a touch of Donne's wit, the tone of Hall's stoicism, and much of the character-book's style, contaminated by the craze for parentheses. Most, if not all, of the fashions, prejudices, and manners of the age are anatomized; important books, reputations, and ideas are discovered; Bacon and the new rationalism are shown to be gaining ground; Donne mingles with Charron in the new scepticism; the influence of the Roman Silver Age is brought out, especially with regard to Seneca, Tacitus, and their advocate Lipsius. There are many allusions to English writers, including one which says that man's '*speculations* are but a *comedy* of *Errors*, and his *Imployments Much ado about Nothing* to borrow our *Comedians titles*'.[1] And some of the subjects include 'The Peoples Physitian', 'The Teares of the Presse', 'The Best Furniture', 'The Politick Weather-Glasse', 'The Magnetick Lady',[2] 'The Grand Schismatick', 'The Fifth Element', 'False Reformations Shipwrack', and 'The Grand Experiment'.[3]

Modern criticism of *Zootomia* is almost nonexistent, but this verdict was pronounced in 1830:

'This worthy doctor labours to be witty and original, till he becomes unintelligible; expressing a good meaning in terms so unconnected and far-fetched that it is often difficult to discover his allusions. Yet his style and manner of quoting much resemble those of his contemporary, Burton, in his

---

[1] *Zootomia* (London, 1654), Second issue, p. 318.

[2] A defence of women which cites Agrippa's defence, praises the Duchess of Newcastle, and refers to Donne as 'that rare *Beauties* (I, or *vertues*) *Hilliard*, and masterly *Painter*' as well as 'our best of Poets'.

[3] A final peroration on the set theme of the Jacobean age—death; but new enough to cite 'Sir *Kenhelm Digby's* Rapture in his Treatise of the *Immortality of the Soule*'.

Anatomy of Melancholy, this also being an Anatomy.'[1]

This was not Lluelyn's opinion, but it contains a not un-just censure, which would lose most of its point if *Zootomia* were edited according to the suggestions of the Guildhall copy. The present verdict gives us something like the deep thoughts and abstruse language which Dryden divided between Donne and Cleveland. But in Commonwealth times it would be hard to find a book of the same kind that had equal merit. Even today it retains an unusual variety of interest for the reader of seventeenth-century literature. Historically it is important for the light which it throws upon the intellectual concerns of the fellows of All Souls College at about the time that Milton plunged into the Puritan rebellion.

And it is the intellectual connections of *Zootomia* that have the greatest interest for a student of this period. For this book helps us to learn what a friend of men like Jasper Mayne, Henry Birkhead, Martin Lluelyn, and John Birken-head was reading and thinking in Commonwealth times. The intellectual bearings of *Zootomia* are perhaps best dis-covered by its informal relation to the attack upon learning and academies which broke out around the middle of the century. In the same year that *Zootomia* appeared, the more formal defence of the universities was published in *Vindiciae Academiarum*, which John Wilkins helped Seth Ward to write. Here Webster's *Academiarum Examen* was formally answered and briefer castigations were accorded the efforts of Hobbes and Dell. Prominent tendencies, as well as their confusion, in the learning of the time emerge when Ward descends upon Webster for proposing, among his remedies, the study both of Bacon and of Fludd:

'How little trust there is in villainous man! he that even now was for the way of strict and accurate induction, is fallen into the mysticall way of the *Cabala*, and numbers formall: there are not two waies in the whole World more opposite, then those of the L. *Verulam* and D. *Fludd*, the one founded upon experiment, the other upon mysticall Ideal

[1] *The Bibliographical and Retrospective Miscellany* (London, 1830), p. 136.

Richard Whitlock, Learning's Apologist

reasons; even now he was for him, now he is for this, and
all this in the twinkling of an eye, O the celerity of the
change and motion of the Wind.'[1]

With evident respect but equal severity Ward pilloried
the learned Hobbes between 'a Friar and an Enthusiast'.[2] It
should be remembered that it was not merely the lowly
Puritan, but even the lofty Milton, who was unkind to the
universities.[3] The warning of John Wilkins in *Ecclesiastes*
(1646) that 'enthusiasm' could not take the place of learning,
even for the preacher, fell on deaf ears. After all exceptions
have been made, the testimony is still too great for us to
deny that not uncommonly the Puritan had little use either
for art or for learning. In these respects Whitlock was a
Cavalier and defender of the things dear to his friends and
fellows of All Souls College; on the other hand, he was

[1] *Vindiciae Academiarum* (Oxford, 1654), p. 46. The extreme Puritan view
aimed at the destruction rather than the reformation of learning.
[2] Wilkins regards Hobbes as 'a person of good ability and solid parts, but
otherwise highly magisteriall', and he concludes: 'It were not amisse, if he were
made acquainted, that for all his slighting of the Universityes, there are here
many men, who have been very well versed in those notions and Principles
which he would be counted the inventer of, and that before his workes were
published. And though he for his part may think it below him to acknowledge
himselfe beholding to Mr *Warners* Manuscripts, yet those amongst us who
haue seen and perused them must for many things give him the honour of
precedency before Mr *Hobbs'* (*Vindiciae*, p. 7).
[3] Their criticism was not without cause, but Wilkins objected to a common
charge in these words: 'Whereas those that understand these places, do know
that there is not to be wished a more generall liberty in point of judgment or
debate, then what is here allowed. So that there is scarce any Hypothesis, which
hath been formerly or lately entertained by Judicious men, and seems to have
in it any clearenesse or consistency, but hath here its strenuous Assertours, as the
Atomicall and Magneticall in Philosophy, the Copernican in Astronomy &c.
And though we do very much honour *Aristotle* for his profound judgment and
universal learning, yet are we so farre from being tyed up to his opinions, that
persons of all conditions amongst us take liberty to discent from him, and to
declare against him, according as any contrary evidence doth ingage them,
being ready to follow the Banner of truth by whomsoever it shall be lifted up.'
(*Vindiciae*, p. 2)
As Wilkins and Glanvill were later associated in the Royal Society, it is
piquant to recall Glanvill's attack on Aristotelianism in the *Vanity of Dogmatizing*, where he gives this definition of a School-man: 'A *School-man* is the
Ghost of the *Stagirite*, in a Body of condensed Air: and *Thomas* but *Aristotle*
sainted.' (1661, p. 152)

morally not unfitted to 'run with the times of Usurpation'. It is because of his character that the intellectual connections of *Zootomia* take on peculiar interest, uniting moral earnestness with the castigation of 'Ignorance in Fashion'. From a book of this character and scarcity, it will be useful and not improper to quote without remorse rather than to 'defecate' its language in a modern paraphrase.

III

Whitlock's literary ambitions and reading find their apology in his preface to *Zootomia*, which is one of his liveliest pieces of writing. There he uses 'Mountaignes Apology *in his* Essay *of* Books' to excuse the informal learning and desultory manner of his own book:

'*I know not how, but as* Montaigne *saith of himselfe,* Tracts *of a* continued Thread *are tedious* to most Fancies, *which of it selfe indeed is of that* desultory *nature, that it is pleased with* Writings *like* Irish Bogs, *that it may* leap *from one* variety *to another, than* tread *any* beaten Path.'[1]

Among many kinds of writings he finds 'Plutarchs *most inviting Imitation for the* form, (*call them* Discourses, Essays, *or what you will*) *nor behinde any for matter; if mixt sometimes with those* Mucrones Sermonum, Enlivening Touches *of* Seneca *full of* smart Fancy, solid sense *and* accurate reason'. His frequent use of Seneca on morals is intended '*even to* shame *our* Christian dulness'. For politics he makes Tacitus his text, for no other reason than this, '*never any better cast* Practise *into* Precept, *or made* History Politicks *in fuller and closer* Observations'.[2]

The matter of *Zootomia* belongs to what Bacon calls 'Satyra Seria' rather than to what he calls 'Interiora Rerum':

'*That I on this* Score *tearm it an* Anatomy of the Living by the Dead, *or of* Practicall Errours (*though in the particulars I decline the* Nauseating *of a* continued Allegory) *doth not much misrepresent* my purpose; *while in the* latitude *of my* Discourses (*and according to the* destin'd Bulk *of this* Tract) *I deliver my*

---

[1] *Zootomia* (London, 1654), Second issue, sig. a1r.   [2] Ibid., sig. a1v.

Richard Whitlock, Learning's Apologist

Judgment (*made out of the* seriousness *of others, or* casualties *of my own Observations) of* mens misapprehendings, *or things* Misapprehensions, *whereby the* Glitter *of things oft passeth for* Gold, *while some things* enduring touch (*but* dull *to the eye*) *arise not to an* Esteem *equall with* counterfeits, *as in nothing more appeares than our* Opinion *of the* World *and its* Desirables *in grosse, dreaming of* life *in a* Carkass, *and of* Perpetuity *in a* blast; *and having high* conceits *of our* vain Projects, *deare ones of our* vexations, *and* doting ones *of falsely admired* Contemptibles. *But come we to* particulars, *and it is* undeniable *but that there are in* (*even the most* familiar) Passages *between* man *and* man, *neglected* (*but on enquiry easily discoverable*) *false* Principles, Erroures *and* causes of Miscarriage, *and in many things* inner parts *unobserved by the* carelesse world, Erroures Vulgi, vulgar Errors *reaching to the* Morals *of men as well as their* Philosophy. . . .'[1]

These discourses, not overlooking the inner parts of things, were written without so much as casting an 'Eye *on* Books *of the* like nature (*without it were my Lord* Bacons Interiora Rerum) *till they were* compiled', and they do not presume to deal with 'Errors *of* Faith'. If any of them seem paradoxical, it is because one main end of his writing was to let the world know that he thinks not as she thinks, and yet thinks never the worse of himself. 'Exactness *of writing on any* Subject *in* Poetick heights *of* Fancy, *or* Rhetoricall Descants *of* Application,'[2] he leaves to others:

'*For my own part I may say, as* Lipsius *in his Epistle*; Rationem meam scribendi scire vis? fundo, non scribo, nec id nisi in Calore & interno quodam Impetu, haud aliter quam Poetae. *Would you know* (*saith he*) *my manner of writing? it is a kind of voluntary* Tiding of, *not* Pumping for; Notions flowing, *not* forced; *like* Poets unconstrained Heats *and* Raptures: *such is* mine, *rather a* running Discourse *than a*

---

[1] Ibid., sigs. a2r–a2v. His book of 'vulgar errors' had been preceded by Dr. James Primrose's *De Vulgi Erroribus* (1639), which was translated into English by Dr. Wittie in 1651, and by Sir Thomas Browne's *Pseudodoxia Epidemica* (1646), which also reveals the influence of Bacon in its 'Kalendar of popular errors' and its method of 'dubitation'.

[2] The Guildhall copy changes 'Descants' to 'Descents'.

Grave-paced Exactnes; *having in them this* Formality of Essayes (*as Sir* W. Cornwallyes *saith of his*) *that they are* Tryals *of bringing my* hand *and* Fancy acquainted *in this using my* Paper, *as the* Painters Boy *a* Board *he blurs with* Tryals.'[1] In short, Whitlock follows the newer fashion of 'Lipsius his hopping stile',[2] and so belongs to the Senecan rather than the Ciceronian school of prose.

As for his quotations, he has used them to confirm some of his 'Descants'; '*besides such is the* peevishnesse of present times, Contemporaries *speaking even the words of the* Ancients, *have no* Authority, *unlesse they* disown them *by* Citation'.[3] Other writers, besides those already mentioned, whom he has more than once to disown by citation are Dr. Primrose, Donne, Charron, Rabelais, Sir Thomas Browne, George Herbert, Theophrastus, Agrippa, Aristotle, Strada, Horace, Martial, Juvenal, and Erasmus; some who appear at least once are Boccalini, Balzac, Shakespeare, Jonson, Carew, Davenant, Hobbes, Duchess of Newcastle, and Sir Kenelm Digby; but neither list begins to exhaust his citations. Of English writers Bacon is the most pervasive authority, and Donne the most common poet, though he is not always cited for his poetry. An interesting literary influence appears in his frequent use of the emblem and emblematic thought. Emblems are introduced by such remarks as, 'I finde in the *Schoole of Nature* no better *Embleme*,' or, 'I know not a better *Hieroglyphick*'; in 'The Divine Prospective', one of the divine essays, '*Galileus his Glasse*' becomes 'this *Paradoxicall glasse*' of faith. It should be added that no inconsiderable part of his reading is to be found in the classics or in the works of the church fathers.

Whitlock is also a defender of that 'Ternary of Fancies Sisterhood', poetry, music, and painting. His general atti-

---

[1] Op. cit., sig. a5r.
[2] This is still insufficiently recognized in the prose of this period; cf. the strange misunderstanding of Ursula Kentish-Wright in her edition of Nicholas Breton, *A Mad World My Masters, and Other Prose Works* (London, 1929, I, 151), where she explains 'A Lipsian stile, terse Phrase' by the note, 'Lipsian: lip salve, flattering speech'. See my *Senecan Amble,* Faber & Faber, 1951.
[3] Op. cit., sig. a5v.

tude may be suggested by the fact that he attempts to 'silence the dull, and more Grave, than wise Coxcombs, that call all Musick fidling'. The thrust at the Puritans becomes more cutting in these lines:

'But here mee-thinks the thread-bare scoff at Devotion Piping hot, seemeth to deny any use of Musick, in that where David chiefly used it, in the Service of God. But for my part, that the wel-ordered Musick of former Ages did not better tune Devotion, and to higher Pitches (or Ela's) of Zeale, than Tunes began by an out-of-tune Clerk, is one of those many Postulata, Assertions taken for granted, that I cannot play Assent to at first sight. . . .'[1]

Nor at any later sight, we may add. But he is most eloquent on poetry, 'Profane Inspirations Plea, or Poetry's Preheminence.'

'Poetry wings Notions to a flight above the low and muddy conceptions of Ignorance, or Dulnesse: and although it may seem to rob Truth of her best Ornament, Nakednesse (as it is commonly objected to Poetry) yet it furnisheth her with an advantageous Dresse of taking Pleasance, even to those that care not so much for Truth it self. Thus Herbert saith excellently.

> A Verse may finde him who a Sermon flies,
> And turn Delight into a Sacrifice.'[2]

Whitlock does not forget that he is appealing to those who do not believe that 'Pleasure must be the preachers study, as well as the Poets.' So he offers a witness who finds poetry in Scripture:

'But for the Honour of Poesie, let Doctor Donnes Observation plead (in his Essay of Divinity among his Fragments) concerning that Song of Moses which was made (saith he) by God himselfe; for though every other Poetick part of Scripture

---

[1] Ibid., p. 484.

[2] Ibid., p. 469. In so far as the Puritans associated truth with nakedness as opposed to an advantageous dress they furthered the revolt against rhetoric, but in so far as they indulged in 'enthusiastic' language they inspired the revolt against enthusiasm which conditioned the new plain style of the Restoration. Cf. my 'Restoration Revolt against Enthusiasm', in this volume.

be also *God's word*, and so made by him, yet all the rest were Ministeriall and Instrumentally *delivered* by the *Prophets*, onely *enflamed* by him. But this which himselfe calls a *Song*, was *immediately* made by himselfe. . . .'[1]

Than this, Whitlock believes, there can be no greater testimony that 'there is *something* more than *humane* in *Poetry*', for 'the flat *Hudles* of *Prose* were too rude, and of *lower flight*, than fitted the *Heights* of *Devotion*: for *Zeale* knowes no flatter *Figures* than *Hyperboles*, gracefully set to *number*, and *measure*.'[2]

But poetry has also a very human usefulness: 'its *Excellency*, and use through all the *three Regions* of *Men* (as excellently Mr. *Hobs*) the *City*, *Court*, and *Country*'; particularly in 'the *Dramatick* part of *Poetry*, inferiour to none for *usefulnesse*; to which *Heathens* (and some *Sermon-shunning Christians*) owe much of their *Discretion*, *Civility*, and *Reclaimes* as to *Morall Honesty*'. In fact, Whitlock makes drama a rival to divinity, and defends plays against those who 'through some *misbecoming* (and no lesse *mistaken*) *Gravity*, think them *below* their *use*'. He concludes that '*Poetry* was the *wisdome* of the *Ancients*, and its contempt is the *Folly* of the *Moderns*'. In these matters we may regard Whitlock as something of a spokesman for his colleagues of All Souls College.

IV

But it is in the role of apologist for learning that Whitlock assumes his most important character. In 'Learnings Apology' he defends learning chiefly against the religious fanatic, but also against the 'selfe-conceited Polititian' and 'Rustick Ignorance'. To him its real enemies are the devil and the ignorant world. His apology opens on this tack:

'In the shape of a Creature without *Reason*, the *Tempter* tempted us to *Knowledge*: In the shape of an *Angel of Light*, he would now bring in *Darkness*: At first the Lyer told us

[1] Ibid., p. 471.
[2] Ibid., p. 472. This notion explains much of the hyperbolic poetry, and why the revolt against 'Zeale' brought a distaste for its 'Figures'.

we knew not enough; now he would perswade us we *know too much*. . . . He is still endeavouring to bring Goodnesse and Piety into scorne with *Learned men*, or *Learning* into contempt with *Good men*.'[1]

There is not a little shrewdness in this approach to conciliation, but there is even more in the conclusion that 'since he first divorced *knowledge* and *practice* in our first Parents, he is loath they should ever *marry* againe'. While this notion supplies one of the main themes of his book, it is here directed against those who believe 'no *Universities* necessary in new *Canaan*, where all the Lords people are Prophets'.

Among such people fine language is not tolerated. 'If a man cloath his discourse in a Language that is not second hand English, or but one degree above the offensiveness of Caterwauling, why he is affected.' Whitlock knows not 'how it cometh to passe, but many speak to God as they would not speak to men; and preach to men in courser phrase, than they would sell their Wares'.[2] Much more, however, is required of 'Gods Embassadours':

'*The Preacher sought to find out acceptable words* . . . words as good as one would wish, such as would please and delight; to be upright, and true, (which is the latter part of the Verse) it seemeth is not al, though the main required in them; but they must be words sought out (not *Extempore*) and acceptable, they must not defie the Polishings of Art, but must be drest in some taking Garbe sutable to the Audience, *Utile dulci*, Profit, and Pleasure must be the Preachers study, as well as the Poets: And whence such Dresses are to be had but from Learnings Wardrobes, I know not.'[3]

If those who oppose and those who favour learning in religion were 'impartially compared', he concludes, 'there might be some hopes, our Librarys might be repreived, and our Colledges unsequestred'.[4] From these acts Whitlock, presumably, had suffered.

But 'Learnings usefulnesse in the defence of Truth' goes

---

[1] Ibid., p. 138. It soon appears that the 'Angel of Light' brings 'New Lights'.
[2] Ibid., p. 143.   [3] Ibid., pp. 144–5.   [4] Ibid., p. 149.

beyond eloquence: it has enabled the Church of England to answer Rome better than any other reformed church.[1] Much more dangerous than Rome, however, is the fact that truth has a precarious existence among the ignorant. 'To say truth, though some call their profound Ignorances, New Lights, they were better Anabaptised into the Appellation of Extinguishers; carryed about with every winde.'[2] Any ordinary sophistry turns their brains; indeed, nothing but winds of doctrine can be expected from those who 'swound at a Syllogisme, purge both wayes at a Dilemma and are ready to make their own Testament, if they see a Greek one'.

To help silence the political enemies of learning, Whitlock turns to Bacon, 'so often in this Discourse mentioned and yet so necessarily'.[3] But he 'would not be thought to excuse the Cynicall Solaecismes of any Schollers Behaviour, that remembreth not that he is among men, and not in a Desart or Platonick Common-wealth'.[4] His general conclusion 'that Rebellion against Knowledge, is but Allegiance to the Prince of Darknesse', leaves 'blind Zeale, mistaken Policy, or rustick Ignorance' very little to stand upon in Common-wealth times.

'The Apologists Apology' pleads that 'the visible ruine of Learning begun by some (and by more desired) may serve for my just defence . . . since it cannot bee objected I feare shadowes, or defend what none opposeth'. And it is neces-sary 'to let the world know I voted not with those Phili-stines, that plotted the putting out our *Sampsons* eyes, once seeing *Englands* (as it may be called, and hath appeared here-tofore, against all the Enemies of Truth)'.[5] But in 'The

[1] Ibid., p. 163.

[2] Ibid., p. 160. It is not impertinent to recall that Glanvill in his 'Epistle Dedicatory' to the *Vanity of Dogmatizing* (1661) could remark that his '*Vindica-tion of the* use *of* Reason *in matters of* Religion' was '*rendered less necessary by his Majesties much desired, and seasonable arrival*', and so remained unpublished.

[3] Ibid., pp. 178–9.

[4] Ibid., p. 187.

[5] Ibid., pp. 190–1. 'Large is *Cornelius Agrippas* Regiment of *Declamatores contra scientias* (as a worthy Imposer of names calleth him) Railers against all humane Arts and Sciences, though his Followers do it in a worse sense than he.' (p. 192)

Happy Match' he develops the moral implications of the
decline of real knowledge into 'meer Speculation':

'. . . I cannot but bewaile (not admire, or reverence) the
so much boasted Light, in Deeds of darknesse-dayes; or
those two sad Divorces, that excellent French man, *Charron
de la sagesse*, hath bewailed before mee: viz. Of Probity and
Piety, coming from the first divorce of Knowledge and
Practise, or (as he termeth them) *Science & Sagesse*, that is,
Knowledge, and Wisdome, be it humane or divine; whiles
separated from Morall, or Christian conformity in Affections, Passions, and Actions.'[1]

Whitlock is as morally earnest as Milton in his belief that
preachers should practise what they preach. 'Our former
complaints,' says Whitlock, 'were against times of Popery,
because zealous without knowledge; our latter and present
may be against Popery inverted, or knowledge without
zeale; but hard it is to determine which is sadder, their blind
zeale, or our lame knowledge'.[2] His moral seriousness will
not permit him to overlook the lameness of the knowledge
which he so ardently defends against the contemporary
'blind zeale'; knowledge without 'works' seemed as empty
as 'dark zeale' was blind. It is this moral earnestness that
makes his defence of the universities actually more serious
than Ward's *Vindiciae Academiarum*.

V

Perhaps the most interesting aspect of Whitlock is the

[1] Ibid., pp. 192-3. That Charron could insinuate sceptical doctrine where
Montaigne would have been denied a hearing may be illustrated in the 'Epistle
Dedicatory' which Marmaduke James wrote for his *Everlasting Covenant, As it
was Delivered in a Sermon at St. Paul's* (1659). James had decided not to publish
because of his disgust at the printing craze of the time, but 'afterwards being
wearied with the many Why-nots' of his acquaintances, he relented: 'I almost
repented the retracted purpose; and beginning to reflect upon the Mode of the
Times, found my self in an errour, if the Directions of that Wise Man of
France [Charron] to his Scholar be true, to wit, That 'tis a great point of
Wisdom, most precisely to obey the Customs of the place and age wherein we
live, to prevent misprision and popular disdain, however irrational they may
seem to us.' His perplexity is solved by good sceptical doctrine of the Montaigne variety.   [2] Ibid., pp. 193-4.

temper of his mind, which is characterized by a rationalism that is checked both by the skeptical vein of Charron and by the experimental vein of Bacon.[1] This temper receives explicit formulation in his essay on 'Reasons Independency'. The keynote is set by the opening sentence:

'It is no lesse *Prerogative* of that noble Creature, *Man*, that no worldly *Force* from *Men*, or *Angels*, can *command* or conquer his *Assent*, than that his *Will* cannot be *compel'd*, to choose or dislike.'[2]

This was not an innocent remark. Free-will is proved both by 'Patrons' and by *'Experiments* in every ones own *breast* in all premeditated Acts of the Will'.

'But this *Liberty of Judgement* is neither maintained, nor ordinarily observed and seemeth allmost lost, either in *Lazy*, or *blinde Sequacity* of other mens *Votes*: Our *Opinions* comming more by *Contagion* than on *Deliberation*; thus breaking our Allegiance to that sole Commandresse of our Reason, Truth. . . .'

We 'sweare submission of *Judgement*, or Assent, to every one that *Invadeth* our *understandings* with those great Names, *Aristotle, Plato, Democritus,* &c. Whereas it were a *Temper* not only leading to *Wisdome*, but were wisdome it selfe, to read all Authors, as *Anonymo's*, looking on the *Sence*, not *Names* of Books'. Referring to Bacon, Whitlock concludes:

'Hence that Learned *Iconoclastes*, that *Image-breaking* Enemie to *Intellectual Idolatry* knew no better *Furniture* for *Truths Temple*, than the broken *Images* of *Aristotle, Plato, Democritus*; or any other of the Antients set up in mens Mindes, as the only *Idoliz'd Oracles* of Truth.'[3]

In human learning he appeals 'to every Mans own impartiall Breast, whether he can boast an *unbiassed Judgement*: and why not?' Then he proceeds to give the causes of intellectual slavery, of which the first is 'the *Marriage*, (or Espousall, as the sage *French-man*) of our *Fancy*, or *Judgement* to some

---

[1] If this compound seems paradoxical, we must remember that Glanvill exhibited a similar compound.

[2] Op. cit., p. 207.

[3] Ibid., pp. 208–9.

Notions, or *Men*; and this hath begot that peevish *Morosity* among men; that the more *knowing Man*, is to the very *Ignorant*, *Hereticall*, and to the *Smatterer* in Knowledge, *Paradoxicall*.'[1]

The allusion is to Charron, and the passage is followed by a sketch of the dogmatist 'lazily sleeping on *Traditions* Pillow, into a *Lethargy* of *Ignorance*'. For the next cause Whitlock leans heavily upon Bacon:

'A second Cause is mistaking *Authority*: what more familiar, than to call the worlds *Infancy*, *Antiquity*? and its true *Senium*, or Age, *Novelty*? which if it be the *Brand* of this my *Assertion*, I have a *Patron* that took it from Reason. But it may be, according to my Assertion, his *Name* will sooner still *opposers* than his *Reasons*: to them I name that *oculatissimus Bacon* (*Learnings Chancellour*, more than *Englands*) but to the Rationall I set down his *Reason*, with uncontroulable *Demonstration*; proving that which we call *New*, and upstart, to be the *truest Antiquity*.'[2]

He then quotes the *Novum Organum*, Book I, Aphorism 84. As for the third cause, there is 'no taking one anothers *words* nor *Hands*, in *Disquisitions* of *Reason*; and where the *Diffidence* is not the Child of *Ignorance* or *Pride*, it is·more commendable than easy *Credulity*, which is the third cause of Intellectual slavery.'[3]

The fourth cause is quite the opposite of easy credulity:

'But another *extreame* to this, & a fourth Cause of this *slavery* of our understandings, is *obstinate adhaesion* to false rules of beliefe, and *Topicks* of Probation: and that either taken from *others* or our *selves*.'[4]

The 'most spreading Infection' originates in the fact that 'men raise their beliefe and Assent, from what is *oldest in them selves*; and hath been longest by them believed'.[5]

To light, therefore, on the 'healthfull neutrality', Whit-

---

[1] Ibid., p. 210. Glanvill's *Vanity of Dogmatizing* provides the closest parallel to 'Reasons' Independency', and also refers to 'the wise Monseur *Charron*' who 'hath fully discourst of this *Universal liberty*, and sav'd me the labour of inlarging' (1661, p. 234).
[2] Ibid., p. 211.   [3] Ibid., p. 214.   [4] Ibid., p. 216.   [5] Ibid., p. 217.

lock 'will observe the Polititians Rule; (as being usefull in the Imperiall Court of *Reason*) to steere a steddy course between *deforme obsequium*, unbecomming servility & *abruptam contumaciam*, & abrupt obstinacy':

'*Last writers* are not, because *Last*, the *best*, but so farre as they have *perused the old*, and so truly stand upon their shoulders: otherwise dreams of the *Ignorant*, or *whimseys* of the *Smatterer* in Learning, might be stampt for currant. It is an observation even here usefull, as well as in Divinity, to obey that Text, *Jerem.* 6. 16. *Stand in the way, and enquire for the old paths.* Stand in the old wayes, or enquire for them, before we enlarge our Discoveries of new. And that inimitable Poets Rule is true in al mending of our Intellectualls.

> ————*Doubt wisely, in strange way*
> *To stand inquiring right, is not to stray:*
> *To sleep, or run wrong, is*————

'*Augmenta Scientiarum*, Advancements of Learning are not meerly *Destructive* of the old, but for the most part additionale, *Progressive*, not deviating.'[1]

Besides employing Donne, Whitlock borrows significantly from Bacon in this passage, even sharing with him the text from *Jeremiah*. The meaning of scepticism for Whitlock and his time is elaborated by what follows.

'If *Copernicus* move the *Earth*; it shall not presently *turne* my Head with Astonishment at it; because *Opinion* hath fixed it (it may be more than its Creatour) no, we shall do well thus to carry our selves to things *Existences*, or their *Causes*; to the first, let us not affirm their existence, and ὅτι on the *Fallacies* of Sense. . . . I am perswaded nothing hath more continued such an Ignorance in the World, as Mens setting these terminating Bounds, and Pillars to their Discoveries, *My Sense, My Reason*; So farre will I go, and no further: calling *Obstinacy* to an Opinion, *Solidity*; and

---

[1] Ibid., pp. 218–19. Here and elsewhere Whitlock draws upon Bacon's analysis of the diseases and errors of learning in the first book of his *Advancement of Learning*.

humble *Ductility* after further Reason, and Discovery, *Sceptick Inconstancy*.'[1]

Two further cautions are enjoined: 'secondly, as to the Causes of things, how warily must we conclude their *Identity*, from a *Homogeneity* or Likenesse of *Effects*'; 'lastly, let us avoid that denying of Experiments, or Existence unquestionable of Effects, because their Causes, or their *modus operandi* (which is but the Application of the Cause to the Effect) doth not fall under *Demonstration*'.[2] Whitlock is willing to agree that 'it is an uselesse *Peevishnesse* to be too strict in *Disquisitions* and *trackings* of *Nature*, where shee will be hid'. The '*Acatalepsia*, impossibility of certainty', to which Bacon objected that it 'doomed men to perpetual darkness',[3] seems to Whitlock at least to leave men in partial darkness, even as to Nature; and this admission places him on the road between Bacon and Glanvill.

As a kind of summary of this sceptical rationalism (to use a paradoxical phrase for a paradoxical thing) Whitlock concludes:

'A *Learned Ignorance*, indeavouring Knowledge, is all our knowledge; and our reason dischargeth its duty, if it neither *sleep nor serve*. But now for its deportment to *Moralls* or *Politicks*, (and its assent, or Approbation, respective;) That *Liberte a' Esprit*, that *Charron* mentions, is the best Temper, a true Patron, and President of this *Independency* of *Reason*, and that *freedome of Spirit*, is that deserving Author of *Religio Medici*, with whom in this I agree.'[4]

[1] Ibid., pp. 219–21. This passes beyond Bacon into the realm of Sir Thomas Browne. For the *Religio Medici* without the sceptical temper see John Collop's *Medici Catholicon*, which was published by Moseley two years later than *Zootomia*.

[2] Ibid., pp. 221 and 222.

[3] Cf. *Novum Organum*, Book I, Aphorisms 67, 75, 126. It will be thought, says Bacon, that 'I maintain a sort of suspension of the judgment and bring it to what the Greeks call *Acatalepsia*,—a denial of the capacity of the mind to comprehend truth. But in reality that which I meditate and propound is not *Acatalepsia*, but *Eucatalepsia*; not denial of the capacity to understand, but provision for the understanding truly; for I do not take away authority from the senses, but supply them with helps; I do not slight the understanding, but govern it' (Aph. 126).

[4] Op. cit., pp. 223–4.

The consequence of 'its deportment to *Moralls* or *Politicks*' is that he will look on all the changes of the world 'but as a *Masse* of *Uniforme Deformities*: and that without *espousing* my *Reason* so to any one, as to think it already so good, as none other like it; or may not be (if he hath not been already) bettered: this suspence, *Surseance de Judgement* (as that excellent Frenchman) *Mette L'Esprit a L'Abri de tous Inconveniens*, it *shadeth* the *minde* from the inconveniences of *Quarrells, Disputes, Sidings* with Opinions, being cheated by Sophistry, &c. . . . It is a liberty maintaining the understanding *Chast*, neither *prostituting* her selfe to, or *suffering a Rape* from any Opinion.

Nullius jurare in verba Magistri.'[1]

The allusion to Charron ('*de Sagesse. Lib. 2. c. 2.*') again connects Whitlock with the scepticism of Montaigne which was disseminated by Charron; the Latin tag points to the motto of the Royal Society, '*Nullius in Verba*'. All of this is significant, among other reasons, because *Zootomia* was published in the days of Cromwell, twelve years after the *Religio Medici* but seven years before the *Vanity of Dogmatizing*, neither of which reveals the pervasive influence of Charron.

To enforce his sceptical approach Whitlock anatomizes the infirmities of readers in 'A Lecture for Readers', in which every one past his 'Horne-booke' is concerned. The Puritans again suffer the 'reply churlish'; for 'with ruder Ignorance, and blind zeale, what is above the *levell* of extempore *Non-sense*, is *Popery*, and Learning such an *Idoll*, that *Bell* and the *Dragon* were but *Puppets* to it':

'Such Readers must have bald sense, and course language, which they cry up with, *This tendeth to edification, this a man may understand,* &c. They call contracted Sense *Obscurity*, avoiding of *Tautologies, affected* Phrase, Language of a finer Dresse, *Ends* of Playes, as if there were no *medium* between *High-shoon* Language, and that of the *Buskin* and *Stage*: or if you will be above their understanding, they will best like it, or believe it; according to that of *Tacitus*, Hist. I. *Cupidine Ingenij humani libentius obscura credi*, In words that never did, never can, nor ever will signifie any thing; so they be new and in Fashion. . . .'[1]

'Again,' says Whitlock, 'too many there are that are resolved to like nothing from the *Pulpit*, or *Presse* that smelleth of the *Lampe*, that cost the Author paines, because it upbraideth their *Lazinesse*. . . . Give them *Sermons* easie as *familiar talke*, and printed Labours like those Sermons.'

But he leaves these 'Readers with *nothing* in their Heads', and comes to those 'with *too much*, the Severest Censurers of Authors'. Such heads are filled with 'those Principles of Prejudice (the true english of the Lord *Bacons Idola* . . .) which are either *falsly receptive*, or *morosely exclusive*'.[2] Here Bacon's 'idols' once more become sceptical criteria of knowledge, but Whitlock proceeds to amplify the two categories to which he has reduced them:

'1. Falsely receptive, that corrupt any Notions mingled with them: of these true is that Aphorisme. *Habet unusquisque (praeter Aberrationes Naturae humanae in genere, seu Idola Tribus) Specum sive Cavernam quandam individuam, quae lumen naturae frangit & corrumpit*, every one hath a secret and individuall *Caverne*, or dark *Cell* in his understanding, which breaketh the Rayes of the *light of Nature*, and falsify the *shives of Truth*. . . .'

To particularize this form of prejudice, he adds, 'among which that is no small one, to set up one *particular Science* for a common-place Book of all our Notions: to espouse our selves so to one part of truth, as to *endowe* her with all our

---

[1] Ibid., p. 251. If the Puritans objected to 'contracted Sense', the Cavaliers objected to 'enthusiastic' language without any meaning whatever.' Whitlock's own view of wit appears apropos of a passage from Strada: 'In which that no wit may be wanting, the *gingling Eare*, or *Fancy*, with whom *Quibbles* are the best *Wit*, may have *Patterns exceeding* ordinary *Imitation*, or *Friblings of Wit*. But (to return of some of Stradas instances) that his commanding *Fancy* could *vary* on the same *thing* (the *Mastery of Wit*) view in the above mentioned place: The severall names for a *Slave*, used, *threatned*, or *deserving* to be *beaten*' (pp. 474–75). Whitlock had read both Davenant and Hobbes on wit, but he approved the 'thesaurus' wit exemplified in the poetry of Crashaw and Cowley.

[2] Ibid., p. 253.

Assent, bringing almost all other Notions to this for their Passe'. There remains the principle of prejudice which is 'morosely exclusive':

'2. To come to the second Bench of *Censurers*, fitted with peevish exclusive Notions, or *Idola* made by *Education*, *Tradition*, &c. (of which somewhat hath been said in the *Essay* of *Reasons Independency*) Look how, what you write, agreeth with these ["their *Creed of Notions*"]. . . .'[1]

In short, 'in *Divinity*, *Morals*, and *Naturals*, true is that rule of the Lord *Bacon*, in his *Novum Organum*, *Aphorisme* 49, *lib*: I, *Intellectus humanus Luminis Sicci non est.* . . . We receive onely those things for Truths we have a mind to. . . . So many waies doth Affection stain our understandings.' And this was also the later 'scepsis scientifica' of Glanvill.

Whitlock concludes that readers must 'bring *Rasae Tabulae*, clean Tables to every Author . . . a good course therefore it is to *spunge* out prejudicate *Notions*, or *Opinions*, received on any ground, but that *Scientificall Syllogisme*, where *Reason* is the *Major*, and *Experiment* the *Minor*: In making of which, all our life will not exclude any new reason, or experiment, but it will help to make the *Conclusion* so much the truer, though we come not to the *Ergò* of our knowledge untill we come to the conclusion of our *daies*, and *studies*.'[2]

Between Browne and Glanvill, Whitlock seems to be the chief spokesman for the scepticism which penetrated England through Montaigne and Charron, though for Whitlock the real medium was Charron. Like Browne, Whitlock finds the Baconian idols useful criteria of reason; like Glanvill, he is more interested in checking dogmatism than in destroying rationalism by means of a thorough-going Pyrrhonism. He illustrates the cautious rationalism which comes from Bacon and passes into the Royal Society, and he has more in common with the early 'Academic' scepticism of Dryden than with his later Pyrrhonism. To his defence of learning as well as to his attack upon religious

[1] Ibid., p. 255. The Guildhall copy changes 'fitted' to 'filled'.
[2] Ibid., pp. 258–9.

fanaticism, Whitlock brought a sceptical temper of mind and an earnest moral character. These qualities he carried from All Souls College to a little parish in the Church of England, but in a way not suspected by Anthony Wood he 'had run with the times' which issued in critical rationalism.

IX

The Restoration Revolt Against Enthusiasm

★

Why imagination was regulated and emotion restrained in Restoration style is a question that has received both recent and able answers from scholars and critics. And yet I, for one, am not satisfied with the answers. Once or twice a scholar has passed over what, to me, is very nearly the centre of the problem; at least, he has disappointed me with what seemed to be little more than a passing recognition. I do not think that anyone has, in the old sense, 'prevented' me in what I wish to add in answer to this fascinating question.

Briefly, perhaps too briefly for conviction, I shall try to present my answer. It is inevitable that the answer to such a question should be complicated, but the necessities of space may throw part of that complication upon my reader, for I must centre my answer round the one word, *Enthusiasm*. The revolt against Enthusiasm will not explain every phase of style during the third quarter of the seventeenth century, but it will do much to explain the change of temper out of which the neo-classical style developed. The revolt against Enthusiasm, which is the immediate cause of this change of temper, is itself the culmination of the thought of the first half of the century, however its manifestation may vary in religious, scientific, or literary style.

The Restoration Revolt against Enthusiasm

What I have to say about Enthusiasm, its relation to style, and its effect of crystallizing the classical temper is not really new. If there is anything novel in it, I think such novelty will be found, not in a perversion of facts, but in making again at least one correlation which the Restoration made and which we have neglected. We are accustomed to think of the English classical temper as one that minimized the emotional and imaginative content of literature; we sometimes call its product a literature of reason. Some have gone so far as to deny it emotion and imagination in the creative sense; but we have outgrown such views. While we feel that such statements are a rough outline of the reorganization which took place in the literary mind during the Restoration, we do not always trouble ourselves to account for such a reorganization, except perhaps to think of it as a result of foreign influence or as a 'restoration' of native elements in the English temper. Foreign influence we may admit, and yet it is not enough. But a restoration of what? Professor Wood has given one answer.[1] But what was restored was something new, born again in a new mental pattern, a new temperament. The Anglican Church in the mind of Tillotson was not the Anglican Church which had coloured the mind of Andrewes; in dogma perhaps, but not in mood. Events coming between the two had created a new temper even in this house of tradition; it was no longer possible to think and feel in it in quite the same way. To account for this change I wish to make a correlation of which the Restoration was conscious and of which we are often negligent.

I

A search for the fundamental grounds upon which imagination was tempered and emotion restricted in Restoration style will carry us back to the man whose shadow falls across the entire seventeenth century, Francis Bacon. When Bacon, following his age, referred poetry to imagination

[1] P. S. Wood, 'Native Elements in English Neo-Classicism', *Modern Philology*, XXIV (1926), 201–8.

and then proceeded to divorce poetry from the real and true by making it mere 'play', he began a train of thought which realized its implications before 1660. In a mind represented by the Royal Society rather than by Spenser, Bacon's notion that poetry submitted 'the shows of things to the desires of the mind; whereas reason doth buckle and bow the mind into the nature of things',[1] presented formidable implications. These implications were reinforced by the psychology of the first half of the century, which Bacon also reflected. On the basis of this psychology Bacon defines imagination as a messenger between sense and reason, and reason and voluntary motion, 'who may come also to rule in his turn. For we see that, in matters of Faith and Religion, we raise our Imagination above our Reason; which is the cause why Religion sought ever access to the mind by similitude, types, parables, visions, dreams. And again, in all persuasions that are wrought by eloquence, and other impressions of like nature, which do paint and disguise the true appearance of things, the chief recommendation unto Reason is from Imagination.'[2]

Thus imagination finds its real 'work' in rhetoric. According to Elizabethan psychology, Bacon seems to have confused imagination and understanding in religion, but he corrected this in *De Augmentis*; certainly he justifies much Jacobean and Caroline preaching. The 'chief recommendation', rhetoric, is necessary because of 'the continual mutinies and seditions of the affections', but 'if the affections in themselves were pliant and obedient to reason, it were true there should be no great use of persuasions and insinuations to the will, more than of naked proposition and proofs. . . .'[3]

And to Bacon the perturbations of the affections were 'infirmities of the mind', to which he would add ungoverned

[1] *Advancement of Learning*, Everyman ed. (London, 1915), pp. 82–3; also pp. 120–1, and *De Augmentis*, V, 1.

[2] Ibid., p. 121. For the best analysis of Bacon's view of imagination, poetry, and rhetoric, see M. W. Bundy, 'Bacon's True Opinion of Poetry', *Studies in Philology*, XXVII (1930), 244–64.

[3] Ibid., p. 147. Imagination is ancillary to reason.

imagination. For him the rule of reason was disturbed by three things, sophistry, imagination, and the affections.[1] With such notions Bacon not only established the relation of imagination and rhetoric to literature and religion, but he also formulated the ideas that were to discredit imagination and emotion for the sake of reason when the Commonwealth had learned to distrust persuasions 'which do paint and disguise the true appearance of things'.

In these notions Bacon was supported in the main by the psychology of his time. We have only to turn to such a popular manual as Thomas Wright's *Passions of the Minde*, 1601, to find a similar view of the passions;[2] and Wright, like Bacon, argues against the Stoics that the passions are not to be extinguished, but moderated.[3] Dr. Anderson has summed up the Elizabethan psychology with which we are concerned in these words:

'The doctrine that the faculties of the soul are likely both by arrangement and by nature to rebel against reason is fundamental in Elizabethan thinking. . . . In the final analysis strife is largely a matter of conflict between reason and the powers of action, more specifically, between reason and the affections; for the senses and the imagination work disaster particularly through their power to command the affections, and the affections entice will from following reason.'[4]

To this age the strongest elements of disorder were the affections and the imagination; in literature they united through the instrumentality of rhetoric. Bacon has given us a literary psychology not altogether free from elements of discord, as time will prove. Both Bacon and Shakespeare

[1] Ibid., p. 146. Poetry is rather a 'play of wit than a science', rather 'manna' than 'food of the mind'. *De Augmentis*, V, 1. For the Elizabethan confusion of poetic and rhetorical theory see D. L. Clark's 'Rhetoric and Poetry in the Renaissance', New York, 1922. Bacon continued this confusion at the same time that he spoke for a sounder rhetoric.

[2] London, 1604, pp. 2–3; issued in 1601, 1604, 1621, 1630.

[3] Ibid., pp. 17–19.

[4] R. L. Anderson, *Elizabethan Psychology and Shakespeare's Plays* (Iowa City, 1927), pp. 138–9; also chaps. I, IV, VIII.

assigned poetry to the imagination, which continued to be primary in the literary faculty or 'wit' throughout the first half of the century; and in Elizabethan psychology the supremacy of the imagination, or of the affections, is always dangerous.[1] Wright's view of rhetoric is much the same as Bacon's;[2] he regards rhetoric as a 'two-edged sword', but necessary 'to batter downe the walles of wilfull affections', however it may lend itself to 'cover stincking matters with fragrant flowers'; in fact, he devotes a whole chapter to the 'Discoverie of Passions in Writing', which is of great interest in this connection. I quote a passage of unusual significance for the future:

'Who of purpose writeth obscurely, peruerteth the naturall communication of men; because we write to declare our minds, and he that affecteth obscurity, seemeth, not to be willing that men should conceiue his meaning. The holy Scriptures I always except, which for many causes admit some obscuritie. But for men, in their writing to follow such a phrase as hardly you can vnderstand what they say, cannot but proceed either from confused vnderstanding, because a cleere conceit breedeth perspicuous deliuerie, or affectation of learning, which springeth from pride. . . .

'To use many Metaphors, Poetical phrases in prose, or inckepot tearmes, smelleth of affectation, and argueth a proud childish wit. To be peremptorie and singular in opinions, to censure ill, or condemne rashly, without rendring some sound and strong reason, for the most part proceedeth from singular selfeloue, and a defectuous judgement.'[3]

If such doctrine, involving such psychology, could be preached in a popular manual at the beginning of the century, we need not be surprised if it eventually took effect. But Wright also taught the art of playing upon the emotions through the imagination;[4] and this office of imagination became one of the chief dogmas of seventeenth-century rhetoric, a dogma that brought imagination under suspicion.

[1] Ibid., p. 172.
[2] See Wright, op. cit., pp. 99, 185, 192-3.
[3] Ibid., p. 141.
[4] Ibid., pp. 185 ff.

Nor does Wright neglect the power of the poet in this respect.[1]

At this point we may hazard a forward glance. In 1682 Dryden, in his preface to *Religio Laici*, writes:

'The Expressions of a Poem designed purely for Instruction ought to be Plain and Natural, and yet Majestic: for here the Poet is presumed to be a kind of Law-giver, and those three qualities which I have nam'd are proper to the Legislative style. The Florid, Elevated, and Figurative way is for the Passions; for Love and Hatred, Fear and Anger, are begotten in the Soul by shewing their Objects out of their true proportion; either greater than the Life, or less; but Instruction is to be given by shewing them what they naturally are. A Man is to be cheated into Passion, but to be reason'd into Truth.'[2]

In *Religio Laici* Dryden hoped that he was imitating Horace's *Epistles*; the 'Figurative way' was the way of Heroic poetry. Dryden, always the voice of his age, is here not less so, for witnesses to this statement are numerous. While we may recognize that this passage divides Sidney's poet, and may ponder its final significance, we cannot misconstrue the concluding sentence, which goes back to the office of imagination as we have seen it in Bacon and Wright. The connection between imagination and emotion is here the same, but the implications have been realized. Bacon's notion of the imagination as a distorter, even an ideal distorter, of the nature of things here comes full circle, and its deception is set on one side with passion as against reason and truth on the other.

Before 1650 there are a few other comments on style which I should like to notice. In Hakewill's *Apologie or Declaration of the Power and Providence of God*, we find this interesting passage:

'Sr Henry Savill sharply censures [Tacitus] for his style, taking occasion from those words in the life of *Agricola*,

---

[1] Ibid., pp. 292 ff.

[2] *Poems of John Dryden*, ed. Sargeaunt (London, 1929), p. 29. The *doctrina* and *eloquentia* of medieval poetics are here separated according to the aims of poetry.

bonum virum facile crederes, magnum libenter: at te (saith he)
*Corneli Tacite bonum historicum facile credimus, bonum oratorem
crederemus libenter,* were it not for this & some other sayings
of the like making: *Fuit illi viro,* saith Tacitus, (judging of
Seneca as we may of him) *ingenium amaenum, & temporis
illius auribus accommodatum:* How that age was eared long or
round I cannot define, but sure I am it yeelded a kinde of
sophisticate eloquence and riming harmony of words;
where-under was *small matter* in sense, when there seemed
to be most in appearance, and divers instances he brings out
of *Tacitus. . . .*'[1]

Here we are reminded of Bacon's description of the
Senecan style, which was popular in his time, as *'paulo
sanius'* than the Ciceronian.[2] This style Bacon had set down
as the latest distemper of learning in matters of style.

At least as early as 1640 we find a beginning of the revolt
against the citation of authorities, and in a significant place.
It is found in the preface to Gilbert Wats's English version
of the *De Augmentis Scientiarum*:

'These considerations invited me to Marginal Citations.
These reasons set apart, I cannot approve this weake ambition; and doe, not without censure, read Moderne Authors
prostitute to humane allegations; as if the *Truth* they deliver,
were to be tried by voices; or having lost its primitive Inno-
cence, must be cover'd with these fig-leaves; or as if the
Authors themselves were afraid that it should make an
escape out of their text, if it were not beset in the Margin
with Authorities as with a watch.'[3]

And yet Wats thinks that his 'Times are learned, so
(which too frequently falls out) somewhat confident'; but
that they could profitably fall 'off from many aery speculations, to the solid simplicity of the Ancients'.

---

[1] London, 1635, p. 285.

[2] See *Works of Francis Bacon*, ed. Spedding & Ellis (London, 1857), I, 452. In
1630 Randolph alludes to these styles in this fashion: 'the fire being blown with
the long-winded blast of a Ciceronian sentence, and the whole confection
boiled from a pottle to a pint in the pipkin of Seneca'. Randolph's *Works*, ed.
Hazlitt (London, 1875), I, 44.

[3] *Of the Advancement and Proficience of Learning* (Oxford, 1640), sig. Gg 2.

The Restoration Revolt against Enthusiasm

In another quarter we find Alexander Ross falling upon the author of *Religio Medici* with these words:

'The Gentleman, who at last acknowledgeth himselfe to be the Authour of this Booke, tells us, that many things in it are not to be called unto the *rigid test of reason*, being delivered Rhetorically: but, as I suspect that friendship, which is set out in too many Verball Complements; so doe I that Religion, which is trimmed up with too many Tropicall pigments, and Rhetoricall dresses.'[1]

Here we see that some of the implications in Bacon's rhetorical doctrine are being realized. Ross also falls upon Browne in an '*O altitudo!*' with the statement that metaphors 'cast a mist upon the thing defined; every Metaphor being more obscure then proper words'.[2] And Ross tells Browne that it is his duty to show young gentlemen 'that there is some danger in reading your Book, without the *spectacles* of judgement: for, whilst they are taken with the *gilding* of your phrase, they may swallow unawares such *pills*, as may rather kill then cure them.'[3]

But Kenelm Digby, later of the Royal Society, comes in for just as heavy a shelling at the hands of Ross in his *Philosophicall Touchstone*:

'If you lay the fault of this upon your *Rhetoricall* expressions, I must answer you, that *Rhetorick* in such a subject may well be spared: use your *Rhetorick* when you will work upon the *affections*, but not when you will informe the understanding; for in this regard you do but cloud, not cleere the intellect.'[4]

Let us remember the rhetorical dogma that is summed up in the passage which I quoted from the preface to *Religio Laici*. Ross lends greater emphasis to the ideas which I have been outlining by such remarks as '*naked truth* cares not for such *dressings*'.

And John Wilkins, deploring the ignorance of contemporary preachers, in the midst of what he called 'that great intermission of University studies and breeding, occasioned

---

[1] *Medicus Medicatus* (London, 1645), sigs. A3–A4. [3] Ibid., p. 80.
[2] Ibid., pp. 20–1. [4] London, 1645, p. 92.

by these unhappy Warres', dared to say of education and learning,

'These common Gifts are not now bestowed upon men, by any speciall infusion, but must be acquired, by the usuall ways of study and labour: A man may as well expect to be inspired with the gift of Tongues, as with the gift of Preaching.'[1]

This is the anti-enthusiastic attitude which later prevails in style.

Evidently the fundamental ideas of the Restoration transformation of style were not unknown to the earlier part of the century. Doubtless Stoicism had something to do with the tendency to repress emotion and elevate reason; doubtless Cartesianism contributed to method and a mathematical plainness; doubtless French *mondanité* played its part; but, without these, the change of style would have come about for other good and sufficient reasons, among which will be found Baconian science.

II

We may now turn to Hobbes and his view of imagination, emotion, and rhetoric. In the *Leviathan* Hobbes analyzes imagination into kinds, such as simple and compound; but it is necessary to insist that for him the act of imagination includes not only images as 'decaying sense', but also the 'Trayne of Imaginations' as acted upon by the *Naturall Wit*, which consists chiefly of 'Celerity of Imagining' and 'steddy direction to some approved end'.[2] The faculties which operate upon this 'Trayne of Imaginations' in poetry are Fancy and Judgment, of which 'the Fancy must be more eminent', but must be disciplined by Judgment.[3] A '*Good Fancy*' or a '*Good Wit*' must have not only judgment, which is not so much reason as discretion or a sense of propriety, but also a sense of design or direction to an end.[4]

[1] *Ecclesiastes* (London, 1646), sig. A2.
[2] See *Leviathan, Everyman* ed. (London, 1914), Part I, chapters 1, 3, 8.
[3] Ibid., p. 34.   [4] Ibid., p. 33.

The Restoration Revolt against Enthusiasm

Wit is commonly used for *Fancy* when it designates an unusual ability to observe similitudes in the 'Trayne of Imaginations', in which a '*good Judgement*' will observe dissimilitudes that are not easy to discern.

When Hobbes expressed these ideas in the *Answer to Davenant*, he terminated his chain of 'begats' with the notion that 'Memory begets Judgement and Fancy: Judgment begets the strength and structure, and Fancy begets the ornaments of a Poem'. But, as he explains, fancy is a swift seeker in the stores of memory, which judgment orders; and fancy has no small part:

'All that is beautiful or defensible in building . . . is the workmanship of Fancy but guided by the Precepts of true Philosophy. But where these precepts fail, as they have hitherto failed in the doctrine of Moral vertue, there the Architect, *Fancy*, must take the Philosophers part upon her self.'[1]

What Hobbes means by the 'strength and structure' of a poem is here explained and modified; his aphoristic and paradoxical tendency, as well as his admiration for judgment, sometimes causes him to overstate himself. Judgment and fancy as they govern expression consist 'in two things, which are, *To know well*, that is, to have images of nature in the memory distinct and clear, and *To know much*. A signe of the first is perspicuity, property, and decency, which delight all sorts of men. . . . A signe of the latter is novelty of expression, and pleaseth by excitation of the minde. . . .'[2]

The interplay of these two faculties is necessary to poetic expression and the creative act; and the truth is that Hobbes does not displace imagination, or fancy, from its proper eminence, although his explanation is mechanical; but he does emphasize strongly the rational element in artistic expression. Two further restraints he imposes on the poet: he insists on 'resemblance with the natural' in expression, and on 'the *possibility* of nature' in fiction; hence 'the Resemblance of truth is the utmost limit of Poeticall

[1] See Spingarn, *Critical Essays of the Seventeenth Century*, II, 60.
[2] Ibid., II, 63.

211

Liberty'.[1] In his insistence upon judgment, Hobbes seems to be attempting to validate the truth of imagination, which is open to suspicion in Bacon and finds that suspicion in writers both before and after Hobbes.

In his chapter on the 'Trayne of Imaginations', Hobbes speaks of the train of thoughts as of two sorts, the 'unguided' and the 'regulated'. After remarking of the former, the associational, that 'in this wild ranging of the mind, a man may oft-times perceive the way of it, and the dependence of one thought upon another', he goes on to say of the latter,

'In summe, the Discourse of the Mind, when it is governed by designe, is nothing but *Seeking*, or the faculty of Invention. . . . Sometimes a man seeks what he hath lost. . . . This we call *Remembrance*, or Calling to mind. . . .

'Sometimes a man knows a place determinate, within the compasse whereof he is to seek; and then his thoughts run over all the parts thereof, in the same manner, as one would sweep a room, to find a jewell; or as a Spaniel ranges the field, till he find a sent; or as a man should run over the Alphabet to start a rime.'[2]

With this and the foregoing matter in mind, let us look at Dryden's preface to *Annus Mirabilis*, published in 1667:

'The Composition of all Poems is or ought to be of wit; and wit in the Poet, or wit writing (if you will give me leave to use a School distinction), is no other than the faculty of imagination in the Writer; which, like a nimble Spaniel, beats over and ranges through the field of Memory, till it springs the Quarry it hunted after, or, without metaphor, which searches over all the Memory for the Species or Ideas of those things which it designs to represent. Wit written, is that which is well defin'd, the happy result of Thought, or product of Imagination. . . . So then, the first happiness of the Poet's Imagination is properly invention, or finding of the thought; the second is Fancy, or the variation,

---

[1] Ibid., II, 61–2.

[2] *Leviathan*, edition cited, chap. III, p. 10. Dryden reveals his knowledge of this passage in 1700; see *Essays*, ed. Ker, II, 248.

deriving or moulding of that thought as the Judgment represents it proper to the subject; the third is Elocution, or
the Art of clothing and adorning that thought so found and
varied, in apt, significant and sounding words: The quickness of the Imagination is seen in the Invention, the fertility
in the Fancy, and the accuracy in the Expression.'[1]

This, the finest description of the poetic process as seen by
the Restoration, incorporates in the mind of a poet the
psychology and teaching of Hobbes, which make for control. Certainly Hobbes and Dryden illuminate one another.
Dryden's later definition of wit as 'a propriety of thoughts
and words; or, in other terms, thoughts and words elegantly adapted to the subject' is only another description of
'wit written'.[2] As we see, in Dryden judgment does not
usurp the place of imagination, but it does exert a discipline
upon its product. And this is its real function in neo-
classical theory.

'As for *acquired Wit*,' says Hobbes, 'there is none but
Reason; which is grounded on the right use of Speech.'[3]
Under his four abuses of speech, Hobbes lists the inconstancy of the signification of words, by which men deceive
themselves; and the metaphorical use of words, by which
they deceive others.[4] The first necessitates the method of
geometry, the settling of significations, or definition;[5] the
second renders the use of metaphors, tropes, and other
rhetorical figures, instead of proper words, inadmissible to
the pursuit of truth.[6] For, says Hobbes,

'To conclude, The Light of humane minds is Perspicuous
Words, but by exact definitions first snuffed, and purged
from ambiguity; *Reason* is the *pace*; Encrease of *Science*, the
way; and the Benefit of man-kind, the *end*. And on the contrary, Metaphors, and senselesse and ambiguous words, are

---

[1] *Poems of John Dryden*, ed. Sargeaunt (London, 1929), pp. 20–1.
[2] *Essays of John Dryden*, ed. Ker (Oxford, 1926), I, 190. This definition was
written only ten years later, in 1677.
[3] *Leviathan*, ed. cit., p. 35.
[4] Ibid., p. 13.
[5] Ibid., p. 15.
[6] Ibid., p. 21.

like *ignes fatui*; and reasoning upon them, is wandering amongst innumerable absurdities; and their end, contention, sedition, or contempt.'[1]

It is evident that Hobbes's view of language as related to truth or philosophy looks both before and after; many of his contemporaries would subscribe to the last sentence as a summary of the immediate past.

As for the emotions, to Hobbes 'Madnesse is nothing else, but too much appearing Passion,' of which melancholy is one form. He even goes so far as to say, 'And if the Excesses be madnesse, there is no doubt but the Passions themselves, when they tend to Evill, are degrees of the same.'[2] The other cause of madness to Hobbes is 'Private Spirit', or Enthusiasm; and of people possessed by this, he writes with an eye upon his times, 'if there were nothing else that bewrayed their madnesse; yet that very arrogating such inspiration to themselves, is argument enough'.[3] He deprecated the claim to inspiration even in the poet.

This madness is connected with the use of metaphors and other *ignes fatui* of language, and is referred by Hobbes particularly to religious illusions. Thus we can see how Hobbes ties up deceits of speech with the passions and imagination, and how they all connect with the past thought of the century. And finally when Hobbes ascribes one source of madness to Enthusiasm, we are prepared for the revolt against Enthusiasm which will crystallize the thought and feeling of the Restoration into a new temper; and this temper, deriving something from the past and something from a revulsion of feeling, will command the future.

III

In 1655 and 1656 two books were levelled at Enthusiasm, one by Meric Casaubon and the other by Henry More; in fact, one may say that hostility toward Enthusiasm then be-

---

[1] Ibid., p. 22.
[2] Ibid., p. 36. 'Passions unguided' are the object of his attack.
[3] Ibid., p. 37.

came quite general. Sir William Temple, looking back from 1690, could stop in the course of refuting divine inspiration in poetry to offer this general view:

'And I am sorry the Natural History or Account of Fascination has not imployed the Pen of some Person of such excellent Wit and deep Thought and Learning as Casaubon, who writ that curious and useful Treatise of *Enthusiasm*, and by it discovered the hidden or mistaken Sources of that Delusion, so frequent in all Regions and Religions of the World, and which had so fatally spread over our Country in that Age in which this Treatise was so seasonably published. . . . I think a clear Account of Enthusiasm and Fascination from their natural Causes would very much deserve from Mankind in general as well as from the Commonwealth of Learning, might perhaps prevent many publick disorders, and save the Lifes of many innocent deluded or deluding People, who suffer so frequently upon Account of Witches and Wizards. I have seen many miserable Examples of this kind in my youth at home; and tho' the Humor or· Fashion be a good deal worn out of the World within Thirty or Forty Years past, yet it still remains in several remote parts of *Germany*, *Sweden*, and some other Countries.'[1]

Since Temple is engaged with the confusion of poetic inspiration and Enthusiasm, and is largely indebted to Casaubon for his solution, his relating this problem of neo-classicism to the Restoration past throws the books of Casaubon and More into a position of great importance. Bacon had defined *Fascination* as 'the power and act of imagination intentive upon other bodies than the body of the imaginant', had condemned the school of Paracelsus for exalting 'the power of the imagination to be much one with the power of miracle-working faith', and had included Enthusiasm under the head of *Divination*, with the general conclusion that 'it is not known how much of them is verity, and how much vanity'.[2] The seriousness of the problem to Temple is evident; it is a problem related to imagination and emotion, as we saw in Hobbes. In short, it is a funda-

[1] Spingarn, op. cit., III, 76.   [2] Bacon, op. cit., pp. 118–20.

mental literary and psychological problem of the seventeenth century, and as such deserves our careful inspection. The relevance of the problem to what Temple calls 'Natural Magick' in poetry is not far to seek, and its relevance to the shifting ground of belief is borne out by the whole century.

The first book against Enthusiasm to be published was Meric Casaubon's 'Treatise concerning *Enthusiasme*, as it is an Effect of *Nature*: but is mistaken by many for either *Divine Inspiration*, or *Diabolical Possession*', dated 1655. Before we examine this book we must pause for a contemporary definition of Enthusiasm. In Blount's *Glossographia* of 1656, the most popular dictionary of the age, we find this definition: '*Enthusiasm* or *Enthysiasm* (*enthysiasmus*) an inspiration, a ravishment of the spirit, divine motion, Poetical fury.' Casaubon's own definition, with deference to true religion, refers to his proper subject in these words: 'By natural *Enthusiasme*, I understand an extraordinary, transcendent, but natural fervency, or pregnancy of the soul, spirits, or brain, producing strange effects, apt to be mistaken for supernatural.'[1]

Casaubon asserts that his *Treatise* 'is no idle philosophical speculation, but of main consequence both to truth in highest points, and publick welfare'.[2] He observes that in ancient times 'every mans religion was his phansy', and poets were thought to be divinely inspired; he declares that 'Tertullian had never been an Heretick, had he been a better Naturalist'. The degree of awareness with which Casaubon regarded Enthusiasm is apparent in his analysis of it into such types as 'Divinatory', 'Contemplative', 'Rhetoricall', 'Poeticall', and 'Precatory'. More than once Casaubon finds Enthusiasm to be an effect of melancholy;[3] or compares it very unfavourably with reason, as 'sound Reason and a discerning spirit is a perpetual kind of Divination'.[4] He declares Plato to be an enthusiast and his language obscure;[5] he

---

[1] *Treatise concerning Enthusiasme* (London, 1655), p. 17.
[2] Ibid., p. 4.   [4] Ibid., p. 47.
[3] Ibid., pp. 39, 68, 82, for instance.   [5] Ibid., pp. 52–3.

analyzes ecstasies as a peculiar cause of Contemplative En-thusiasm;[1] calling Behmen a fanatic, he points out the dangers of astrology and mystical theology, which is apt to turn all religion into mere fancy.[2] He finds that imagination infects the understanding with Enthusiasm;[3] that 'natural *ardor* or *fervency*' is the principal cause of Enthusiasm, the peculiar advantage of rhetoric, the *ignis fatuus* of divine in-spiration, and a common source of ambiguity; and that 'there is not any thing more natural unto man, as he is a man (that is a rational creature), then *Reason*'.[4]

Casaubon's remarks on rhetoric need to be inspected more closely; as a central passage we may take the follow-ing:

'Rhetorick (or rhetorical speech) is a speech dressed with certain devices and allurements, proper to please and to per-swade. The use of such devices and allurements, is sometimes good, by the advantage of some sensual delight, the more powerful to inforce, or to insinuate somewhat that of it self is true, right, or reasonable. However, it is a very disputable point, whether bare speech, if well handled, be not sufficient, nay most available to perswade, in things of most weight. For those actions are best grounded, that are grounded upon judgement, upon which bare Speech hath most direct in-fluence; as Rhetorick hath upon the Affections: and the fruits of a convicted judgement by calm reason, are likely to be more durable then those that are the effects of any passions, or affections, stirred up by rhetorical powers.'[5]

This is old doctrine now directed against Enthusiasm, and it is interesting to note how explicitly bare speech is coming to be the speech of judgment. Of the use of figures and ornaments, Casaubon remarks:

'But this very reason that makes them so pleasing in ordinary language, hath brought *Metaphors* out of credit with Philosophers, that seek not the pleasures of the senses, but the naked truth of things.'[6]

He says that Seneca allows them to philosophers, and the

[1] Ibid., Chap. III.   [3] Ibid., pp. 88–9.   [5] Ibid., p. 140.
[2] Ibid., pp. 126–31.   [4] Ibid., p. 139.   [6] Ibid., pp. 181–2.

Scripture uses them, as a concession to the dulness of human understanding; he comments on one who condemns the 'sweet cadency and collocation of words' with the remark, 'I wish there were no worse Doctrine ever heard out of our Pulpits';[1] he even analyzes the 'mystical' effects of rhetoric, its power of incantation.[2]

While all of these statements have their relation to Enthusiasm, we must not neglect one or two special applications which Casaubon makes. He declares that it was a common opinion of Quintilian's time 'that Rhetorick and good lines came more by *Enthusiasme* then otherwise'; and, having quoted a passage from Seneca, he comments:

'Here is perfect *Enthusiasme*, with allusion to the *Sibylls*, and such others as were generally conceived to be possest. Yet, whether *Seneca* himself did believe so much, as his words seem to import, is a question: it being his manner, to be very high and tumid in his expressions; which neverthelesse a sober reader will not allwayes take to the utmost of what they will bear.'[3]

This should be connected with the general cultivation of the Senecan style in the first half of the century, and with the other criticism of that style which we have noticed.

Of the art of *extempore* speaking, and the chief end of rhetoric in Quintilian's age, Casaubon makes this application to his own time:

'Which being so rare a thing in our dayes, that a man, if he can utter any thing, which may seem to be *extempore*; though perchance it do but seem so, and that it be performed but very meanly; is by many, (who therefore upon that account, swallow down pure non-sense sometimes, with better content, then they will hear much better and more profitable matter, that is delivered with some studie and premeditation:) by many deemed, I say, no lesse then inspired.'[4]

In days when cobblers laid down their awls at the behest of Enthusiasm and fell to preaching, this had a special per-

[1] Ibid., p. 172.   [2] Ibid., pp. 174 ff.   [3] Ibid., p. 145.
[4] Ibid., pp. 158-9.

tinence. Indeed, Hobbes had said that the poet as well as the divine, though 'enabled to speak wisely from the principles of nature and his own meditation, loves rather to be thought to speak by inspiration, like a Bagpipe.'[1]

The second big attack on Enthusiasm came from the pen of Henry More in 1656, and carried this title: 'Enthusiasmus Triumphatus, or a Discourse of the *Nature, Causes, Kinds,* and *Cure* of Enthusiasme.' To More '*Enthusiasme* is nothing else but a misconceit of being *inspired*'.[2] A 'misconceit' due to imagination:

'Wherefore it is the enormous strength of Imagination (which is yet the Soul's weaknesse or unwieldinesse whereby she so farre sinks into Phantasmes, that she cannot recover her self into the use of her more free faculties of Reason and Understanding) that thus peremptorily engages a man to believe a lie.'[3]

This, says More, is 'the Originall of such peremptory delusions as mankind are obnoxious to'; and as such we may expect it to invite a rigorous discipline from the reason.

More confesses that it is hard to define what thus captivates the imagination, but he fastens upon melancholy as the general cause, and refers to Burton as one affording examples.[4] The connection with imagination is demonstrable, according to More, from the very nature of melancholy:

'Whence it is a strong temptation with a Melancholist, when he feels a storm of devotion or zeal come upon him like a mighty wind, his heart being full of affection, his head pregnant with clear and sensible representations, and his mouth flowing and streaming with fit and powerfull expressions, such as would astonish an ordinary Auditorie to hear; it is I say a shrewd temptation to him to think that it is the very *spirit of God* that then moves supernaturally in him, when as all that excess of zeal and affection and fluencie of words is most palpably to be resolved into the

---

[1] Spingarn, op. cit., II, 59.
[2] *Enthusiasmus Triumphatus* (London, 1656), p. 2.
[3] Ibid., p. 5. More was actually a friend of genuine mystical 'illumination'.
[4] Ibid., pp. 10–11.

power of Melancholy, which is a kind of *naturall inebriation.*'[1] The reduction of this state, which for Casaubon was produced by 'natural ardor or fervency', to melancholy or a powerful coalition between emotion and imagination is a significant fact in the formation of the new sensibility. From this picture of the enthusiastic preacher we turn to the poet, but not to a different kind of inspiration.

In More's account the poet, enthusiast, and rhetorician are significantly mingled. While discussing the mixture of sanguine and melancholy humours, More concludes:

'From this complexion are *Poets*, and the more highly pretending *Enthusiasts*. Betwixt whom this is the great difference, that a *Poet* is an *Enthusiast in jest*, and an *Enthusiast* is a *Poet in good earnest*; Melancholy prevailing so much with him, that he takes his no better then Poeticall fits, and figments for divine inspiration and reall truth.'[2]

While this is designed to put the Enthusiast in his place, it cannot be said to raise poetic imagination above the place to which it was assigned by Bacon. A later passage gives us a more detailed relation of Enthusiasm to eloquence:

'Whatever credit the *Enthusiast* may conciliate to himself from his moving Eloquence, his mysterious style and unexpected notions, they are easily to be resolved into that principle of Melancholy above named, the sense of which complexion is so deep and vigorous, that it cannot fail to inable the Tongue to tell her story with a great deal of life and affection; and the imagination is so extravagant that it is farre easier for her to ramble abroad and fetch in some odde skue conceit from a remote obscure corner, then to think of what is nearer and more ordinarily intelligible.'[3]

After this vivid analysis of enthusiastic style, we ought not to be surprised if 'what is nearer and more ordinarily intelligible' becomes the norm of Restoration style. It is interesting to note the odd pertinence of this description to the Metaphysical style. But of course More's chief quarrel concerns the very relationship between religion and eloquence which Bacon established through the imagination.

[1] Ibid., p. 16.   [2] Ibid., p. 20.   [3] Ibid., p. 57.

The Restoration Revolt against Enthusiasm

As three delusions yet to be mentioned, More considers *'Mystical interpretations of Scripture, Quakings,* and *Visions'*, all attributable to melancholy with its high passion and imagination.[1] For the first he reminds us that he has 'already shown that Melancholy as well as Wine, makes a man Rhetoricall or Poetical; and that *Genius* how fancieful it is, and full of allusions and Metaphors and fine resemblances, every one knows.'

The right sort of interpretation More finds that Sir Francis Bacon 'has admirably wel performed in his *Sapientiae Veterum,* without any such peculiar or extraordinary illapses of a divine Spirit into him, a business, I dare say, he never dreamt of, and any man that understands him will willingly be his Compurgatour.'
In his reading of Bacon on the poetic imagination More has the advantage of us, who have been rather loath to be Bacon's 'Compurgatour' in this respect. And the fact that More, like Bacon, was charmed by the rational appeal of 'parabolic' poetry is not irrelevant to our study.

The grand corrective for all these delusions is reason. More recalls Bacon by saying that he should be very much amazed at the madness of the school of Paracelsus, did he 'not remember that they are *Enthusiasts* and follow not the guidance of Reason, but the strength of Fancy'.[2] We are to suspect 'any discovery of Truth by an Enthusiastick spirit . . . because that temper that makes men Enthusiastical is the greatest enemy to Reason'.[3] The most sovereign medicine against Enthusiasm is a *'Composition* of *Three* excellent *Ingredients,* to wit, *Temperance, Humility,* and *Reason'.* And More adds,

'By *Reason* I understand so setled and cautious a Composure of mind, as will suspect every high flown and forward fancy that endevours to carry away the assent before deliberate examination; she not enduring to be gulled by the vigour or garishnesse of the representation, nor at all to be borne down by the weight or strength of it; but patiently to trie it by the known Faculties of the Soul, which are

[1] Ibid., pp. 24–9.   [2] Ibid., p. 47.   [3] Ibid., p. 50.

either the *Common notions* that all men in their wits agree upon, or the *Evidence of outward Sense*, or else a *cleer and distinct Deduction from these*. What ever is not agreeable to these three, is *Fancy*, which testifies nothing of the *Truth* or *Existence* of any thing, and therefore ought not, nor cannot be assented to by any but mad men or fools.'[1]

I think I need not insist upon the importance of this definition of a new sensibility; the italicized words form an admirable summary of what the Restoration held to be real and true. We do not require More's words to be persuaded how powerful a curb reason will henceforward be upon 'the exorbitant impressions and motions of Melancholy and Enthusiasme'; but it is well to remember that his voice was one of the most authoritative in his time.

Certainly the Restoration had cause to distrust the passions and to be suspicious of the imaginative rhetoric that worked upon them. In this connection we should do well to pay more attention to the popularity of books on the passions in this period. Although these books did afford instruction to those seeking to learn how to play upon the passions, their primary purpose was to teach control by reason. Probably the most important of native books on this subject in the first half of the century was Thomas Wright's *Passions of the Minde*. But Charron's *Of Wisdome*, as it appeared in English, surpassed Wright in popularity, and held a view of the passions and imagination similar to the one we have been examining. In the second half of the century Senault, Descartes, and Charleton were among those read on the passions, and of these Senault was probably the most important.[2] Monmouth's translation of Senault, *The Use of Passions*, appeared in 1649 and was reprinted in 1671. The consensus of the teaching of such books is, in Monmouth's words, that

'Reason is the proper utinsill of man; all other things are but as strangers to him, he may lose them without im-

---

[1] Ibid., pp. 53–4.
[2] See *Essays of John Dryden*, ed. Ker, I, 220, on the need of the poet to study the passions.

poverishing himself, and as long as he is master of Reason, he may still vaunt himself to be man.

'Since this is the chief of all that is good we must disperse it through all the parts of man, and make even the meanest faculties of our soul capable thereof; doubtlesly it may make for our security, if it be well husbanded.'[1]

Here we have one of the major problems of the seventeenth century, one which only grew more pressing after the emotional explosion of the Civil Wars, and one which eventually told against emotion and imagination. Here we are at the heart of the belief which led into neo-classicism. It was always a part of seventeenth-century thought, but it required the tergiversation of Enthusiasm to transform it into a dogma. Feeling and emotion in literature are altered, and may even be diminished, by whatever an age believes to be real or true. And that is why the revolt against Enthusiasm seems to me so important, so necessary to an understanding of the altered feeling, the modified tension of the emotions, the tempered imagination, the dominance of the plain style, and other features of the literature of the Restoration.

IV

To support this correlation between the revolt against Enthusiasm and the formation of the Restoration temper, I could call upon a host of minor witnesses; but I shall restrict myself to such central figures as Glanvill, Parker, and Sprat, in order that I may complete my study within the limits of a paper. In the *Vanity of Dogmatizing*, 1661, Glanvill launches another attack upon Enthusiasm, in which he finds imagination and the affections to be principal causes of ignorance and error. He writes of Enthusiasm as one who has been 'prevented' by the 'Triumph' of Dr. More on that subject, and so he rather ignores the problem of rhetoric which More presents. Perhaps he was not yet sensitive to

[1] *The Use of Passions. Written in French by J. F. Senault. And put into English by Henry Earl of Monmouth* (London, 1649), pp. 6–7.

its full significance; at any rate, he strikes home on the way in which Enthusiasm deceives the understanding:

'To impose names is part of the *Peoples* Charter, and I fight not with *Words*. Only I would not that the *Idea* of our *Passions* should be apply'd to any thing without us, when it hath its subject no where but in our selves. This is the grand deceit, which my design is to detect, and if possible, to rectifie.'[1]

Glanville is writing about the senses, but this is, as he says, 'the grand deceit' which it is his purpose to detect in its various manifestations. In his chapters on the ways in which the affections distort the reason, he suggests one of the appeals of mathematical reasoning to this age:

'And as Mr. *Hobbs* observes, the reason that Mathematical demonstrations are uncontroverted, is; because *Interest* hath no place in those unquestionable *verities*. . . .'[2]

Interest engages the affections, and the affections, Glanvill implies, are fatal to science; but Hobbes had pointed out the way to minimize such distortions by geometrical definitions.

In Chapter XI Glanvill attacks the fallacy of imagination, and particularly the 'composing' imagination, which produces the 'misconceits' of Enthusiasm that are so absurd to an 'unpassionated *reason*'. Thus Glanvill concludes:

'There is yet another as deplorable a deceit of our *Imagination*, as any: which is, its impressing a strong perswasion of the Truth of an *Opinion*, where there is no evidence to support it. And if it be such, as we never heard question'd or contradicted; 'tis then held as indubitate, as *first principles*. Thus the most of mankind is led by *opinionative* impulse; and *Imagination* is praedominant. Hence we have an ungrounded *credulity* cry'd up for *faith*; and the more vigorous impressions of *Phancy*, for the *Spirits* motions. These are the grand delusions of our Age, and the highest evidence of the *Imaginations* deceptions. This is the *spirit*, that works in the

---

[1] *Vanity of Dogmatizing*, for 'The Facsimile Text Society' (New York, 1931), p. 91.
[2] Ibid., p. 133.

children of *Phancy*; and we need not seek to remoter resolutions. But the excellent Dr. *H. More* hath follow'd *Enthusiastick effects* to their proper *Origine*, and prevented our endeavours of attempting it.'[1]

This view of imagination has both positive and negative connections with Bacon and Elizabethan psychology, while it lends emphasis to Enthusiasm as the main cause of the grand delusions of the age. Glanvill's whole book seeks to invalidate 'Enthusiastick effects', deceiving imagination and distorting emotion, at the same time that it advances the new gospel of 'unpassionated reason'. Of course the story of the *Scholar-Gypsy* exhibits the extraordinary power of the imagination, and is an example of what Bacon and Temple call *fascination*. If 'Imagination is predominant' in the Enthusiastic temper—a dangerous psychological state according to their manuals—the conclusion is obvious for the Restoration sensibility, which discovers itself in opposition to the former. The Restoration mind will follow More in suspecting 'any discovery of Truth by an Enthusiastick spirit', and Senault in dispersing reason, the chief good, through all the parts of man. Of course imagination will continue to be recognized in literature, but as a rational power rather than as a divine inspiration.

The influence of Hobbes upon his time was, we admit, very considerable; but I wonder if we often stop to think how important Hobbes makes the problem of communication in the first part of the *Leviathan*, or how deeply he succeeded in planting that problem in the mind of the Restoration. However Glanvill may praise Descartes, those early chapters of the *Leviathan* made their dent upon him. In the case of Samuel Parker, later Bishop Parker, they form the basis of an attack upon the language of Platonism in *A Free and Impartial Censure of the Platonick Philosophie*. This book antedates Sprat's *History of the Royal Society* by one year, and is interesting to us chiefly for its vigorous assault upon enthusiastic language of various sorts. Besides showing us how nearly synonymous Enthusiasm and the corruption of

---

[1] Ibid., pp. 104–5.

language as a conveyer of truth had become, Parker shows us that it was Hobbes who provided the chief criteria with which to solve the problem of communication that now troubled so many minds. It is from this point of view that he criticizes the language of Enthusiasm:

'And therefore I conclude that the office of Definitions is not to explain the Natures of things, but to fix and circum-scribe the signification of Words; for they being Notes of things, unless their significations be settled, their meaning must needs be Equivocal and uncertain; that is, unless it be determined of what things such particular Names are signs, no man shall be able to signifie his Thoughts to another, because he will use uncertain signs.'[1]

And of course this position is that of Hobbes in his chapter 'Of Speech' in the *Leviathan*, although Parker is writing as a member of the Royal Society. He criticizes Plato and his followers for their language, in which the words lack defini-tion and the powers of imagination are so great as to create ambiguity, with the result that the words are unfit 'to express the Train of any mans thoughts to Another'.[2] Hobbes again. Parker then attacks similar excesses in 'our late English *Rosie-Crusians*', 'for there is so much Affinity between *Rosi-Crucianisme* and *Enthusiasme*, that whoever entertains the one, he may upon the same Reason embrace the other; And what Pestilential Influences the Genius of *Enthusiasme* or opinionative Zeal has upon the Publick Peace, is so evident from Experience, that it needs not be prov'd from Reason.'[3]

As the social consequences of Enthusiasm were felt by all, so an anti-enthusiastic temper and a desire for peace are con-nected here as they are fifty years later in the 'peace of the Augustans'. Other great distorters of language and truth, in Parker's eyes, were the Cabbalists.

But Parker's revolt against Enthusiasm rests upon a broader basis than that of a dislike for certain sects:

'I that am too simple or too serious to be cajol'd with the

---

[1] *A Free and Impartial Censure* (Oxford, 1666), p. 63.
[2] Ibid., p. 68.   [3] Ibid., pp. 72–3.

frenzies of a bold and ungovern'd Imagination cannot be perswaded to think the Quaintest plays and sportings of wit to be any true and real knowledge.'[1]

In this the implications of Bacon's conception of the imagination are fully realized, the new notions of the real and true are set in opposition to imagination, and the antimony between philosophy and poetry which troubled the Elizabethan mind has become explicit. These conclusions are clarified by later passages in Parker, as when he asserts that 'true Philosophie is too sober to descend to these wildnesses of Imagination, and too Rational to be cheated by them. She scorns, when shee is in chase of Truth, to quarry upon trifling gaudy Phantasms: Her Game is things not words.'[2]

Such statements are only particularized when he calls Plato 'the first Author of Amorous Romances'. Parker explains the precise grounds for his criticism in the following passage:

'Now to Discourse of the Natures of Things in Metaphors and Allegories is nothing else but to sport and trifle with empty words, because these Schems do not express the Natures of Things, but only their Similitudes and Resemblances, for Metaphors are only words, which properly signifying one thing, are apply'd to signifie another by reason of some Resemblance between them. When therefore any thing is express'd by a Metaphor or Allegory, the thing it self is not expressed, but only some similitude observ'd or made by Fancy.'[3]

This notion of language and communication goes back to Hobbes's chapter 'Of Speech', but of course it also connects with the programme of the Royal Society. To the language of Enthusiasm, Whichcote, no less than Hobbes, could reply: 'If you say you have a revelation from God, I must have a revelation from God too before I can believe you.' Parker makes it evident that the beliefs of the Restoration and the idea of a true and correct language are intimately related, and that both are realized largely in opposition to

---

[1] Ibid., p. 73.   [2] Ibid., p. 74.   [3] Ibid., p. 75.

Enthusiasm. Thereafter the content of literary style, the sensibility which informs it, is as different from that of Sir Thomas Browne as well could be.

Sprat's *History of the Royal Society* owes its importance in the history of style to the fact that it presented a definite and positive programme of style that corresponded to the new beliefs and embodied the negative criticism which we have seen hurled upon various offenders in language. Among these offenders Sprat includes the alchemists, of whose 'chase of the *Philosopher's Stone*' he writes:

'This secret they prosecute so impetuously, that they believe they see some footsteps of it, in every line of *Moses*, *Solomon*, or *Virgil*. The truth is, they are downright *Enthusiasts* about it. And seeing we cast *Enthusiasm* out of *Divinity* it self, we shall hardly sure be perswaded, to admit it into Philosophy.'[1]

This hardly persuades us that scientific impetus was necessary to cast Enthusiasm out of pulpit oratory.

The corruption of language Sprat places in the time of the Puritan *interregnum*; witness this brief sketch of language from the time of Henry the Eighth:

'From that Age, down to the beginning of our late *Civil Wars*, it was still fashioning, and beautifying itself. In the Wars themselves (which is a time, wherein all Languages use, if ever, to increase by extraordinary degrees; for in such busie, and active times, there arise more new thoughts of men, which must be signifi'd, and varied by new expressions) then I say, it receiv'd many fantastical terms, which were introduc'd by our Religious Sects; and many outlandish phrases, which several *Writers* and *Translators*, in that great hurry, brought in, and made free as they pleas'd, and with all it was inlarg'd by many sound, and necessary Forms, and Idioms, which it before wanted.'[2]

A corruption, as we see, not unmixed with advantage, but for that very reason, as Sprat continues, requiring purging and correction. While the weight of the blame seems to fall upon the religious sects, the whole passage is best under-

[1] *History of the Royal Society* (London, 1702), pp. 37–8.   [2] Ibid., p. 42.

stood in relation to Sprat's discussion of wit at the end of the *History*.

The dangers of rhetoric, which science felt to be 'a most profest enemy', and for which Sprat said that '*eloquence* ought to be banish'd out of all *civil Societies*, as a thing fatal to Peace and good Manners', come under the 'Ornaments of speaking', which Sprat describes as follows:

'They were at first no doubt, an admirable Instrument in the hands of *Wise Men*: when they were onely employ'd to describe *Goodness, Honesty, Obedience*; in larger, fairer, and more moving Images: to represent *Truth*, cloth'd with Bodies; and to bring *Knowledg* back again to our very senses, from whence it was at first deriv'd to our understandings. But now they are generally chang'd to worse uses: They make the *Fancy* disgust the best things, if they come sound, and unadorn'd: they are in open defiance against *Reason*; professing, not to hold much correspondence with that; but with its Slaves, the Passions: they give the mind a motion too changeable, and bewitching, to consist with *right practice*. Who can behold, without Indignation, how many mists and uncertainties, these specious *Tropes* and *Figures* have brought on our Knowledg?'[1]

This is not a new diagnosis, but rather the sum of all that we have examined, both criticism and psychology; the 'motion too changeable' belongs to the latter part of this paper. Doubtless Bacon's imagination was designed to give 'larger, fairer, and more moving Images', if only as a 'play of wit'. This is the background which forced the Royal Society to seek 'the only Remedy, that can be found for this *extravagance*', in their familiar programme of style, 'and that has been, a constant Resolution, to reject all the amplifications, digressions, and swellings of style: to return back to the primitive purity, and shortness, when men deliver'd so many *things*, almost in an equal number of *words*. They have extracted from all their members, a close, naked, natural way of speaking; positive expressions, clear senses; a native easiness: bringing all things as near the Mathe-

[1] Ibid., pp. 111–12.

matical plainness, as they can: and preferring the language of Artizans, Countrymen, and Merchants, before that, of Wits and Scholars.'[1]

Against the background which we have been considering, this assumes a richer significance than we have been accustomed to see in it. The reasons for the rejections are sufficiently summarized in the preceding passage from Sprat. The 'return' brings the Royal Society to its definition of Wit: 'so many *things*, almost in an equal number of *words*'. For the most part these and the ensuing words are only a return to Hobbes, who had first made a positive attack upon language and the problem of communication in the early chapters of the *Leviathan*. Nobody had insisted so much as Hobbes upon the reference of 'words' to 'things'; it was also Hobbes who first stressed the equivalence of words and things, when he condemned not only the obscurity of words, but also 'the ambitious obscurity of expressing more then is perfectly conceived, or perfect conception in fewer words then it requires'.[2] The 'close, naked, natural way of speaking' is not unlike a scientific adaptation of the Senecan style; but 'positive expressions, clear senses' are certainly lessons from Hobbes's 'settling of significations'. And who had insisted so much as Hobbes upon 'bringing all things as near the Mathematical plainness' as possible? Plain not so much because unadorned, as defined or lucid. It was also Hobbes who gave what amounts to a definition of style for philosophy: 'Seeing then that *truth* consisteth in the right ordering of names in our affirmations, a man that seeketh precise *truth*, had need to remember what every name he uses stands for; and to place it accordingly. . . .'[3]

In other words, 'the right words in the right places'. It is not a far cry to Dryden's 'propriety of thoughts and words'; but the interval measures the distance between the Royal Society's definition of wit, 'so many things, so many words', and the literary wit of the Restoration as found in Dryden's prose. And 'preferring the language of Artizans'

---

[1] Ibid., p. 113.   [2] See Spingarn, op. cit., II, 63.
[3] *Leviathan*, edition cited, p. 15.

has an illuminating connection with Sprat's appendix on Wit.[1]

Sprat divides the matter of *wit* into two main kinds: the 'improvable' and the 'exhausted'. The *wit* that connects with the 'language of Artizans' he describes as follows:

'The *Wit* that is founded on the *Arts* of mens hands, is masculine and durable: It consists of *Images* that are generally observ'd, and such visible things which are familiar to mens minds. This therefore I will reckon as of the first sort, which is still improvable by the advancement of *Experiments*.'

Truly, there was a reason for the Royal Society's preference; and in this, no doubt, Sprat instructed the neoclassicists. But Sprat has not exhausted the subject, for he continues:

'And to this I will add the *Works* of *Nature*, which are one of the best and most fruitful soils for the growth of *Wit*. It is apparent, that the defect of the *Antients* in *Natural Knowledge* did also streighten their Fancies.'

Sprat goes on to develop the use of experiments to this purpose, and to praise Bacon for his skill in 'this way of *Wit*'. The other ways of wit I shall note briefly:

'The *Wit* of the *Fables* and *Religions* of the *Ancient World* is well-nigh consum'd. . . .

'The *Wit* which is rais'd from *Civil Histories*, and the Customs of *Countries*, is solid and lasting. . . .

'The Manners, and Tempers, and Extravagances of men are a standing and eternal foundation of *Wit*. . . .

'The *Wit* that may be borrow'd from the *Bible* is magnificent, and inexhaustible. . . . The very *Enthusiasts* themselves, who are wont to start at such *Wit* as *Atheistical*, are more guilty of its excesses than any other sort of men. . . .'

The next type of wit Sprat must have had particularly in mind when he contrasted the 'language of Artizans' with 'that of Wits and Scholars':

'The *Sciences* of mens Brains are none of the best Materials for this kind of *Wit*. Very few have happily succeeded in *Logical, Metaphysical, Grammatical*, nay even scarce in

[1] See op. cit., pp. 413–19.

Mathematical Comparisons; and the reason is, because they are most of them conversant about things remov'd from the Senses, and so cannot surprise the *fancy* with very obvious, or quick, or sensible delights.'

To none could this apply more than to the Metaphysical poets; and Donne, who first outmoded mythology, is himself here partially outmoded. It will be seen that Sprat allows more licence to literary wit than to scientific expression, but at the same time he does not hesitate to advance the possibilities of science as a source of wit, of a wit in which Bacon was admirable. And such wit is 'founded on the Arts of mens hands', whence comes the language preferred by the Royal Society.

The last point that I shall consider in Sprat brings me to a larger aspect of the revolt against Enthusiasm. After years of intense introspection, haunted by the chimeras of Enthusiasm, men turned gratefully to science as an extraverting influence upon the mind. Science, which offered them a criticism of reality, was the opposite of Enthusiasm; it embodied notions of truth and reality that were objective rather than subjective in character. Sprat expresses this mood very well.

'But now since the *King's* return, the blindness of the former *Ages*, and the miseries of this last, are vanish'd away: now men are generally weary of the *Relicks* of *Antiquity*, and satiated with *Religious Disputes*: now not only the *eyes* of men, but their *hands* are open, and prepar'd to *labour*: Now there is an universal *desire*, and *appetite* after *knowledge*, after the peaceable, the fruitful, the nourishing *Knowledge*: and not after that of antient Sects, which only yielded hard indigestible *arguments*, or sharp *contentions* instead of food. . . .'[1]

This food was to be found in Experimental Philosophy, which, says Sprat, 'has commonly in mens Censures, undergone the imputation of those very faults, which it endeavors to correct in the *Verbal*. That indeed may be justly condem'd for filling mens thoughts, with imaginary

[1] Ibid., pp. 152-3.

Ideas of Conceptions, that are no way answerable to the practical ends of Life: But this on the other side (as I shall shortly make out) is the surest guide, against such Notional wandrings: opens our eyes to perceive all the realities of things: and cleers the brain, not onely from darkness, but false, or useless Light.'[1]

The chief 'false or useless Light' was Enthusiasm, and *Verbal* not only denominates a philosophy, but also embraces most of what the Restoration revolted against. And Sprat holds that Experimental Philosophy not only can provide real food, but it also inculcates a better substitute for religious discipline than Speculative Science.[2] With this contribution Sprat leaves hardly any human need unministered to by the new experimental science. In the larger thought of the age science held a high place not because it was science, but because it validated most of the beliefs of the age. These beliefs More summarized as rational tests for the truth or existence of anything, 'which are either the *Common notions* that all men in their wits agree upon, or the *Evidence of outward Sense*, or else a *clear and distinct Deduction from these*. What ever is not agreeable to these three, is Fancy.'

And Samuel Parker summed up a half century of experience in these words:

'At least when our knowledge proceeds in an Empirical way 'tis solid and palpable, and made so undoubtedly certain from the plain and most undoubted Testimony of Sense and Experience, as undeniably to convince *Scepticism* of a pitiful and ridiculous Obstinacy. But when we begin our knowledge from Notions within our selves . . .'tis doubtless that Generalities are not capable of so palpable and convictive an Evidence, as single and particular Observations. And therefore my *Lord Bacon* has well noted it as none of the least obstructions to the advancement of knowledge, that *Men have sought for Truth in their own little Worlds, and that withdrawing themselves from the Contemplation of Nature, and the Observations of Experience, they have tumbled up and*

[1] Ibid., p. 26.   [2] Ibid., p. 367.

*down in their own Speculations and Conceits; And so have by
continual meditation and agitation of Wit urged, and as it were,
invocated their own Spirits to Divine, and give Oracles unto
them, whereby they have been deservedly and pleasingly deluded*
(*Advancement of Learning*, L. 1, c. 5).'[1]

If this had seemed true to Bacon a half century before, it
seemed doubly true to Parker and Sprat in the Restoration.
With the comments of More and Sprat, nothing could sum
up better the mental revolution which made the Restoration
so different from the preceding age. Here we can see what
each age believed to be real and true, how the passage from
introspective to objective truth was made, and why it
seemed imperative, if scepticism were not to be the general
end of all. After the religious upheavals of the Civil Wars,
this had a poignancy of meaning that we are apt to lose,
particularly if we forget the reign of Enthusiasm, which had
given oracles to so many men.

In one respect at least Donne had been typical of his age,
and had expressed the main psychological problem of the age
to come. That problem is repeated by Henry Tubbe in 1659:

'Nothing is so full of change and alteration as man.
Proteus never knew so many various shapes. Our Passions
turn us round in a perpetual circle of vicissitude.'[2]

Donne's youthful motto, *Antes muerto que mudado*, though
perhaps inscribed on his portrait in a moment of bravado,
expressed, nevertheless, one of the profoundest desires of his
age. If it be said that Tubbe merely voiced one of the eternal
problems of religion, the answer is that no age felt it more
than the first half of the seventeenth century. The religious
effort to attain stability, to reach a truth outside of man,
arrived at an unprecedented chaos during the Common-
wealth, when men found themselves more than ever
'tumbled up and down in their own Speculations and Conceits', with what result we see in Parker. And the whole age
felt the Protean element in man to be the passions. Shakespeare had analyzed them in poetry; Bacon had given them
a colder dissection; psychologies and devotional manuals

[1] Parker, op. cit., p. 57. [2] *Meditations Divine & Morall* (London, 1659), p. 173.

had taught their control; Stoicism had found favour in their discipline; character-writing had drawn their features; sermons had exhorted them; the Puritans, at least, had feared them even in their devotions. But the greatest vicissitude of the passions came in the days of Enthusiasm, and concluded in violent tergiversation.

The appeal to experience upon which alone the Restoration felt that it could ground the real and true, did not, as we have seen, conclude in the limits of a narrow empiricism (as seems to be suggested by Parker), but permitted a 'palpable and convictive' truth to such notions as were verified by the common reason of man. Reason, more or less uniform in all men, was allowed to supply, in fact to be, the 'Touchstone of Experience'; but emotion was definitely discredited, and therefore restrained in literature; while imagination was suspected, and therefore tempered by judgment. To say 'tempered' is to allow imagination a partial escape from the implications in Bacon which became serious condemnations before 1660, but it is a mitigation warranted by the facts and by the reception of Hobbes in 1670.

What Hobbes's ideas about esthetics and the wits of men came to mean to the Restoration can be seen very clearly in Dr. Walter Charleton's discourse *Concerning the Different Wits of Men*, which details many of the ideas of Hobbes, and is said to have been much consulted by Locke. In 1669 Charleton describes the famous distinction between Fancy and Judgment as follows:

'By *Judgement* we distinguish subtility in objects neerly resembling each other, and discerning the real dissimilitude betwixt them, prevent delusion by their apparent similitude. . . .

'By *Imagination*, on the contrary, we conceive some certain similitude in objects really unlike, and pleasantly confound them in discourse: Which by its unexpected *Fineness* and allusion, surprising the Hearer, renders him less curious of the truth of what is said.'[1]

[1] *Two Discourses* (London, 1669), pp. 19–21; reissued with changes in 1675 and 1692.

The last effect, says Charleton, is very evident in the use of tropes and figures. It is interesting to note the stress here on preventing and producing delusion. Even plainer than in Hobbes appears the complementary nature of fancy and judgment, and something like a balance of the two gives Restoration literature its distinctive quality. But Charleton still bears witness to the primacy of imagination in the poet:

'From *Celerity* of Imagination there ariseth a twofold difference of Wit. *Some* are naturally inclined to indulge their thoughts the liberty of *Ranging*, and love not to confine them: *Others* delight in fixing their mind upon one subject, and narrowly examining it. The *former* sort are allowed to have *Laudabilem Phantasiam*; and have a Genius disposed to Poesy and Invention: unless their Phansie be immoderately quick and ranging: for then it passes into *Folly*. . . .'[1]

This is indebted to Hobbes, but it clarifies his significance:[2] to prevent 'immoderate ranging' was the proper function of Restoration judgment. Charleton also follows Hobbes in declaring that 'in *Poets*, both Phansie and Judgement are required; but Phansie ought to have the upper hand'.[3] The relation between the two faculties is made very pointed by Charleton in style:

'For, that which gives due sharpness and grace to the *Stile* of a Writter, and recommends it to the present and succeeding Ages, is exquisite and elaborate Judgement; which is very rarely conjoyn'd with natural fluency of speech.'[4]

Thus judgment not only restrains the immoderate ranging of the imagination, but it sharpens and refines the expression. In 1675 Charleton adds to his *Discourse* the notion that since 'Passions are generally stronger in those men, who excell others in fineness of Wit and quickness of Imagination,' it is 'No wonder then, if . . . men of airy fancies and ranging Wits, are prone to commit errors in judgement and action; as apt to be seduced by the specious suggestions of their exorbitant passions. . . .'[5]

---

[1] Ibid., pp. 23–4.
[2] See *Leviathan*, Part I, chap. 8.   [4] Ibid., pp. 70–1.
[3] Ibid., p. 25.   [5] *Two Discourses* (London, 1675), p. 59.

And so the very nature of the poet makes imagination more susceptible to error, and its correction by judgment more imperative. This is how Hobbes was understood by the Restoration nearly two decades after he had written; the revolt against Enthusiasm has if anything sharpened his distinctions, and yet it has not displaced the imagination as the rightful province of the poet.

But as a result of early seventeenth-century thought, a new psychology of communication, shifts in belief, the disaffection with rhetoric, and their general aggravation by Enthusiasm, we get a new complex of thought and feeling, a new temper in the literary mind, marked chiefly by a discipline of feeling and imagination, and expressed in a refinement of language. Bacon, you will recall, after referring poetry to the imagination, allowed imagination to dominate in two provinces, religion and eloquence; in these two, imagination operated through the power of rhetoric, which was directed upon the emotions; since the emotions were refractory to reason, persuasions 'more than of naked proposition and proofs' were required. I have shown how and why the modification of this scheme took place. Let me venture a brief summary. Enthusiasm discredited emotional appeal; but imagination, acting through rhetorical devices, was regarded as the chief agent of such appeal. Hence, Enthusiasm discredited imagination as well, and brought reason into a more commanding position. But the revolt against Enthusiasm did not hold all th · ground it seemed to win, and so the final result was to temper imagination and restrict emotion in literature, rather than to create a literature of reason—a monstrosity. Undoubtedly, imagination, from one point of view, lost something of the serious relation with truth which it had in Sidney's day; but, from another point of view, it acquired a new sense of truth through its alliance with judgment. The brunt of the attack upon imagination fell upon its office of stirring the passions through rhetoric.

If this argument seems but to repeat an old story, it is for the purpose of suggesting the importance of the revolt against Enthusiasm in altering the beliefs which, in turn, altered the emotional content of literature. If this only illuminates what Professor Grierson calls the 'spiritual emptiness' of Dryden, it will have served its purpose. Professor Grierson believes that Dryden 'had no sense of the ideal, the poetical aspect of any subject on which he wrote'; he says, 'With all his great gifts Dryden was not a great poet, because he believed in nothing.'[1] Arnold's distinction 'between genuine poetry and the poetry of Dryden' has been criticized of late, says Professor Grierson, by 'an age that is disposed to exalt once more wit and cleverness at the expense of imagination and feeling'.

For this age Mr. Mark Van Doren speaks in a criticism of Dryden in which Professor Grierson sees chapter and verse for Arnold's view:

'Dryden was most at home when he was making statements. His poetry was the poetry of declaration. At his best he wrote without figures, without transforming passion.'
And this is just, for it involves not only Dryden's but his Age's conception of truth. You will recall the passage from *Religio Laici* which I quoted, and part of which I quote again:

'The Florid, Elevated, and Figurative way is for the Passions; for Love and Hatred, Fear and Anger, are begotten in the Soul by shewing their Objects out of their true proportion; either greater than the Life, or less; but Instruction is to be given by shewing them what they naturally are. A Man is to be cheated into Passion, but to be reason'd into Truth.'

So Dryden felt when fired by thoughtful matters rather than by heroic passions. It will be seen that Dryden is conscious of Professor Grierson's point of view, and indeed often wrote from it, but at his best he wrote from another belief. It may be that Dryden's ideal of truth was not so high as that of Wordsworth, to whom Professor Grierson turns for a definition of poetry; but it was not a thing of wit and

[1] See *Cross Currents in English Literature of the 17th Century* (London, 1929), pp. 321–8.

cleverness. It is an irony of criticism that Dryden has become a candidate for his own invention, the 'Doctoral Degree of Wit'. Even in wit, Dryden might add, 'an image which is strongly and beautifully set before the eyes of the reader, will still be poetry when the merry fit is over, and last when the other is forgotten.'

If I have misled my reader by promising brevity, it is because discretion is the better part of brevity. But the emphasis of 'statement' in Dryden's poetry brings us to the end of our study. No word could better sum up the temper of the Restoration and its natural poetic expression, as well as its prose. *Statement* epitomizes the insistence begun by Hobbes on the reference of words to things and their equivalence, or denotation. In poetry this brought prose virtues, or classical qualities, which enhanced poetry's power of statement, and no poetry can state as satisfyingly, as nobly, with such a bronze ring, as Dryden's. It brought lucid feeling, precise imagination, and the energy of thought. In prose it made the 'plain' style. And, most of all, it incorporated an ideal of truth. If Dryden believed in nothing, his art must have been truly great, for no man ever wrote in English a more 'honest' language than Dryden at his best.

X

The Rhetorical Pattern of
Neo-Classical Wit

★

The creation patent of the neo-classical couplet offers as
many difficulties as Charles II presented Dugdale in the
Baronage of England. Where the seventeenth century settled
upon Waller and his second, Denham, we have wavered
from Waller to Sandys, Jonson, Drayton, Sir John Beaumont, and others. If we cannot determine the author of this
'invention', then our indecision itself may be significant, for
it suggests that the urges of the neo-classical couplet were in
the air, and manifested themselves occasionally in various
poets, being most persistent in Waller. To explain the coming of age of the neo-classical couplet, perhaps the most
significant fact is that when the earlier writers approached
this couplet they betrayed the literary and rational impulses
which were to command the future, and so indicated the
verse form in which the Restoration could explore its own
mind. Waller became the focal point at which these impulses were concentrated rather than the poet in whom
they were born. The development of poetry still led from
Jonson to Dryden, though by way of Waller; and the con-
necting link was less the couplet itself than the informing
force of the couplet, which was a manner of saying things
ultimately derived from Latin rhetoric.

The Rhetorical Pattern of Neo-Classical Wit

It is common to describe the neo-classical decasyllabic verse as couplets of a thoroughly distichic character, almost uniformly end-stopped both in rhythm and in sense, or what we may call 'serried' verse. Of these couplets there are two varieties to be found in Dryden and Pope: the balanced, antithetic sort, employing a strong medial caesura, which divides the line into balancing parts; and the less patterned sort, with a weaker caesura (or even none at all), which moves more freely within the line and accompanies a slight concession to overflow. Although there is no strict division of labour, the highly patterned sort, with its oscillating movement, is more suitable to reflective verse; while the less patterned sort, with its freer design, admits the forward movement which narrative verse requires.[1] But it is with the highly patterned verse that we are concerned, since the less patterned is only a relaxed form of the more patterned, which contains the concentrated form of neoclassical wit.

In neo-classical verse this wit has two formal aspects which betray its origin. One is on the side of prosody, and the other on the side of syntax; their union in the form of the verse itself suggests the union of two developments which go back to the early seventeenth century, if not before. These developments are the maturing of a prosodic tradition which leads from Puttenham to Bysshe, and the growth of a new style of wit relying for its pattern upon certain rhetorical figures. A union of the two trends was effected in the work of certain individuals, whose influence over the later seventeenth century is indisputable. This union is represented in theory by Puttenham's *Arte of English Poesie*, with its prosody and its rhetoric; it is represented in practice, with something like selective genius, by the work of Jonson and Waller. It will be instructive to see (so far as we can within our limits) how these two lines of development are brought together in the early seventeenth century, and how they are thenceforth distinguished in the rhetorical pattern

[1] On the metric of heroic couplets see Egerton Smith's *Principles of English Metre* (Oxford, 1923), chaps. iv, xii, xx.

of the couplet which became neo-classical. Not all poets who might claim a place can be discussed, but only the most prominent or the most significant.

I

Let me indicate, first, the trend of prosodic thinking from Puttenham to Bysshe. Puttenham, whose metrical ideas have much in common with those of James VI before him and Beaumont after him, deals with 'Proportion Poetical' in Book II of his *Arte of English Poesie* (1589).[1] In English, says Puttenham, measure or meter consists 'in the number of sillables, which are comprehended in euery verse, not regarding his feete, otherwise then that we allow in scanning our verse, two sillables to make one short portion (suppose it a foote) in euery verse'.[2] Here we have syllable-counting and feet, so far as he will recognize them, only of the dissyllabic sort. The '*rithmos* or numerositie' which secured harmony for the Greeks 'grew by the smooth and delicate running of their feete, which we haue not in our vulgare, though we vse as much as may be the most flowing words and slippery sillables, that we can picke out'.[3] Hence it is that Puttenham stresses the 'tunable consentes in the latter end of our verses': '. . . so in our vulgar Poesie . . . your verses answering eche other by couples, or at larger distances in good [cadence] is it that maketh your meeter symphonicall. This cadence is the fal of a verse in euery last word with a certaine tunable sound which being matched with another of like sound, do make a [concord].'[4]

Puttenham is very particular about rhyme, and declares that 'there can not be in a maker a fowler fault, then to falsifie his accent to serue his cadence, or by vntrue orthographie to wrench his words to helpe his rime'. The

---

[1] I call the author of this book Puttenham for convenience; the case against Puttenham is argued by B. M. Ward in the *Review of English Studies*, I (1925), 284–308.

[2] *Arte of English Poesie*, ed. Arber ('English Reprints'), p. 81.

[3] Ibid., p. 91.

[4] Ibid., p. 93.

measures of best proportion in English fall between four and twelve syllables; 'and euery meeter may be aswel in the odde as in the euen sillable, but better in the euen'.[1] The reason why meters in odd syllables are allowed is thus explained: '. . . . the sharpe accent falles ypon the *penultima* or last saue one sillable of the verse, which doth so drowne the last, as he seemeth to passe away in maner vnpronounced, and so make the verse seeme euen: but if the accent fall vpon the last and leaue two flat to finish the verse, it will not seeme so: for the odnes will more notoriously appeare . . . like a minstrels musicke. . . . This sort of composition in the odde I like not, vnlesse it be holpen by the *Cesure* or by the accent as I sayd before.'[2]

Not until Bysshe will one find a stronger devotion to dissyllabic feet with the accent on the even syllables.[3] 'The meeter of ten sillables,' declares Puttenham, 'is very stately and Heroical, and must haue his *Cesure* fall vpon the fourth sillable, and leaue sixe behinde him thus.

> *I serue at ease, and gouerne all with woe.'*

Such a view of measure, accent, and rhyme, if imposed upon verse, would certainly develop a more or less rigid pattern, in which rhyme would have a decidedly structural effect.

Until Bysshe, Puttenham is unique in his extensive and explicit treatment of the caesura. 'There is,' says he, 'no greater difference betwixt a ciuill and brutish vtterance then cleare distinction of voices': '. . . also the breath asketh to be now and then releeued with some pause or stay more or lesse: besides that the very nature of speach (because it goeth by clauses of seuerall construction and sence) requireth some space betwixt them with intermission of sound, to th'end they may not huddle one vpon another so rudly and

---

[1] Ibid., p. 84.

[2] Ibid., pp. 85–6. The relation of the caesura to an odd number of syllables is an advance upon Gascoigne.

[3] Although Puttenham considers the adaptation of classical feet to English verse, he concludes (p. 141) against such 'mincing measures'.

so fast that th'eare may not perceiue their difference.'[1]

It is apparent that Puttenham recognizes a rhetorical pause as well as a metrical pause. Asserting that 'if there be no *Cesure* at all, and the verse long, the lesse is the makers skill and hearers delight', he proceeds to mark the musical pause for each meter, placing it in heroic verse, as we have seen, upon the fourth syllable. In verse of six syllables and under, no caesura is needed 'because the breath asketh no reliefe: yet if ye giue any *Comma*, it is to make distinction of sense more then for any thing else: and such *Cesure* must neuer be made in the middest of any word, if it be well appointed'.[2] After accusing Chaucer and his contemporaries of seldom observing the caesura and of letting 'their rymes runne out at length', he again insists that 'in euery long verse the *Cesure* ought to be kept precisely, if it were but to serue as a law to correct the licentiousnesse of rymers, besides that it pleaseth the eare better, and sheweth more cunning in the maker by following the rule of his restraint'. The caesura distinguishes the musical sections of the line, or, as Puttenham would say, keeps words from huddling upon the ear. Altogether Puttenham enjoins a rule of restraint upon the license of rhymers that would insure both the distinction of voices and the distinction of parts which mark the neo-classical couplet.

Such a scholar as Mr. Omond finds that by the close of the seventeenth century 'Elizabethan freedom was replaced by mechanical exactness; the syllable-counters had triumphed'.[3] But he does not take into serious account the one book after Puttenham which shows most definitely this passage from freedom to mechanical correctness: that is Joshua Poole's *English Parnassus* (1657), which contains 'A short Institution to English Poesie' by J. D. Not only does Mr. Omond call Bysshe's *Art of English Poetry* (1702) 'the first modern book of its kind', but he declares that 'from

---

[1] Ibid., p. 87. Puttenham often speaks of verse by analogy to the music of his time.

[2] Ibid., pp. 88–9.

[3] T. S. Omond, *English Metrists* (Oxford, 1921), p. 31.

what immediate sources Bysshe derived his doctrine does
not appear'.[1] And yet one source of Bysshe's doctrine would
have appeared if Mr. Omond had not slipped Poole into the
appendix. The important part of Poole is the preface by
J.D., who may have been John Davies, but who was, at any
rate, unusually aware of prosodic trends.[2] J.D. mentions
Sidney and Daniel on poetry, and the treatises, but not the
names, of Campion and Puttenham; he obviously knows
Daniel[3] and Puttenham best, and his 'Institution' develops
primarily the theories of Puttenham. J.D. declares that
'harmony, in *prose*, consists in an exact placing of the *accent*,
and an accurate *disposition* of the words. . . . In *Poesie*, it consists besides the aforesaid conditions of Prose in *measure*,
proportion and *Rhime*.'[4] In turn Bysshe begins his first
chapter with this statement: 'The Structure of our Verses,
whether Blank, or in Rhyme, consists in a certain Number
of Syllables; not in Feet compos'd of long and short Syllables, as the Verses of the *Greeks* and *Romans*.' This principle of 'numbers' is of course a positive return to Puttenham, who, like Bysshe, preaches the doctrine of the 'Structure of the Verse', determined by the 'Seat of the Accent'
and the 'Pause', together with the 'Rhyme'. For Bysshe 'the
true Harmony of Verses depends on a due Observation of
the Accent and Pause'.[5] J.D. makes a significant middle
term in this prosodic descent.

[1] Ibid., p. 32.
[2] The British Museum copy is signed *Jn Dn*, which signature 'may be that of
Dryden'.
[3] The few observations on prosody in Daniel's *Defence of Rhyme* belong to
this school, and supply matter for this preface (cf. Omond, pp. 29-30).
[4] *English Parnassus* (London, 1657), sig. a2ᵛ; reprinted 1677. Dryden's early
view of metrics appears in *An Essay of Dramatic Poesy* (1668): for him blank verse
is but measured prose; measure alone does not constitute verse. For the Greeks
and Latins verse 'consisted in quantity of words and a determinate number of
feet'. But in the vulgar languages 'a new way of poesy was practised. . . . This
new way consisted in measure or number of feet, and rhyme; the sweetness of
rhyme, and observation of accent, supplying the place of quantity in words. . . .
No man is tied in modern poesy to observe any farther rule in the feet of his
verse, but that they be dissyllables; whether spondee, trochee, or iambic, it
matters not; only he is obliged to rhyme' (*Essays*, ed. Ker, I, 96-7).
[5] Cf. *Art of English Poetry* (London, 1718), pp. 1-3.

The Rhetorical Pattern of Neo-Classical Wit

The chief difference between Puttenham and Bysshe is a shift of emphasis from rhyme to numbers, but J.D. is more nearly balanced between them. While harmony for him consists largely in the disposition of the words 'so as to be pronounced without violence by the accent', yet rhyme is 'that wherein all the symphony and musick of a verse consists'.[1] All three prosodists emphasize the dependence of rhyme upon accent, and all three are concerned about polysyllables that 'come not into verse without a certain violence'. All three declare feminine rhymes too frivolous for the majesty of heroic verse, and only J.D. neglects the importance of the caesura in its harmony and structure. But J.D. does condemn, under the proper disposition of words, 'a certain licentiousnesse, which some *English* Poets have in imitation of the *Greek* and *Latine*, presumed on to *dismember*, and *disjoin* things that should naturally march together; placing some words at such a distance one from another, as will not stand with the English Idiome'.[2] And this censures not only the lapse into 'flat prose' but also 'the sense variously drawn out from one Verse into another', or the elaborate period and overflow, which he illustrates in a passage of heroic couplets. Bysshe obviously models his book on Poole, and sometimes uses J.D.'s preface in formulating his 'Rules for making Verses'. As one instance of such use, observe their common matter on 'the misplacing of the accent', even to the example from Davenant.[3] It is clear, I think, that the Puttenham-Poole-Bysshe line marks a definite tradition of prosodic thinking, which even in Elizabethan days began, in theory at least, to replace freedom by restrictive laws.

II

The rhetorical theory for the style of wit which came to prevail in neo-classical verse may also be found in Putten-

---

[1] Poole, sigs. a5ᵛ and a7ᵛ.

[2] Ibid., sig. a6ʳ. Dryden says (*Essays*, ed. Ker, I, 6) that they were whipt at Westminster if they inverted the order of their words and closed their lines with verbs twice together.

[3] Cf. Poole, sig. a5ᵛ; and Bysshe, p. 6.

ham. It is on the rhetorical side that Puttenham must have appeared at once learned and novel. In 1591 Sir John Harington referred his readers to this treatise, 'where, as it were a whole receit of Poetrie is prescribed, with so manie new figures as would put me in great hope in this age to come, would breed manie excellent Poets', if the author's own verse did not prove the contrary.[1] Only, we know that Jonson had a copy of Puttenham, and that Drayton has been suspected of using him. In Book III, 'Of Ornament', Puttenham divides figures into three ranks: 'auricular', 'sensable', and 'sententious'. The sententious figures, which he also calls 'rhetoricall', seem to him to mingle the virtues of all three sorts, and especially to 'geue sence and sententiousness to the whole language at large'.

'[Your rhetorical figures, says Puttenham,] doe also conteine a certain sweet and melodious manner of speech, in which respect, they may, after a sort, be said *auricular*: because the eare is no less rauished with their currant tune, than the mind is with their sententiousness. For the eare is properly but an instrument of conueyance for the minde, to apprehend the sence by the sound. And our speech is made melodious or harmonicall, not only by strayned tunes, as those of *Musick*, but also by choice of smoothe words: and thus, or thus, marshalling them in their comeliest construction and order. . . .'[2]

The ordering breeds 'no little alteration in man'. If Jonson could find some justification in Puttenham for his inclination to believe 'that verses stood by sense without either colours or accent', Waller could find in him something like his whole poetic creed. There is reason to suspect that Neo-classical poets discovered what Puttenham here asserts, that sententious figures do also contain or induce a certain 'current tune'.

Under 'Figures sententious' Puttenham first describes seven kinds of repetition which are really *figurae dictionis*, and are used commonly by Spenser;[3] these are sometimes

[1] See Puttenham, p. 13.   [2] Ibid., pp. 206–7.
[3] See *Shepheards Calendar*, ed. C. H. Herford (London, 1925), pp. lxiv–lxvi.

connected with what Dryden later calls the 'turn of thoughts'. Of the sententious figures proper I wish to single out only five, for three of them will provide the rhetorical pattern of neo-classical verse and inform its characteristic movement of thought, while the other two suggest its ideal form in the didactic mode.

The form which the neo-classical couplet approaches as an ideal is the epigrammatic. It is foreshadowed in the sententious development of the couplet in the Elizabethan sonnet and play, or in the Jacobean epigram; Pope, of course, sets this inclination. Sententious figures that provide such an ideal framework are the *epiphonema* or 'close' and the *sententia* proper. The *epiphonema* or acclamation, says Puttenham, is especially appropriate to the epigram, and 'may seeme a manner of allowance to all the premisses'. As illustration he quotes Sir Philip Sidney very prettily closing up a ditty in this sort:

> *What medcine then, can such disease remoue,*
> *Where loue breedes hate, and hate engenders loue.*[1]

Sententiae, according to Puttenham, are witty sentences, 'such as smatch morall doctrine and teach wisedome and good behauiour', which he illustrates from Queen Elizabeth:

> *Neuer thinke you fortune can beare the sway,*
> *Where vertues force, can cause her to obay.*[2]

The important thing to notice is the inevitable tendency toward closure which a didactic function or an epigrammatic urge imposes upon the couplet. As Joseph Warton in his *Essay on Pope* long afterward admits, 'Rhyme may be properest . . . for pieces where closeness of expression and smartness of style are expected'; and these ideals, the desiderata of aphoristic form, are finally responsible for shaping the neo-classical couplet.

---

[1] P. 225. The second line uses *antimetabole*, which we shall discuss in connec- with the rhetorical pattern commonly found within such a framework.
[2] Ibid., p. 243.

The Rhetorical Pattern of Neo-Classical Wit

But closeness of expression and smartness of style are effectively secured within the couplet chiefly by three rhetorical figures, which have long been recognized as the properties of neo-classical verse syntax. In Puttenham these figures are set down as *antimetabole* or repetition with inversion, *antitheton* or antithesis, and *parison* or parallelism and balance; they are considered by Puttenham as structural figures which affect the sense, not as merely verbal schemes.

Antimetabole, says Puttenham, 'takes a couple of words to play with in a verse and by making them to chaunge and shift one into others place they do very pretily exchange and shift the sence'. He regards it as a witty figure and quotes, among other illustrations, this couplet:

> *In trifles earnest as any man can bee,*
> *In earnest matters no such trifler as hee.*[1]

Without the identity of words this becomes the simple inversion, or a figure of emphasis and concision. In its strict form this figure appears—for instance, in *Cooper's Hill* —as a 'turn':

> *Sure there are Poets which did never dream*
> *Upon* Parnassus, *nor did tast the stream*
> *Of* Helicon, *we therefore may suppose*
> *Those made not Poets, but the Poets those.*
> *And as Courts make not Kings, but Kings the Court,*
> *So where the Muses & their train resort,*
> Parnassus *stands; if I can be to thee*
> *A Poet, thou* Parnassus *art to me.*[2]

Seldom is this figure so often repeated as in the opening of this poem, and we may be sure that this passage afforded Dryden the 'beautiful turns of words and thoughts' which Sir George Mackenzie taught him to appreciate in Waller and Denham. The normal inversions of neo-classical verse reinforce its antitheses, contribute to the closeness and smartness of its expression, and emphasize its ideas by throwing the strong words into rhyming positions. It should be

---

[1] Ibid., p. 218.   [2] Notice how the figure enjoins a medial caesura.

remembered that poets could hardly avoid such lessons in the rhetorical instruction of the time.

Of *antitheton*, the 'contentious' figure, Puttenham gives an illustrative couplet 'where one speaking of Cupids bowe, deciphered thereby the nature of sensual loue':

> *His bent is sweete, his loose is somewhat sowre,*
> *In ioy begunne, ends oft in wofull howre.*[1]

'*Isocrates* the Greek Oratour,' adds Puttenham, 'was a litle too full of this figure, and so was the Spaniard that wrote the life of *Marcus Aurelius*, and many of our modern writers in vulgar, vse it in excesse and incurre the vice of fond affectation: otherwise the figure is very commendable'.[2] After this reference to Euphuism, it is interesting to ask whether the antithesis which helped to tighten up our prose did not also help to tighten up our verse. Even in Puttenham's examples one can observe how antithesis in the couplet develops a witty force or sense of thrust, of half-line against half-line, and line against line.

In *parison* we find the third structural element in neo-classical verse. And this Puttenham calls 'the figure of euen, because it goeth by clauses of egall quantitie, and not very long, but yet not so short as the cutted comma: and they geue good grace to a dittie, but especially to a prose'. This may be illustrated by these lines out of Puttenham:

> *Our life is loathsome, our sinnes a heauy lode,*
> *Conscience a curst iudge, remorse a priuie goade.*
> *Disease, age and death still in our eare they round,*
> *That hence we must the sickly and the sound.*[3]

Of course *parison* involves the notion of balance as well as

---

[1] Puttenham, p. 219. The analytic suggestion is interesting.

[2] This contradicts T. K. Whipple's contention that sixteenth-century opinion did not connect Isocrates with euphuistic figures (cf. 'Isocrates and Euphuism', *Modern Language Review*, XI [1916], 25–6).

[3] P. 222; notice the medial caesura. If this description of *parison* sounds like a description of *isocolon* or 'Egall members' (cf. Wilson's *Arte of Rhetorique*, ed. Mair, p. 204), we should remember that English rhetorics did not distinguish carefully between them; frequently they were lumped as *compar* (cf. John Smith, *Mysterie of Rhetorique Unveil'd* [London, 1665], p. 203).

parallelism, for it means similarity of *form* between the equal rhythmic members of *isocolon*. And balance and parallelism, one need hardly say, are the chief adjuncts of antithesis; in the stopped couplet, moreover, they entail short members and imply the medial pause, which Puttenham and Bysshe thought one of the principal means to harmony.

As Puttenham has connected both antithesis and parallelism with prose, it will be proper at this point to relate the rhetorical mode which I have been describing to the Senecan prose of this period. To illustrate their connection it will be sufficient, I believe, to point out the traits which Professor Croll has so admirably distinguished in this prose. It is to the 'curt' rather than to the 'loose' form of Senecan prose that the antithetic mode in verse is related. In the curt form we find a cultivation of sententiousness, antithesis, point, and in general the figures of thought; 'this style is always tending toward the aphorism, or *pensée*, as its ideal form'.[1] It is significant that Bacon compiled *antitheta* as a 'preparatory store for the furniture of speech and readiness of invention'. He followed this suggestion in the *Advancement of Learning* with an extended list of *antitheta* in his *De Augmentis*; their form depends upon antithesis, parallelism, and balance, and a great many of them will be found in the *Essays*.[2] While the antithesis is chiefly a figure of sound in Lyly, it becomes a figure of thought or wit in Bacon; and a similar shift from a stress on wordplay to a stress on play of thought is recognized when we pass from Elizabethan to Jacobean verse. Although the curt period in prose tends to be asymmetrical, the curt period in verse (the stopped couplet) tends to employ figures of symmetry, and thus to vary from its prose

[1] M. W. Croll, 'The Baroque Style in Prose', *Studies in English Philology* (University of Minnesota Press, 1929), p. 435. On this prose see also his 'Attic Prose in the Seventeenth Century', *Studies in Philology*, XVIII (1921), 79–128.

[2] See *Philosophical Works*, ed. J. M. Robertson (London, 1905), pp. 129 and 545 ff. 'And the best way of making such a collection,' says Bacon (p. 545), 'with a view to use as well as brevity, would be to contract those commonplaces into certain acute and concise sentences'; however, he now disparages his own *antitheta*, not as examples of Senecan style, but as products of youth (p. 557).

counterpart; but they both like to use symmetry to emphasize cunning departures from it. As Professor Croll has shown, the character of this prose derives from the imitation of Silver Latin writers; the same may be said of the verse, for verification can be had not only in its special rhetoric, but also in the cultivation of the Roman epigram, and in the predominant taste for Silver Latin poets reflected in the editing of the noted Thomas Farnaby. At the same time the general favourite among poets of the Golden Age was certainly the antithetic Ovid, whose influence had been strong upon writers of the Silver Age.

To point the Senecan turn in prose, there is Professor Croll's objection to the use of antithesis to characterize Euphuism:

'It may be a figure of words, or sound, on the one hand, and a figure of thought (*figura sententia*), on the other. In the latter use, it is one of the most important *differentia* by which we recognize the style of the Anti-Ciceronian movement which arose at the end of the sixteenth century in reaction from the various forms of ornate, formal style in the preceding age, such as Euphuism itself, Ciceronian imitation, and so on.'[1]

In the development of the kind of wit with which this paper is concerned, this figure of thought is the central rhetorical doctrine. The 'points' of this wit generally depend upon an antithesis, open or veiled, which provides an unexpected turn of thought. Such wit may be recognized in the characteristic ingenuities of many writers in this mode: if it is Bacon, 'Men in great places are thrice servants'; if Jonson, 'And whisper what a proclamation says'; if Dryden, 'But Shadwell never deviates into sense'; and if Pope, 'Damn with faint praise, assent with civil leer.' In short, Silver Latin imitation in Jacobean prose and verse developed an antithetic turn of mind which left decisive marks upon its literary product.

When rhetorical ornament was generally dropped, antithesis, parallelism, and balance were carried over to both the

[1] Lyly's *Euphues*, ed. Croll and Clemons (London, 1916), p. xvii.

The Rhetorical Pattern of Neo-Classical Wit

simplified prose and the simplified verse of the Restoration. These are the main rhetorical forms employed, less obtrusively in the prose and more obtrusively in the verse, after the Restoration. With ideals of clarity and comprehension, Restoration writers could not fail to see that antithesis and parallelism positively assist comprehension and carry a suggestion of logical form; they perhaps did not realize that these figures may give even nonsense an air of comprehensibility. Moreover, these figures not only had appeared with a subtle and evasive grace in the King James Version, but had turned with new cunning in the couplets which Sandys fashioned for many of his Biblical paraphrases.[1] It ought not to be forgotten that the curt Senecan style, the Biblical style, and the stopped couplet have not only these characteristic figures in common,[2] but also a similar shortness of members in their periods. And with such shortness predicated, these figures, aided by inversion, are the principal means to variety; but if obtruded, they make in their more obvious effect for uniformity. Of all figures they are, moreover, those which most decidedly affect sentence structure, or the pattern of thought; and they induce a simpler, more uniform rhythm than is to be found in the ornate prose and verse of the seventeenth century.

These shaping figures produce the antithetic pattern of the curt Senecan period and the neo-classical couplet; they are most brilliantly displayed in the Character-writing and occasional verse of the seventeenth century. If not decisive, neither is it irrelevant that Puttenham had supplied a manual for occasional verse, giving 'a whole receit of Poetrie' distinguished by its emphasis on the contemporary rhetoric of figures; it is at least suggestive that Jonson owned this book. Upon the sententious figures which we have

[1] His couplets are shaped by Ovidian and Biblical turns. In 1700 Dryden declared that the poet who has arrived the nearest to giving Ovid the same turn of verse that he had in the original 'is the ingenious and learned Sandys, the best versifier of the former age' (*Essays*, ed. Ker, II, 247).

[2] John Smith's *Mysterie of Rhetorique Unveil'd* (1665) illustrates the typical use of these figures in Scripture. The relative simplicity and ornateness of Scriptural style was long a matter of dispute.

examined, occasional verse depends for closeness and smartness of expression, for point and sharpness of wit; in the heroic couplet, with the attendant caesura, they give distinction of parts, emphasis, and neatness to the pattern, and likewise simplify the rhythm. In verse an antithetic wit, for which these figures supply the pattern, is adapted above all to satire, panegyric, argument, or portraiture; and wherever pointed contrast, sharp definition, novel turns, or critical poise are in demand, this wit will find a place. I do not mean to say that this is the only form of neo-classical wit or verse, but rather that the 'set' is definitely toward this pattern.

III

When Donne and Jonson reacted against the diffuser graces of Spenserian poetry, they began to cultivate a closer texture in verse, they put more into their lines. But it was Jonson who made most of the couplet; believing in discipline, he embodied in the couplet both the cast of mind and the rhetorical artifice that were to determine its neo-classical pattern. With his decided preference for the couplet went a realization of the part played in it by the caesura: he can use the pause to punctuate thought in the manner of the Neo-classicists. In the neo-classical couplet the caesura, although an element in the sound pattern, becomes an element in the rhetorical pattern by serving to turn the antithetic balance and point of the ideas. Bysshe not only makes the pause divide the verse into two parts, but asserts that 'the Construction of Sense should never end at a Syllable where the Pause ought not to be made';[1] the pause, in short, ought to offer violence neither to the ear nor to the sense. The sententious, antithetic, parallel, and pointed forms of Jonson's thought, which are concentrated in his *Epigrams*, have been illustrated convincingly by Professor Schelling;[2] and it is

---

[1] Op. cit, p. 6.
[2] See 'Ben Jonson and the Classical School', *PMLA*, XIII (1898), 221–49. For these forms as imitated from Martial see T. K. Whipple, 'Martial and the English Epigram', *University of California Publications in Modern Philology*, X

this antithetic mode of thinking and feeling that informs the couplet which connects with the future. If we recall Jonson's criticism of Spenser, his style of prose, and his expressed habit of writing his poetry first in prose, we shall realize that in cultivating such forms of thought he was actually recalling poetry to prose norms. It is no accident, then, that the trends of poetry and prose in this time parallel one another, or that Jonson wrote the verse he did when he expressly desired to employ the 'language such as men do use', which poetry deserts to its own cost.

To look for the remarks of Jonson which bear upon the heroic couplet is to find the most significant statements that he ever made about metrics. While most of them are made to Drummond, we cannot suppose, in the light of Jonson's character, that they were made to Drummond alone. In the *Conversations* we learn that Jonson had an epic 'all jn Couplets, for he detesteth all other Rimes', and that 'he had written a discourse of Poesie both against Campion & Daniel especially this Last, wher he proves couplets to be the bravest sort of Verses, *especially when they are broken, like Hexameters* and that crosse Rimes and Stanzaes (becaus the purpose would lead him beyond 8 lines to conclude) were all forced'.[1] To Drummond he criticized Donne 'for not keeping of accent' in his *Anniversarie*; likewise he declared his preference for stopped verses by remarking that 'some loved running Verses plus mihi com(m)a placet'.[2] Related to this is that passage in the *Discoveries* about composition:

'Others there are, that have no composition at all; but a

(1925), 400–3; their place in rhetoric and poetry has appeared in Puttenham. For a similar influence of Ovid upon Drayton and Heywood see J. S. P. Tatlock, 'The Origin of the Closed Couplet in England', *Nation*, XCVIII (9th April 1914), 390.

[1] *Ben Jonson*, ed. Herford and Simpson (Oxford, 1925), I, 132. The italics are mine, to mark Jonson's preference for caesural break. His opposition to Daniel was no doubt inspired partly by the confession that to 'mine own ear those continual cadences of couplets used in long and continued poems are very tiresome and unpleasing' (*Defence of Rhyme*).

[2] Ibid., p. 143. Daniel preferred 'sometimes to beguile the ear with a running out, and passing over the rhyme'.

kind of tuneing, and riming fall, in what they write. It runs and slides, and onely makes a sound. . . .

> *They write a verse, as smooth, as soft, as cream;*
> *In which there is no torrent, nor scarce streame.'*[1]

Altogether these are notions of the couplet, of observing caesura, of keeping accent, and of composing rather than 'running' verses, which, if followed, could result in little short of Waller. It is true that Jonson has 'A Fit of Rhyme against Rhyme,' but here also he discloses his regard for caesura:

> *Vulgar languages that want*
> *Words, and sweetness, and be scant*
> *Of true measure,*
> *Tyrant rhyme hath so abused,*
> *That they long since have refused*
> *Other cesure.*

If Jonson detested all rhymes except couplets, he was ready to prove couplets the bravest sort of verses; and his dislike of other rhymes, and of the wants which rhyme supplied, must not have been lost on men like Waller. 'In verse and prose alike,' say his latest editors, 'he sought brevity, terseness, emphasis; sentences not loosely connected or vaguely continuous, but sharply detached.'[2] With such aims his requirements for the couplet are thoroughly consistent.

After the praise lavished by Courthope and Saintsbury upon Sir John Beaumont's poem to King James 'Concerning the true forme of English Poetry,'[3] it may seem ungrateful to suggest that it could have been written out of Jonson's *Discoveries* and *Conversations*. But since Beaumont was printed first, we must conclude that his ideas about verse were held in common with others; one of whom, as he suggests, was King James; and Puttenham may be considered another. A third, Jonson, offers a more puzzling

---

[1] *Discoveries*, ed. G. B. Harrison ('Bodley Head Quartos' [1923]), p. 30.
[2] *Ben Jonson*, ed. Herford and Simpson, II, 412.
[3] Reprinted in Chalmers, *English Poets*, VI, 30–1.

parallel; for instance, compare the foregoing 'torrent' couplet from Jonson with this one from Beaumont:

> *When verses like a milky torrent flow,*
> *They equal temper in the poet show.*

Other lines of Beaumont which make us return to Jonson are these:

> *Vneuen swelling is no way to fame,*
> *But solid ioyning of the perfect frame:*
> *So that no curious finger there can find*
> *The former chinkes, or nailes that fastly bind.*

Although a common source is possible, still Jonson does assert that composition 'rests in the well-joyning, cementing, and coagmentation of words; when as it is smooth, gentle, and sweet; like a Table, upon which you may runne your finger without rubs, and your nayle cannot find a joynt; not horrid, rough, wrinckled, gaping, or chapt'.[1] When Beaumont enjoins 'pure phrase', we remember that Jonson loved 'pure and neat language', 'phrase neat and pick'd'; and so we might continue to match parts. Aside from a common praise of couplets, such agreements as these serve to remind us that neo-classical precept was growing in consequence. Whether or not Beaumont was merely echoing Father Ben's opinions, we can rest assured that critical sanction was not lacking for the verse of Waller, and that even a motive was supplied (or confirmed after the fact) by Beaumont's condemnation of Metaphysical obscurity, 'halting feet', and 'ragged' poems. As Aubrey recounts Waller's refinement of poetry, the story goes that 'when he was a brisque young sparke, and first studied poetry, "Methought," said he, "I never sawe a good copie of English verses; they want smoothness; then I began to essay" '.[2] With all the stress on

---

[1] *Discoveries*, p. 79. M. Castelain, in his edition (p. 106), finds a source in Vives, but Vives lacks the simile. Jonson, however, confesses a 'Beaumont's booke to bee/The bound, and frontier of our poetrie' (cf. his Elegy for Beaumont).

[2] *Brief Lives*, ed. A. Clark (Oxford, 1898), II, 275.

composition and 'keeping of accent' that we have noticed, it is hard to believe Waller original in his aim, whatever we may think of his 'essay'.

It would be superfluous, after Professor Schelling's essay, to demonstrate again that Jonson has a rightful place in the Waller-Dryden-Pope line because of his unusually large use of caesured, stopped couplets and the antithetic mode. 'In Jonson's hands,' says Professor Schelling, 'the decasyllabic couplet became the habitual measure for occasional verse, and sanctioned by his usage, remained such for a hundred and fifty years. But not only did Jonson's theory and practice coincide in his overwhelming preference for this particular form of verse, but the decasyllabic couplet as practised by Jonson exemplifies all the characteristics which, in greater emphasis, came in time to distinguish the manner and versification of Waller and Dryden.'[1] At most we should have to mitigate this statement only by widening the sanction and by adding the forces which lent vitality to that sanction. That Jonson's sanction was effective cannot be proved, but it can be urged by a comparison of the verses which Lord Falkland and Sidney Godolphin contributed to the 'Elegies upon the Author' (Donne) and to the later *Jonsonus Virbius*. A just comparison of the two pairs of elegies, which ought to be examined entire, would show that the verse in which both poets honour Jonson is much more neo-classical than that in which they honour Donne. Although their verse to Donne will show that their homage is also a homage of style, it is offered by 'Sons of Ben'.

I shall quote a passage from Falkland in honour of Jonson not for the sake of comparison, but to suggest the kind of verse written by those who were left his heirs:

> *Then for my slender reed to sound his name,*
> *Would more my folly than his praise proclaim,*
> *And when you wish my weakness sing his worth,*
> *You charge a mouse to bring a mountain forth.*
> *I am by nature formed, by woes made, dull,*

---

[1] 'Ben Jonson and the Classical School', *PMLA*, XIII (1898), 235–6.

The Rhetorical Pattern of Neo-Classical Wit

My head is emptier than my heart is full;
Grief doth my brain impair, as tears supply,
Which makes my face so moist, my pen so dry.
Nor should this work proceed from woods and downs,
But from the academies, courts, and towns;
Let Digby, Carew, Killigrew, and Maine,
Goldolphin, Waller, that inspired train,
Or whose rare pen beside deserves the grace,
Or of an equal, or a neighbouring place,
Answer thy wish, for none so fit appears,
To raise his tomb, as who are left his heirs:
Yet for this cause no labour need be spent,
Writing his works, he built his monument.[1]

While all these writers were not left his heirs in the way of
neo-classical verse, Waller and Godolphin were, and Falkland must be allowed after the tribute of this verse. The
antithetic manner of the verse, it is not unfair to remark, is
striking; and the rhyme (as an obvious and simple test) nowhere does violence to the intimate ties of syntax. As
Jonsonus Virbius was published in 1638, it associated with
Jonson (in Falkland, Cartwright, Godolphin, Waller, and
others) precise suggestions of the neo-classical manner before
the regular publication of Waller. 'The voice most echoed
by consenting men,' is echoed less by Godolphin than by
Waller; still, 'The Muses fairest light,' now ascribed to
Godolphin rather than Cleveland,[2] does definitely echo the
neo-classical mode of Jonson. It is not unreasonable to believe, after such witness, that *Jonsonus Virbius* did in fact
support the sanction which Jonson gave to a certain manner
of writing occasional verse.[3]

[1] *Works of Ben Jonson*, ed. Gifford and Cunningham (London, 1910), III,
499–500.
[2] See *Ben Jonson*, ed. Herford and Simpson, I, 116 n.
[3] By 1646 Martin Lluelyn (*Men-Miracles* [1646], pp. 101–2) can turn satire,
with new emphasis, in this fashion:
   '*When* Laws *and* Princes *are despis'd, & cheape,*
   When High-pitcht Mischeifes *all are in the heap;*
   Returns must still be had; Guilt *must strive more*
   Though not to 'Ennoble, *yet to* Enlarge *her store.*

But the forces which lent vitality to this sanction never appear in a stranger guise than one that has yet to be noticed. The wit of antithesis, paradox, and point not only displayed its turns in the Senecan prose of this age, but even in the Spenserian school. The tendency toward antithetic scoring in verse can be observed in the work of Giles and Phineas Fletcher. It is apparent, for instance, in the opening stanza of Giles Fletcher's *Christs Victorie and Triumph*:

> *The birth of him that no beginning knewe,*
> *Yet gives beginning to all that are borne,*
> *And how the Infinite farre greater grewe,*
> *By growing lesse, and how the rising Morne,*
> *That shot from heav'n, did backe to heaven retourne,*
> *The obsequies of him that could not die,*
> *And death of life, ende of eternitie,*
> *How worthily he died, that died unworthily.*

Of course the play upon Christian paradox simply connects Fletcher with the paradoxical wit of Lancelot Andrewes, and illustrates the obligation of the mind of this age to antithetic patterns in verse and prose.[1] In Jonson this wit was purged, as it were, of the eccentricities of Christian paradox and Metaphysical subtlety. The arts of verbal antithesis and epigrammatic contrast appear likewise in such a passage as this from Phineas Fletcher:

> *Prayers there are idle, death is woo'd in vain;*
> *In midst of death poore wretches long to die:*
> *Night without day or rest, still doubling pain;*
> *Woes spending still, yet still their end lesse nigh:*
> *The soul there restlesse, helplesse, hopelesse lies; .*

> Poor cheape Designes! *the* Rebell *now must flie*
> *To* Packet-Warre, *to* Paper-Treacherie.
> *The* Basiliskes *are turn'd to* Closet-Spies,
> *And to their* Pois'nous *adde* Enquiring *eyes.*
> *As* Snakes *and* Serpents *should they cast their sting,*
> *Still the same* Hate, *though not same* Poison *fling:*
> *And their* Vaine *teeth to the same point addresse,*
> *With the like* Rancor, *though unlike* Successe.'

[1] Cf. W. F. Mitchell, *English Pulpit Oratory* (London, 1932), pp. 151 ff.

The Rhetorical Pattern of Neo-Classical Wit

The body frying roars, and roaring fries:
There's life that never lives, there's death that never dies.[1]

But the further service of Jonson was to associate the art of antithetic scoring with its logical verse form, the stopped couplet. The Fletchers demonstrated that Spenserian discipleship could not harmonize with the mental complexion of the Jacobean age, that ornate and antithetic rhapsody was neither Spenser nor the proper voice of Jacobean minds. They showed even more clearly, by contrast of form, the preoccupation of their age with 'point', the development of wit toward an antithetic cast, and its connection with the theological and metaphysical wit of the preachers and poets.

IV

In consequence of such tendencies of wit and verse, Waller must appear not as an inventor but rather as a consolidator of poetic development and as the acknowledged leader of a restrictive movement. In 1664 Dryden, as we know, first set the seal of authority upon Waller's leadership:

'But the excellence and dignity of rime were never fully known till Mr. Waller taught it; he first made writing easily an art; first showed us to conclude the sense most commonly in distichs, which, in the verse of those before him, runs on for so many lines together, that the reader is out of breath to overtake it. This sweetness of Mr. Waller's lyric poesy was afterwards followed in the epic by Sir John Denham, in his *Cooper's Hill*, a poem which . . . for the majesty of the style is, and ever will be, the exact standard of good writing.'[2]

But shortly before 1670 Samuel Butler concluded his character of *A Quibbler* with a criticism which is also an offence:

'There are two sorts of Quibbling, the one with Words,

---

[1] *The Purple Island*, canto vi, stanza 37; notice the 'turns'.
[2] *Essays of John Dryden*, ed. W. P. Ker (Oxford, 1926), I, 7.

and the other with Sense, like the Rhetoricians *Figurae Dictionis & Figurae Sententiae*—The first is already cried down, and the other as yet prevails; and is the only Elegance of our modern Poets, which easy Judges call *Easiness*; but having nothing in it but *Easiness*, and being never used by any lasting Wit, will in wiser Times fall to nothing of itself.'[1]

It is obvious that Dryden and Butler (who together describe the formal aspects of the new verse) do not agree on what constitutes 'writing easily' or 'easiness' in the poetry of their day. Butler, however, was critizing the current wit, and Dryden confessed in 1693 that he was unacquainted with 'the beautiful turns of words and thoughts' in Waller and Denham 'till about twenty years ago', when he began to study 'those beauties which gave the last perfection to their works'.[2] Later Dennis condemned the figures of point and wit in Denham and Waller, 'whom he came to consider the forerunner of Pope'.[3] When Dryden did become aware of 'turns', he recurred to the subject most frequently in connection with Ovid, whose influence upon the closed couplet has been more than once suggested—and with reason, for the balanced, antithetic style was imitated, by Jonson for one, from Latin poets like Ovid, Martial, and Lucan.

There was no doubt in Butler's mind that a certain poet had stamped modern poetry with the 'Easiness' of quibbles on sense, for he particularizes the two sorts of quibbling in his *Note-Books*:

'The first is don by shewing Tricks with words of the Same Sound, but Different Senses: And the other by expressing of Sense by Contradiction, and Riddle. Of this Mr. Waller, was the first most copious Author, and has so infected our modern writers of Heroiques with it, that they

[1] *Characters and Passages from Note-Books*, ed. A. R. Waller (Cambridge, 1908), p. 90. See Aubrey's remark on Butler (*Brief Lives*, ed. Clark, I, 136): 'He haz often sayd that way (e.g., Mr. Edmund Waller's) of quibling with sence will hereafter growe as much out of fashion and be as ridicule as quibling with words—quod N.B.'

[2] *Essays*, II, 108.

[3] See H. G. Paul, *John Dennis* (New York, 1911), pp. 181, 184.

can hardly write any other way, and if at any time they endeavour to do it, like Horses that are put out of their Pace, they presently fall naturally into it againe.'[1]

The 'expressing of Sense by Contradiction, and Riddle' goes back to the cultivation of antithesis and paradox (or *oxymoron*) which we have examined.[2] Waller turned the balance from paradox to antithesis in the poetic wit which centred in contradiction. In predicting that this mode would fall to nothing, Butler was too hopeful, for it was precisely this 'Elegance' that became the pattern of neo-classical verse. Beginning as a new form of wit derived from the old, it lived to shape the new verse itself; and it is this hypothesis that I have been examining. It may be said that the new pattern of wit, which came at times to depend less on the sense itself than upon the pattern of thought, found its natural verse form in the closed couplet, and that this union opened the way to a development of English verse. As the Elizabethan quibble on words passed into the Metaphysical quibble on sense, so the latter passed into a new style of wit which depended less upon the ambiguity than upon the antithesis of ideas, or less upon startling reconciliations and more upon surprising oppositions. From the surprising opposition of ideas wit passed into verse as oppositions of structure.

It will be useful to regard these witty oppositions in the light of the English rhetorics of Butler's time. One of the most popular English rhetorics, which depend upon their Latin counterparts, was John Smith's *Mysterie of Rhetorique Unveil'd*, first published in 1657. Of the *figura dictionis* and the *figura sententiae* Smith declares that 'the former belongs to

---

[1] *Characters . . .* , pp. 414–15.

[2] Contemporary definitions of these figures will show their common basis in contradiction: *Oxymoron*, 'A figure when the same thing is denyed of it self, or when a contrary Epithet is added to any word. By this figure contraries are acutely and discreetly reconciled or joyned together.' *Antithesis* is 'the illustration of a thing by its opposite . . . and is a Rhetorical Exornation when contraries are opposed to contraries in a speech or sentence; or when contrary Epithets are opposed, as also when sentences, or parts of a sentence are opposed to each other.' (Cf. John Smith, *Mysterie of Rhetorique Unveil'd* [London, 1665].) In one the contraries are reconciled; in the other they are opposed.

the matter, and as it were, to the body of speech; but the latter, to the form, and as it were, to the soul, that is, to the sentence'.[1] And more particularly on the latter he adds:

'Garnishing of the frame of speech, in a sentence, called *Figura Sententiae*, is a figure, which for the forcible moving of affections, doth after a sort beautifie the sense and very meaning of a sentence: because it carries with it a certain manly majesty, which far surpasses the soft delicacy of the former Figures, they being as it were effeminate and musical, these virile and majestical. It is when the ornament lies in the whole sentence, or where the elegancy is diffused through the structure of one, or more sentences.'[2]

The comparison here is with the *figura dictionis*, which was pretty generally outlawed at this time.[3] In this passage Smith permits us to observe the place which Puttenham's sententious figures held in the rhetorics of Waller's generation; in particular Smith remarks of the antithesis in sentences: 'This *Antithesis* marvailously delights and allures.'[4] Such figures might well be taken, both from the example of Latin poets and from the teaching of the rhetorics, as the appropriate ornament of heroic poetry.

It is well known that in 1690 Atterbury declared the indebtedness of the time to Waller 'for the new turn of Verse, which he brought in, and the improvement he made in our Numbers'. After praising the new harmony of Waller as opposed to the older verse of Donne and others, he remarked:

'There was no distinction of parts, no regular stops, nothing for the ear to rest upon. . . . Mr. Waller remov'd all

[1] Ibid., p. 5.

[2] Ibid., p. 7.

[3] See Davenant's detraction of those who think wit 'lyes in *agnominations*, and in a kinde of an alike tinkling of words' (Spingarn, *Critical Essays of the Seventeenth Century*, II, 22); this wit is connected with Euphuism (cf. *Euphues*, ed. Croll and Clemons, p. xxxviii).

[4] P. 164. But Thomas Blount, who deals with these 'sharp and witty' figures in the *Academie of Eloquence* (London, 1654), advises discretion: '*Sententia*, if it be well used, is a Figure; if ill and too much, a Style, of which none that write humorously and factiously, can be clear in these days, when there are so many Schismes of Eloquence' (p. 34).

these faults; brought in more polysyllables, and smoother measures; bound up His thoughts better; and in a cadence more agreeable to the nature of the Verse He wrote in: so that where-ever the natural stops of that were, He contriv'd the little breakings of His sense so as to fall in with them. And for that reason, since the stress of our Verse lies commonly upon the last syllable, you'll hardly ever find Him using a word of no force there.'[1]

By popular consent these were the innovations of Waller, but why and how he could innovate at all should, by this time, be clear to the reader. And Waller's prose is not to be neglected in accounting for his new turn of verse. His prose falls into the mode of 'the English Seneca', Bishop Hall, particularly as it led into the antithetic brilliance which touched Robert South. In the eighteenth century we find Doddridge describing Hall as 'the most elegant and polite writer of his age', but noting that 'he abounds rather too much with antitheses and witty turns'.[2] And this is the style characteristic of Waller's prose, as it may be sampled in a letter 'To my Lady Lucy Sidney' on the marriage of her sister Dorothy, which Waller must have written with at least a touch of outraged feeling:

'May she that always affected silence, and retiredness, have the house fill'd with the noise, and number, of her children; and hereafter of her grandchildren! and then, may she arrive at that great curse so much declin'd by fair Ladies, old age! May she live to be very old, and yet seem young; be told so by her glass, and have no aches to inform her of the truth! And when she shall appear to be mortal, may her Lord not mourn for her, but go hand in hand with her to that place, where we are told there is neither marrying, nor giving in marriage; that being there divorced, we may all have an equal interest in her again! My revenge being im-

---

[1] *Works of Edmund Waller*, ed. E. Fenton (London, 1744), pp. 289–90; this 1690 preface is generally ascribed to Atterbury. In 1718 Prior (*Preface to Solomon*) objects that the couplet has become too confined and the sense too broken, so that every couplet is brought to the point of an epigram,

[2] Cf. W. F. Mitchell, *English Pulpit Oratory*, p. 367.

mortal, I wish all this may also befal their posterity to the world's end, and afterwards!'[1]

Of course this is Waller the wit, but the same style of antithesis and witty turn, with a touch of paradox, may also be found in his speeches. Here, too, Butler could complain of the 'expressing of sense by contradiction and riddle', or of a turn of prose like the new turn of heroics. Antithesis, parallelism, and witty turns, with simple Biblical and classical allusions, these are the chief traits of Waller's prose, as of his verse.

When Hallam objected to Denham's famous apostrophe to the Thames on the ground that 'the lines contain nothing but wit, and that wit which turns on a play of words',[2] he was not far wrong in his diagnosis. These lines, which Dryden celebrated and which became a pattern of neo-classical verse, do actually turn upon the figures that we first saw in Puttenham.

> *Oh could I flow like thee, and make thy stream*
> *My great example as it is my theme!*
> *Though deep, yet clear; though gentle yet not dull;*
> *Strong without rage; without o'erflowing, full.*

The strong pauses, at which Dryden hints while observing the 'sweetness' of the last couplet,[3] could find their sanction in Puttenham and Jonson. But observe the use of balance, antithesis, and cunning inversion within the antithesis of the last line, thereby throwing 'full' under the emphasis of rhyme. It should be remembered that the pattern of this neo-classical pattern probably derived from Cartwright's elegy on Jonson in the *Jonsonus Virbius*, where these lines occur:

---

[1] *Works*, pp. 282–3.

[2] *Introduction to the Literature of Europe* (London, 1842), III, 31 n.

[3] *Essays*, II, 217–18. Although Dryden connects pauses with Malherbe, the caesura had come into English precept as far back as Puttenham and Gascoigne (cf. Egerton Smith, pp. 27–8), and had been imposed upon the heroic couplet.

The Rhetorical Pattern of Neo-Classical Wit

Giv'st the right blush and colour unto things,
Low without creeping, high without loss of wings;
Smooth, yet not weak, and by a thorough care,
Big without swelling, without painting fair.[1]

This is how Jonson wrote, says Cartwright; and this, we may add, employs the same neo-classical devices that we observe in Denham. While this comparison suggests an undue simplification if it is mistaken for a full view of neo-classical descent, it does nevertheless reveal a line of descent that is too often obscured. As to the figures, it can scarcely be doubted that even poets recognized, after Puttenham and Smith, that sententious figures do 'after a sort beautifie the sense and very meaning of a sentence' and make 'for the forcible moving of affections'. And because these figures garnished 'the frame of speech', we may regard them as supplying a pattern of wit.

V

We may now glance at the last phase of the Restoration attitude toward the wit associated with Waller. Dryden's notion of wit as 'a propriety of thoughts and words'[2] was evolved largely in opposition to this other sort of wit. As early as 1667 he began to define wit in this opposition.

' 'Tis not the jerk or sting of an epigram, nor the seeming contradiction of a poor antithesis (the delight of an ill-judging audience in a play of rhyme), nor the jingle of a more poor paronomasia; neither is it so much the morality of a grave sentence, affected by Lucan, but more sparingly

---

[1] Cf. Jonson's *Discoveries* (p. 78) on the middle language: 'There the Language is plaine, and pleasing: even without stopping, round without swelling; all well-torn'd, compos'd, elegant, and accurate. The vitious Language is vast, and gaping, swelling, and irregular; when it contends to be high, full of Rocke, Mountaine, and pointednesse: As it affects to be low, it is abject, and creeps, full of bogs, and holes.' Cartwright would appear to have absorbed Father Ben's teaching before publication, even to a turn of phrase; for he echoes Jonson rather than Jonson's source (cf. Castelain ed., p. 105).

[2] But this, Addison declares (*Spectator*, No. 62), 'is not so properly a Definition of Wit, as of good Writing in general'.

used by Virgil; but it is some lively and apt description, dressed in such colours of speech, that it sets before your eyes the absent object, as perfectly, and more delightfully than nature.'[1]

In this passage Dryden is in agreement with Butler's condemnation of the two sorts of quibbling. But it should be remembered that this was written while proceeding 'from wit, in the general notion of it, to the proper wit of an Heroic or Historical Poem'; and that it is defining the descriptive rather than the reflective sort of neo-classical wit. In 1672 Dryden is still complaining, apropos of heroic plays, that Lucan 'crowded sentences together, was too full of points, and too often offered at somewhat which had more of the sting of an epigram, than of the dignity and state of an heroic poem'.[2] In 1700, in the *Preface to the Fables*, he reviews the 'turns' which were first pointed out to him in Waller and Denham. Though Virgil, he had found, used turns discreetly in heroic poetry, Dryden was never in his own mind at ease with them in serious poetry. Here propriety again comes to the front: 'The thoughts remain to be considered: and they are to be measured only by their propriety; that is, as they flow more or less naturally from the persons described, on such and such occasions.' After praising Chaucer for the justice with which he represents the death of Arcite, Dryden asks:

'What would Ovid have done on this occasion? He would certainly have made Arcite witty on his deathbed; he had complained he was further off from possession, by being so near, and a thousand such boyisms, which Chaucer rejected as below the dignity of the subject. They who think otherwise, would, by the same reason, prefer Lucan and Ovid to Homer and Virgil, and Martial to all four of them. As for the turn of words. . . .'[3]

As may be seen, Dryden's propriety belongs to the concept of decorum, and does not exclude turns of thought, like that put into Ovid's mouth, on suitable occasions. Complaining that 'he was further off from possession by being so

[1] *Essays*, I, 14-15.   [2] Ibid., p. 152.   [3] Ibid., II, 257.

near', is the sort of wit that Butler condemned as the 'expressing of sense by contradiction'.

After such remarks it will be interesting to see what Dryden does with the death of Arcite. This passage from his dying speech to Emily will suffice for our instruction:

> To die, when Heav'n had put you in my Pow'r;
> Fate could not chuse a more malicious Hour!
> What greater Curse cou'd envious Fortune give,
> Than just to die when I began to live!
> Vain Men, how vanishing a Bliss we crave,
> Now warm in Love, now with'ring in the Grave!
> Never, O never more to see the Sun!
> Still dark, in a damp Vault, and still alone!
> This Fate is common; but I lose my Breath
> Near Bliss, and yet not bless'd before my Death.
> Farewell; but take me dying in your Arms,
> 'Tis all I can enjoy of all your Charms:
> This Hand I cannot but in Death resign;
> Ah, could I live! But while I live 'tis mine.[1]

Needless to say, this is not Chaucer; nor is it unfair to say that it is closer to Ovid.[2] For the turn of words, the musical repetition of words (often by their derivatives), Puttenham has rhetorical names; and Spenser used the figures. As for the turn of thoughts, if we do not get the 'boyisms' of Ovid, we do get substitutes for being 'further off from possession by being so near': witness the line, 'Than just to die when I began to live!'; or 'but I lose my Breath Near Bliss, and yet not bless'd before my Death'; or 'but take me dying in your Arms, 'Tis all I can enjoy of all your Charms'. It is impossible not to conclude that the neo-classical cast of verse carried a pattern of wit which was too strong even for Dryden's compunctions. Nothing can be plainer than that

---

[1] *Poems of John Dryden*, ed. Sargeaunt (London, 1929), p. 310.
[2] And yet Chaucer and Ovid are not always opposed in artifice of style, for Chaucer seems to have studied balanced antithesis in the school of Ovid (cf. Mary A. Hill, 'Rhetorical Balance in Chaucer's Poetry', *PMLA*, XLII [1927], 845–61).

this verse is neither Chaucer nor yet what Dryden set himself to write. But what he did write is to be explained, as we have seen, by an antithetic mode of patterned couplets which has important antecedents in the past; it is the new style of wit which Dryden, in part, resisted.

When Addison wrote on 'True and false Wit', he began with Locke's notion of wit as deriving from the resemblance and congruity of ideas, on which he based his discussion. But he could not dismiss the subject without observing 'that as Mr. *Lock* in the Passage above-mentioned has discovered the most fruitful Source of Wit, so there is another of a quite contrary Nature to it, which does likewise branch it self out into several Kinds. For not only the *Resemblance*, but the *Opposition* of Ideas does very often produce Wit; as I could shew in several little Points, Turns, and Antitheses, that I may possibly enlarge upon in some future Speculation.'[1]

One cannot help wondering if Addison were about to set the stamp of academic approval on the wit which Butler had condemned long before. Such would appear to be the case; and if this speculation had been written, it would have included several kinds of true and false wit derived from 'the opposition of ideas'. If we add that Metaphysical wit commonly struck upon resemblance in incongruity, or that Cowley's 'Of Wit' really defines wit as the *discordia concors* of Dr. Johnson, with the stress on the *concors*, we shall have before us the chief mutations of wit in the seventeenth century. While the wit of 'congruity' was directed largely against the Metaphysical wit, so was the wit of 'contradiction' as found in Waller; but Dryden asserted 'propriety' even against the antithetic wit, until Pope came to harmonize the two. If the wit of expressing things by oppositions is not to be regarded as a wit of judgment, of separating differences, it is at least, as Locke says of judgment, 'a Way

---

[1] *Spectator*, No. 62 (11th May 1711). In 1710, however, Addison (*Tatler*, No. 163) had made Ned Softly admire the worst verses of Waller and 'the little Gothic ornaments of epigrammatical conceits, turns, points, and quibbles, which are so frequent in the most admired of our English poets'.

of proceeding quite contrary to Metaphor and Allusion'.

To what extent the wit of opposition became a purely formal thing may be discovered in Pope; for not infrequently in him we find the opposition without the antithesis, as in this passage from *The Rape of the Lock*:

> *On her white breast a sparkling Cross she wore,*
> *Which Jews might kiss, and Infidels adore.*
> *Her lively looks a sprightly mind disclose,*
> *Quick as her eyes, and as unfix'd as those:*
> *Favours to none, to all she smiles extends;*
> *Oft she rejects, but never once offends.*

Here there is an opposition of epithets more seeming than real, and structural rather than significant; the wit has passed into the very design of the verse.[1] On the long road which we have come there are many things, both metrical and rhetorical, that culminate in these six lines; but they are all comprehended in a wit of vibrant oppositions which gave a distinct pattern to the neo-classical couplet. No doubt the Augustan 'antithesis' derived its peculiar authority from the fact that 'it was the verbal equivalent of an ideal', the ideal of 'the mean', which is defined by opposites; but both as structural convention and as attitude of mind it was a development of the past.

---

[1] Even those lines which are not true antitheses have a pattern of words and a rhythmic opposition that beguile the ear. Pope's 'opposites' are not always the 'antithets' of Bailey's *Dictionary* (1728).

XI

The Occasion of *An Essay of Dramatic Poesy*

★

Dr. Johnson introduced the invidious distinction between the general and the occasional in Dryden's criticism, declaring in the *Lives* that his occasional positions are sometimes interested, negligent, or capricious—inconstant to his general precepts. In a less pejorative sense *An Essay of Dramatic Poesy* illustrates the occasional as well as the general, but it is unique in Dryden's criticism because it was published without any visible means of support, not as a pendant to another work. Some ·writers, mistaking the personal apology in the *Defence of an Essay*—which, as a matter of fact, is incident only to the argument about rhyme—have overplayed the occasional bias of the *Essay* with respect to Sir Robert Howard. But one provocation to the *Essay*, to which an unidentified allusion directs us, has been unaccountably neglected. This motivation helps to explain the *Essay*, and even its concern with dramatic principles, without challenging its conformity to its own laws.

When Dryden wrote the *Essay*, the French and English had already clashed in a notable exchange of opinion. The occasion actually led to diplomatic action and the banishment of the offender. The occasion especially concerned the

Royal Society[1] and so provided another reason why Dryden might not be insensitive to the controversy. It is hardly necessary to remark that complimentary allusions to science are a conspicuous feature of the *Essay*, which was probably written before he was dropped by the Society.[2] But it does seem necessary to remark that dramatic poetry had been an issue in this clash. The famous exchange, in which the Royal Society was directly involved, had for its principals Samuel Sorbière and Thomas Sprat, and produced works which long kept a certain notoriety in England. It is, therefore, all the more strange that they have never entered the discussion of circumstances incident to the *Essay of Dramatic Poesy*.

In the same year that Dryden published *The Rival Ladies*, with its prefatory defence of rhyme in serious plays, Samuel Sorbière published his *Voyage to England*[3] and raised a storm of indignation, which was embarrassing to the Royal Society because he had been 'admitted a member'. Thomas Sprat, the official spokesman for the Society, laid down his *History* long enough to write *Observations on Monsieur Sorbier's Voyage into England*,[4] which appeared in 1665. In the

[1] See Vincent Guilloton, *Autour de la Relation du Voyage de Samuel Sorbière en Angleterre*, 1663-1664 ('Smith College Studies in Modern Languages', Vol. XI, No. 4 [Northampton, 1930]).

[2] These allusions seem less random—aside from their place in the argument —when we recall his 'Apostrophe to the Royal Society' in the *Annus Mirabilis* (1667).

[3] *Relation d'un Voyage en Angleterre où sont touchées plusieurs choses qui regardent l'état des sciences, et de la religion, et autres matières curieuses.* (Paris, 1664). Then Dryden said, 'For the French, I do not name them, because it is the fate of our countrymen to admit little of theirs among us but the basest of their men,' etc.

[4] Its apparently official character, though not official in fact, is stressed on the title-page: 'Written to Dr. Wren, Professor of Astronomy in Oxford. By *Thomas Sprat*, Fellow of the Royal Society. London, Printed for *John Martyn* and *James Allestry*, Printers to the Royal Society.' His third paragraph explains his reply: 'For having now under my Hands the History of the *Royal Society*, it will be in vain for me to try to represent its Design to be Advantageous to the Glory of *England*, if my Countrymen shall know that one who calls himself a Member of that *Assembly* has escaped unanswered in the public Disgraces which he has cast on our whole Nation' (cf. Evelyn's letter to Sprat, 31st October, 1664).

same year Sir Robert Howard published his *Four New Plays*, with the preface now remembered chiefly for having started the controversy with Dryden. Meanwhile the Great Plague had broken out, to be followed by the Great Fire in 1666; together they closed the theatres and hindered publication for eighteen months. For these two years Dryden has nothing to show in the way of publication except his collaboration with Howard on *The Indian Queen*, published in *Four New Plays*. But it was in this interval, by his own account, that he wrote *Annus Mirabilis* and the *Essay of Dramatic Poesy*, the first of which certainly appeared in 1667,[1] along with Sprat's *History of the Royal Society*. How Sorbière and Sprat are related to the quarrel about dramatic poetry may now be examined.

In criticizing English drama Sorbière raised issues which remained central to the controversy represented by the *Essay of Dramatic Poesy*. His chief remarks are as follows:[2]

'But the Players [Plays] here wou'd be of little Esteem in *France*, so far short the *English* come of the *French* this Way: The Poets laugh at the Uniformity of the Place, and the Rules of Times: Their Plays contain the Actions of Five and Twenty Years, and after that in the First Act they represent the marriage of a Prince; they bring in his Son Fighting in the Second, and having Travelled over many Countries: But above all things they set up for the Passions, Vertues and Vices of Mankind admirably well; and indeed do not fall much short in the performance. In representing a Miser, they make him guilty of all the basest Actions that have been practised in several Ages, upon divers Occasions and indifferent Professions: They do not matter tho' it be a Hodch Potch, for they say, they mind only the Parts as they come on one after another, and have no regard to the whole Composition. I understand that all the *English* Eloquence

---

[1] Malone believed that the *Essay* was published at the end of 1667 (cf. *Prose Works of Dryden*, I, Part I, 58).

[2] For convenience Sorbière and Sprat are quoted from *A Voyage to England . . . by Mons. Sorbière. As also Observations on the same Voyage, by Dr. Thomas Sprat* (London, 1709); cited hereafter as '*Voyage*'.

The Occasion of An Essay of Dramatic Poesy

consists in nothing but meer Pedantry, and that their Sermons from the Pulpit, and their pleadings at the Bar, are
much of the same Stamp. . . . Their Comedies are a kind of
Blank Verse, and suit an Ordinary Language better than our
Meetre, and make some Melody: They cannot but conceive
it to be a troublesome thing to have the Ear continually
tickled with the same Cadence; and they say, that to hear
Heroick Verses spoken for Two or Three Hours together,
and to recoyl back from one to the other, is a Method of
Expression that is not so natural and diverting: In short, it
looks as if the *English* would by no means fall in with the
Practices and manner of Representation in other Languages; and the Italian Opera's appear more extravagant,
and much more disliked by them than ours. But we are not
here to enter upon a Dispute about the different Tastes of
Men, it's best to leave every one to abound in his own
Sence.'[1]

[1] *Voyage*, pp. 69–71. Compare Sorbière's French for the exact turn of his
remarks, once seriously misrepresented by the English:

'Mais les Comédies n'auroient pas en France toute l'approbation qu'elles ont
en Angleterre. Les Poëtes se mocquent de l'uniformité du lieu, & de la régle
des vingt-quatre heures. Ils font des comédies de vingt-cinq ans, & après avoir
représenté au premier acte le mariage d'un Prince, ils représentent toute d'une
suite les belles Actions de son fils, & luy font voir bien du pays. Il se picquent
sur tout de faire d'excellens characters des passions, des vices, & des vertus; Et
en cela ils réussissent assez bien. Pour depeindre un avare, ils en font faire à un
home toutes les plus basses actions qui se pratiquent en divers âges, en diverses
rencontres, & en diverses professions; Et il ne leur importe que ce soit un pot
pourry; parce qu'ils n'en regardent, disent-ils, qu'une partie après l'autre, sans
se soucier du total.

'J'entends que toute l'Eloquence Angloise est conduite de cette manière; &
que dans la Chaire, & au Barreau, on ne parle pas d'autre façon. . . .

'Les Comédies sont en prose mesurée, qui a plus de rapport au langage
ordinaire que nos vers, & qui rend quelque mélodie. Ils ne peuuēt s'imaginer
que ce ne soit une chose importune d'avoir continuellement l'oreille frappée de
la mesme cadence; ils disent, que d'entendre parler deux ou trois heures en vers
Alexandrins, & voir sauter de cesure en cesure, est une maniere de s'exprimer
moins naturelle, & moins divertissante. En effect il semble qu'elle s'esloigne
autant de ce qui se pratique dans le monde, & par conséquent de ce que l'on veut
représenter; que la manière Italienne de réciter les Comédies en musique,
s'esgare & extravague au delà de la nostre. Mais il ne faut pas disputer des
gousts, & il vaut mieux laisser chacun abonder en son sens,' (*Relation* [Cologne,
1669], pp. 129–32).

The Occasion of An Essay of Dramatic Poesy

The issues raised here concern the rejection of the unities and decorum as well as the use of rhyme. Rhyme is rejected by the English because it is neither natural nor pleasing. The English (although the translated remark about opera misses the point) are open to attack because they are nonconformists to European dramatic standards—a ground of attack calculated to annoy the court of Charles II.

As one who had made a reputation out of English writers, Sorbière was especially offensive to Sprat, who would not have erred as a modern writer has erred, by praising Sorbière for ideas which he probably derived from Hobbes.[1] Hence Sprat takes advantage of 'any disparagement of English literature on the part of Sorbière. On the violation of the unities by the English, Sprat replies by contrasting, in too round figures, the present and the past age:

' 'Tis true, about an Hundred Years ago the *English* Poets were not very exact in such Decencies; but no more then were the Dramatists of any other Countries. The *English* themselves did laugh away such Absurdities as soon as any; and for these last Fifty Years our Stage has been as regular in those Circumstances as the best in *Europe*.'[2]

This contrast, properly dated, appears again in Dryden's *Essay*, together with some concern for European standards.[3] But Sprat, as we shall see, also liberalizes his terms of conformity.

The issue of decorum leads Sprat into a comparison of French and English dramatic poetry, in which he discusses rhymed verse:

'He next blames the *Meanness of* [the] *Humours which we represent.* And here, because he has thrust this Occasion upon me, I will venture to make a short Comparison between the French Dramatical Poetry and ours. . . . I will therefore

---

[1] See Alan M. Boase, *The Fortunes of Montaigne* (London, 1935), pp. 254–5; and compare Hobbes's *Answer to Davenant* on poetry and his *Human Nature* or *Leviathan* on language. If this matter was not available to Sorbière in Latin, still the parallel is unmistakable; the ideas were no accident in Hobbes.

[2] *Voyage*, p. 166.

[3] In the Dedication of *The Rival Ladies* Dryden is worried lest the English seem eccentric by refusing rhyme in drama.

make no Scruple to maintain that the *English* Plays ought to be preferr'd before the *French*: And to prove this I will not insist on an Argument which is plain to any Observer, that the greatest Part of their most Excellent Pieces has [have] been taken from the *Spaniard*; whereas the *English* have for the most part trodden in New Ways of Invention. From hence I will not draw much Advantage, tho' it may serve to balance that which he afterwards says of our Books, that *they are generally stoln out of other Authors*; but I will fetch the Grounds of my Perswasion from the very Nature and Use of the Stage itself. It is beyond all Dispute, that the true intention of such Representations is to give to mankind a Picture of themselves, and thereby to make Virtue belov'd, Vice abhorr'd, and the little Irregularities of Mens Tempers, called Humours, expos'd to laughter. The Two First of these are the proper Subjects of Tragedy, and Trage-Comedy. And in these I will first try to shew why our Way ought to be preferr'd before theirs. The *French* for the most part take only One or Two Great Men, and chiefly insist on some one Remarkable Accident of their Story; to this End they admit no more Persons than will [barely] serve to adorn that: And they manage all in Rhime, with long Speeches, almost in the Way of Dialogues, in making high Idea's of Honour, and in speaking Noble things. The *English* on the other side make their chief Plot to consist of a greater variety of Actions; and besides the main Design, add many other little Contrivances. By this Means their Scenes are shorter, their Stage fuller, many more Persons of different Humours are introduc'd. And in carrying on of this they generally do only confine themselves to Blank Verse. This is the Difference, and hence the *English* have these Advantages. By the Liberty of Prose they render their Speech and Pronunciation more Natural, and are never put to make a Contention between the Rhime and the Sence. By their Underplots they often change the Minds of their Spectators: Which is a mighty Benefit, seeing one of the greatest Arts of Wit and Perswasion is the right ordering of Digressions. By their full Stage they prevent Mens being continually tir'd with the same Objects: And so they make the Doctrine of the Scene to be more lively and diverting than the Precepts of Philosophers, or the grave Delight of Heroick Poetry; which the *French* Tragedies do resemble. Nor is it sufficient to object against this, that it is undecent to thrust in Men of mean Condition amongst the Actions of Princes. For why should that misbecome the Stage, which is always found to be acted on the true Theatre of the World? There being no Court which only consists of Kings, and Queens, and Counsellors of State. Upon these Accounts, Sir, in my weak Judgment, the *French Dramma* ought to give place to the *English* in the Tragical and Lofty Part of it.'[1]

Sprat concludes his comparison with an easy victory in comedy, treating Sorbière to a lesson in humours which he might have learned for himself:

'And now having obtained this, I suppose they will of their own Accord resign the other Excellence, and confess that we have far exceeded them in the Representation of the different Humours. The Truth is, the *French* have always seemed almost asham'd of the true Comedy; making it not much more than the Subject of their *Farces*: Whereas the *English* Stage has so much abounded with it, that perhaps there is scarce any Sort of Extravagance of which the Minds of Men are capable but they have in some measure express'd. It is in Comedies, and not in Solemn Histories, that the *English* use to relate the Speeches of Waggoners, of Fencers, and of Common Soldiers. And this I dare assure *Monsieur de Sorbiere*, that if he had understood our Language, he might have seen himself in all [his] Shapes, as a vain Traveller, an empty Politician, an insolent Pedant, and an idle Pretender to Learning.'[2]

The last shape, of course, was peculiarly annoying to a defender of the Royal Society, which felt that it had been deceived.

For our purpose it may be well to itemize the grounds of

[1] *Voyage*, pp. 167–9. The chief variants of the 1665 text are supplied in brackets, except for the spelling of 'rhime' as 'rhythm'.   [2] Ibid., p. 169.

defence employed by Sprat. In the matter of unities he justifies English drama by European standards; he argues from the nature of drama, defines plays with respect to their ends; he argues from the art by which a play attains its end; he finds that nature is satisfied by blank verse, that variety of plot and character are persuasive means (art) to the end of instruction, surpassing 'the grave Delight of Heroick Poetry', which characterizes French tragedy. Decorum in characters is to be judged by nature, of which a play is an image, and particularly by the kind of nature appropriate to the play. In short, Sprat accepts the unities with qualifications in the interest of delight but rejects the French doctrine of decorum and use of rhyme in the interest of nature. English plays are superior both in nature and in art; the English way to the end of drama is superior because it is more lively, and therefore more persuasive in its instruction. Such an approach, it may be observed, is not uninstructive for the *Essay of Dramatic Poesy*.

While Sorbière and Sprat may be said to have launched the debate officially,[1] they by no means defined all of the issues. If this admission seems to grant them more importance than they deserve, it will suffice to indicate the background for the argument which engages Dryden's 'wits'.[2] The Sorbière incident was at least an event in a controversy wider but now less substantial than Howard's Preface to *Four New Plays*.

[1] Guilloton (pp. 8–9) shows that this debate was restrained: 'Dans une lettre à Louis XIV du 21 juillet 1664—quinze jours après l'arrêt qui condamnait Sorbière—l'ambassadeur Cominges dit au roi qu'il est intervenu auprès de Charles II pour empêcher certains membres de la Société Royale "qui déjà taillaient leurs plumes" pour lui répondre, de riposter au voyageur français. Le roi d'Angleterre a dû menacer "ces Messieurs de l'Académie" pour les obliger à lui apporter les matériaux déjà préparés pour leur réplique.' Nevertheless, Sprat's 'Letter to Wren' (*Observations*) was dated 1st August 1664, and some covert, though partial, replies seem to have been made.

[2] The opening of the *Essay* further characterizes the wits who are introduced in the Dedication. Oddly enough, on 'that memorable day' Eugenius, if he is Buckhurst, presumably shared in the victory over the Dutch rather than in that over the French. The *Essay* is described in the *Defence* as 'a little discourse in dialogue, for the most part borrowed from the observations of others'. Too often 'others' has been restricted to foreign sources.

In that preface Howard devotes his time to a defence of English plays which is no extenuation of his own; rather, as he says with respect to rhyme, his own err by following in part the method which he condemns. Howard debates some issues that were neglected by Sprat but are discussed by Dryden, and in general broadens the argument to include the Ancients, whôm the French imitate. He introduces his defence in these words:[1]

'Yet I shall presume to say something in the justification of our nation's plays, (though not of my own), since in my judgment—without being partial to my Country—I do really prefer our plays as much before any other nation's as I do the best of ours before my own.'[2]

Finding the Ancients deficient in plot and wit, although their comedy has some pretences to both, he proceeds to define the French way in terms of the Ancient pattern. Two aspects of this way, to which the English have become susceptible, are attacked: 'presenting the business in relations' and writing in rhyme. The method of the Ancients was forced upon them by their subjects, but the French commit the error without the necessity. 'If these premises be granted,' he argues, ' 'tis no partiality to conclude that our English plays justly challenge the pre-eminence.'[3] Coming when it did, Howard's Preface must have been read largely as another reply to Sorbière.

But he is ready to admit that the English differ from others less happily in one respect:

'Yet I shall as candidly acknowledge that our best poets have differed from other nations (though not so happily) in usually mingling and interweaving mirth and sadness through the whole course of their plays—Ben Jonson only excepted, who keeps himself entire to one argument. And I confess I am now convinced in my own judgment that it is most proper to keep the audience in one entire disposition both of concern and attention.'[4]

---

[1] For convenience references to Howard and Dryden are made to *Dryden & Howard*, 1664–1668, ed. D. D. Arundell (Cambridge, 1929); cited hereafter as 'Arundell'.   [2] Ibid., p. 6.   [3] Ibid., p. 7.   [4] Ibid., p. 8.

Though such 'pursuing accidents' may be possible, 'they may not be so proper to be presented—an entire connection being the natural beauty of all plays'. To that extent Howard bows to the unities.[1] But, after the French, neither Italian nor Spanish plays offer him anything worthy of imitation. In terms of Dryden's *Essay*, his argument, except for rhyme, is more in accord with that of Eugenius than with that of Crites, but it agrees with Lisideius on tragicomedy. He is against both the Ancients and the French, but allows that the Ancients had reason for their method;[2] among the English he evidently rates the past age, especially Jonson, above the present.

When we come to Dryden, it must be said at once that by defending rhyme he appeared to belong to the French party;[3] in other respects he is neither more nor less ready than other members of the English party to accept elements of the French way of drama. Dryden himself placed the *Essay* in relation to the quarrel with Howard about rhyme, explicitly in the *Defence of an Essay*, and implicitly in the *Essay* by borrowing Howard's arguments. Others have attempted to saddle all of Crites' arguments upon Howard, but such an assimilation does not correspond to the facts; nor does it seem to have been a part of Dryden's purpose, for this allusion in his Dedication applied to no one so well as to Howard:

'Even Tully had a controversy with his dear Atticus; and in one of his Dialogues, makes him sustain the part of an enemy in philosophy, who, in his letters, is his confident of state, and made privy to the most weighty affairs of the Roman Senate.'[4]

In context this remark is part of an apology for his own opinions, 'which were first made public'.[5] Then Dryden

---

[1] Here the unity of feeling, an aspect of the unity of action or of decorum.

[2] Of course, Thomas Rymer became the chief English advocate for the Ancients.

[3] Howard had stigmatized rhyme as part of the French way, but Dryden speaks of his 'adversaries' in the Dedication of the *Essay*.   [4] Arundell, p. 20.

[5] See his recapitulation of the controversy with Howard at the close of the *Defence of an Essay*.

gives this description of the *Essay*: '. . . the relation of a dispute betwixt some of our wits upon this subject, in which they did not only speak of plays in verse, but mingled, in the freedom of discourse, some things of the ancient, many of the modern ways of writing; comparing those with these, and the wits of our nation with those of others.'[1]

Needless to say, the quarrel between the ancient and modern ways of writing is also represented in the quarrel between the French and English. Therefore, Dryden's opening remark to the reader becomes less puzzling to a modern reader: 'The drift of the ensuing Discourse was chiefly to vindicate the honour of our English writers, from the censure of those who unjustly prefer the French before them.'[2] Howard could have made a similar claim for his Preface. Altogether, this remark, like Howard's Preface, suggests an occasion, beyond the quarrel about rhyme, to which such a vindication of the English would be relevant. Sorbière provided such an occasion, if only by making a French party among the English all the more obnoxious.

Dryden's next sentence to the reader emphasizes the occasional aspect of the *Essay* at the expense of its general character: 'This I intimate, lest any should think me so exceeding vain, as to teach others an art which they understand much better than myself.' Despite this protestation, the author of the Preface to *The Duke of Lerma* took the *Essay* as a sign of such vanity in Dryden. But the *Essay* itself bears out Dryden's claim; for it has all the marks of a vindication, weighing the charges which had been made against English drama and marshalling the arguments which had been or could be used to refute them. It is not incidental to this purpose that he, like Howard, also entertains the reader 'with what a good play should be'; it is, however, central to another purpose.

In the *Essay*, rhyme is the issue reserved for final and separate debate, but it was the issue which Dryden first set up, and thereby compromised his native stand. Dryden invokes European example only in support of rhyme, but

---

[1] Arundell, p. 21.   [2] Ibid., p. 22.

even then he asserts English precedent for it—more vigorously in the *Essay*, though he is already anti-French in the
Dedication of *The Rival Ladies*.[1] To his praise in these works
of the perfecters of English rhyme he added, in his enthusiasm, the dedication of the *Essay* to one of those translators
of Corneille's *Pompey* who had provided him with a dazz-
ling argument for English rhymed plays.[2] It has long been
recognized that Dryden put Howard's arguments against
rhyme into the mouth of Crites, but not that Sprat anticipated Howard in arguing against rhyme, especially its un-
naturalness. Therefore Neander is really answering both, as
well as justifying an English use of a prominent feature of
the French way of drama.

The *Essay* ought to be examined for its disposition of
previous argument, apart from rhyme. It will be remembered that Crites and Lisideius are spokesmen for the
Ancients and French respectively, and that Eugenius and
Neander are partners in rebuttal. Just as Eugenius argues
that Ancient plots are deficient, so Neander argues that
French plots are deficient; and as Eugenius argues that the
Ancients did not follow their method rigidly, so Neander
argues that the French have departed from theirs when they
sought variety. The consequence is to render the unities not
indispensable but contingent upon variety.[3] Let us recall
that the issues of plot and wit with which Crites begins the
argument had been raised against the Ancients by Howard.
Although he was probably not the 'late writer' to whom

[1] Jonson provided English precedent not only for rhyme but also for dramatic
regularity. He is very useful to Dryden, even doctrinally, in repudiating
French influence.

[2] See the allusion to *Pompey* in the Dedication. This translation (1664)—
called the 'SMEC' version by a eulogist of Orinda—was a work of the wits, including not only Buckhurst but Sedley and Waller (cf. *Letters from Orinda*
[1705], p. 112, and Dryden's or Tonson's *Miscellanies* [1716], II, 94). Through
these names, and because of this association, Dryden's *Essay* pays still more
homage to rhyme. Crites alone opposes it, but Crites is given an office appropriate to his name and dismissed in the company of Neander rather than of the
wits. If Crites were Roscommon, as has been suggested, he would have
written the prologue to the rival *Pompey* translated by Katharine Philips.

[3] Positively, of course, Dryden argues for both the unities and rhyme as aids
to imitation.

Eugenius refers, Howard had pointed out that the subjects of the Ancients 'were usually the most known stories and fables'—a fact which Eugenius proceeds to develop into a limitation upon variety and delight.[1] On tragi-comedy Lisideius definitely echoes Howard's argument against this mixture, especially as it may frustrate the interest and concern of the audience.[2] Lisideius, moreover, answers Sprat on French plots:

'But I return again to the French writers, who, as I have said, do not burden themselves too much with plot, which has been reproached to them by an ingenious person of our nation as a fault. For he says they commonly make but one person considerable in a play; they dwell upon him and his concernments, while the rest of the persons are only subservient to set him off.'[3]

The actual words of this 'ingenious person of our nation', hitherto unidentified, will be found in Sprat's remarks about the French way in reply to Sorbière. But Lisideius also interprets Sprat's argument in his answer:

'If he intends this by it, that there is one person in the play who is of greater dignity than the rest, he must tax not only theirs, but those of the ancients, and—which he would be loath to do—the best of ours.'

Sprat would not have been loath to tax an opponent with shifting his argument. Again, Lisideius goes to considerable pains to refute Howard's charges against the French method of relations;[4] the nexus becomes obvious when he says, 'But it is objected that if one part of the play may be related, then why not all.'[5]

---

[1] Arundell, pp. 38, 7. Obviously he was not the writer if 'late' means 'lately deceased'. Howard does not develop the consequence mentioned by Dryden; rather he argues that these stories obliged the dramatists to resort to 'relations'. Cowley, now a 'late' writer, characterized these stories in terms similar to those of Dryden, but with respect to epic poetry (Preface to *Poems* [1656]).

[2] Arundell, pp. 47–8, 8.

[3] Ibid., pp. 50–1.

[4] Ibid., pp. 51–5.

[5] Ibid., pp. 53, 7. Howard had said that 'they do by consequence maintain that a whole play might be as well related as acted'. It might be remarked that Howard's show of logic eventually became a little irksome to Dryden.

The Occasion of An Essay of Dramatic Poesy

The argument of Neander agrees in all respects save rhyme with the defence offered by Sprat, including the charge that French plays were based on Spanish plots. Neander refutes the arguments of Lisideius and Howard on tragi-comedy, which he makes a special glory of the English.[1] He follows Sprat when he argues against 'Lisideius and many others' who 'cry up the barrenness of the French plots above the variety and copiousness of the English';[2] he agrees with Sprat on short speeches versus long harangues. It is in the interest of variety that he argues a weakness in Lisideius' answer to Sprat:

'There is another part of Lisideius his discourse, in which he has rather excused our neighbours than commended them,—that is, for aiming only to make one person considerable in their plays.'[3]

' 'Tis evident,' says Neander, 'that the more the persons are, the greater will be the variety of the plot,' and thus supports Sprat.

He is ready to admit, however, that Lisideius has reason in what he says about relations, especially in arguing that all incredible actions be related.[4] Here, of course, he is arguing partly against Howard; but Lisideius is not allowed a victory, for the French have erred grossly in this respect, and a mean between French and English practice is best. Howard had argued that the French used relations without regard to necessity. When Neander argues 'that we have many plays of ours as regular as any of theirs, and which, besides, have more variety of plot and characters',[5] he comes pretty close to summing up Sprat's defence, including regularity as a criterion.

If Sorbière may be said to have initiated the occasion for the *Essay*, and the *Essay* itself may be allowed to reveal an appropriate orientation, the question may then be asked

[1] Ibid., pp. 58, 48, 8.
[2] Ibid., p. 58.
[3] Ibid., p. 61.
[4] Ibid., pp. 61-2. Howard argued that it was impossible to represent some parts of the stories used by the Ancients.
[5] Ibid., p. 66.

why Dryden delayed its publication from 1665-6, the apparent date of composition,[1] until 1668. The most obvious answer is supplied by the Plague and Fire. Actually the *Essay* was entered in the Stationers' Register, 7th August 1667, and thus was probably intended for publication in the same year as the *Annus Mirabilis*.[2] The delay, which is magnified by the publication date, requires no other explanation, since *The Indian Emperor*, though registered 26th May 1665, was not printed until late in 1667.[3] The retrospective note in the Dedication of the *Essay* springs from the same interval, which overlaps Dryden's retirement in the country.[4] On the other hand, because of the interruption of normal life by the Plague and Fire, the loss in timeliness was less than it would seem; Sprat's *Observations* reappeared in 1668. While the king's attempt to prevent any reply to Sorbière may have made Dryden's vindication more indirect, no doubt Dryden wrote the *Essay* chiefly to explore and define his own theories of dramatic art—not without regard to the taste of the Court, to which he owed so much

[1] See the Dedication of the *Essay*. The remark in the Dedication that he has since laid aside the writing of plays in rhyme until he has more leisure seems rather odd when we consider that although he did not defend rhyme in comedy, he laid it aside (after *The Maiden Queen*) only to write comedies.

[2] The Prefatory Epistle to this poem, dated from Charlton, Wiltshire, 10th November 1666, asks Howard to see the poem through the press; it was published early in 1667, and celebrated the late fire as well as the unconcluded Dutch war. *The Maiden Queen*—apparently read by Howard between his 'first perusal' and his 'correction' of the *Annus Mirabilis* (cf. Epistle) and staged early in 1667—was entered in the Stationers' Register at the same time as the *Essay*, and had been published by 18th January 1668, when Pepys bought a copy 'newly printed'. Dryden's remark about laying rhyme aside since that time should make *The Maiden Queen* at least contemporary with the *Essay*.

[3] The interval between registration and publication, even for Dryden's plays, usually was very much shorter. For bibliographical details concerning these works see Hugh MacDonald's *Bibliography* (Oxford, 1939).

[4] The opening sentence of the *Essay*, however, seems to place the *Essay* later than the date assigned in the Dedication; for Dryden's phrase 'in the first summer of the late war' could not have been written much before the entry in the Stationers' Register, since the 'late war' was concluded in the preceding month with the Peace of Breda. This suggests, despite Dryden's protest, revision.

The Occasion of An Essay of Dramatic Poesy

—and his recent success with *The Indian Emperor* encouraged him to undertake it.[1]

Despite the enforced delay, which made 1667 the earliest date for the publication of the *Essay*, there can be no doubt that it was an ambitious work or that it had a dual purpose. All this is clear from the address 'To the reader'. I have already quoted the first part of that address, which intimates the occasional aspect of the *Essay*. The latter part suggests a more general purpose:

'But if this incorrect Essay, written in the country without the help of books or advice of friends, shall find any acceptance in the world, I promise to myself a better success of the second part, wherein the virtues and faults of the English poets who have written either in this, the epic, or lyric way, will be more fully treated of, and their several styles impartially imitated.'[2]

That which has been inadequately treated, or neglected in favour of a party defence, will be the main subject of a second part. This more general purpose Dryden fulfilled, at least in large part, but not as he anticipated; rather in the form of occasional essays attached to other works.[3] For the dramatic way he has many essays to show; for the epic way, several essays and parts of essays; for the lyric way, various miscellaneous passages.

---

[1] *The Maiden Queen*, however, his first attempt to embody his new formula (cf. Prologue), was saved by the king's approval (cf. Preface). In the Preface to *Juvenal* (1693) he speaks of the *Essay* as a product of the time 'when I was drawing the outlines of an art, without any living master to instruct me in it; an art which had been better praised than studied here in England. . . . I was sailing in a vast ocean, without other help than the pole-star of the ancients, and the rules of the French stage amongst the moderns, which are extremely different from ours, by reason of their opposite taste.' He was speaking to the man to whom he dedicated the *Essay*.

[2] Arundell, p. 22.

[3] The groundwork for his later criticism was laid in the *Essay* and the 'Account' of the *Annus*, which overlap on rhyme and the 'proper wit of poetry'. The Preface to *Troilus and Cressida*, for example, is no radical departure from the *Essay*. While the authorities are new—Bossu, Rapin, Longinus—the argument still owes much to Corneille's *Discourses*, particularly on manners and the properties of the action, even to the founding of pity and fear on the chief character—a rule not 'fully enough discovered to us'.

The Occasion of An Essay of Dramatic Poesy

This 'incorrect Essay'—later honoured by revision, though not of its alleged defects—still keeps a place apart in his criticism, but least for its dual motivation, which makes it, like most of his essays, both occasional and general in nature; it keeps that place, aside from merit, for its ambitious programme, dialogue form, and basic principles. Yet even in 'drawing the outlines of an art' Dryden had adjusted his argument both to occasion and to principle.

XII

The Platonic Lady

★

The Platonic cult which flourished in the court of Charles I
and descended to the Restoration under the patronage of
the solemn French romances that succeeded *Astrée* was never
without it opponents, but few of them would have thought it
necessary to purify the cult until Mrs. Katherine Philips came
to found her 'Society of Friendship' in 1651. More congenial
to Restoration ideas of purification, however, was the satirizing
of hypocrisy, and this was provided for the cult by a physician
in ordinary to the late king. Dr. Walter Charleton, who was
perhaps not unmindful of Mrs. Philips's efforts, attacked the
Platonic cult from the naturalistic side in his prose fiction *The
Ephesian Matron*, first published apparently in 1653.[1] As this
work appears never to have been considered in discussions of
the anti-Platonics, it may not be amiss to give a brief account
of the nature of its attack.

The framework of Charleton's satire is the familiar tale out
of Petronius, told to the accompaniment of philosophical reflections that conclude in a discourse upon the nature of love,
to which the narrative *dénouement* is attached. The last section
is called 'Of Platonique Love,' and both it and the prefatory
'Letter,' together with the story itself, are an attack upon such

---

[1] Other editions in 1658, 1659, and 1668; the editions of 1653 and 1658 I
have not seen. It was translated into Latin by Bartholomew Harris in 1665.
The 1658 and 1668 editions were published with *The Cimmerian Matron* by
P. M., Gent.

The Platonic Lady

love. In his prefatory 'Letter' to a person of honour, Charleton leaves the Platonic ladies, adversaries of the matron, 'to consult their grand Oracle *Lilly*, how to find out' his patron's 'most humble Servant.' He also apologizes for the philosophical trappings of his story:

> If I have set her forth in an equipage somewhat too *grave* and *solemn*, according to the fashion of my own phansy, which is most delighted with sad colours, and plain usefull garments; so that she may now seem the Mistresse rather of a *Philosopher* than of a *Courtier*: it was, because I would not have her appear altogether a stranger, and ignorant of the *mode* of the time, wherein the greatest *levity* and *licentiousnesse*, is commonly wrapt up in the most *austere looks*, and sober *formality* of dresse; and *Lasciviousness* generally usurps the long veil of *Modesty*.[1]

Here the satire glances at the Puritans and throws a dubious light upon Platonic love 'as a tradition of courtliness' maintained against 'the dull righteousness of Puritan morality.'[2] Of the matron's religion Charleton is ironically uncertain, 'because (contrary to the custom of her sex) she is very reserved in that particular':

> . . . I should take her to be of old *Epicurus's* Faith, following the simple dictates of mother-Nature, and living by the plain rule of her own *Inclinations; as holding it a contradiction, to be born under one Law, and to another bound:* or else a *Sister of the Family of Love*, which scruples at no freedom with a sanctifi'd Brother, & justifies her familiarity with fervency of zeal, and suggestions of the *spirit*.[3]

Noteworthy in this passage are the familiar intrusion of Epicurus into Charleton's thought and the striking and significant quotation from the double law of Fulke Greville's *Mustapha;* they suggest the libertine interpretation of the Law of Nature which came to mark the Hobbists.[4] But the Ephesian matron does not only differ from the Platonic ladies in her religion:

> Besides that, she is a professed enemy to their darling, *Platonick Love;* and ingenuously confesseth, she knowes no flames, but such as arise from the difference of Sex, and are kindled in the blood, and other luxuriant

---

[1] *The Ephesian Matron* (London, 1659), sig. A4ʳ.
[2] Cf. P.W. Souers, *The Matchless Orinda* (Cambridge, 1931), p. 259.
[3] Charleton, *op. cit.*, sig. A6ʳ. In short, her tendencies are *libertine*; the Familist suggestion is a wicked glance at another devotion of love.
[4] See Chapter II, 'The Libertine Donne,' *supra*, and *Mustapha* 'Chorus Sacerdotum.'

humours of the body: and that her Amours alwaies tend to the propagation of somewhat more Material, than the simple *Ideas of vertue*, of which our Philosophicall Ladies so much talk.[1]

Indeed, the prefatory 'Letter' alone is enough to drive the Platonic ladies to consult Lilly on the identity of an author who did not risk his name on the title-page.

The story of the Ephesian matron as retold by Charleton would give Petronius no occasion for envy, since it is weighed down by satirical reflections which are much the most interesting part of the work. Some of these comments deserve mention. In view of the heroical taste of the age, it is pertinent if by no means novel to learn that 'the tyranny of Love over even Heroical Minds . . . hath given occasion to men to call it the *Heroical Passion*.'[2] But Charleton has little patience with the contemporary wits who find something like virtue in a fatiguing vice or an added zest in the favours of Platonic reserve:

I am not ignorant, there are a sort of Heretiques in Love, who prize no pleasures that come easily; and think it below their Courage to engarrison that Fort, whose Gates are thrown open at first Summons: as if Delight were the more gratefull and transcendent for being difficult and tedious in acquisition.[3]

And he has even less patience with 'the nice Distinction, which *Flattery* hath imagined, betwixt *Love* and *Lust;* as if one were the genuine off-spring of the Mind alone, the other the spurious issue of the Body.'[4] On the contrary, unprejudiced inquirers into that 'which is generally understood to be *Love*, (for, we are not now upon the consideration of *Amity*, or *Friendship*) will not be easily perswaded, that there is any so great Dissimilitude or Disparity betwixt them, as that they may not be deduced from one and the same principle, at least, that they can be divided.'

This, I presume, will be somewhat distastfull to the pure and refined Disciples of the *Platonique* sect, who profess to be inamoured onely on the beauties of the *Soul*, wholly rejecting all respects of flesh and blood, and entirely devoting their Courtship to contemplate, and entranse themselves in admiration of the lovely Idea's of Virtue: nor will the *Ladies* (made, doubtlesse, of a mold much finer and less sulphureous, than other coarser

[1] Charleton, *op. cit.*, sig. A8r.
[2] *Ibid.*, p. 70.   [3] *Ibid.*, p. 72   [4] *Ibid.*, p. 75.

Mortalls are,) be well pleased to hear their sweet and cleanly Flames should be aspersed with the mixture of grosse and sooty Exhalations, such as arise from Ardours of the Body.[1]

The exception of friendship may be in deference to Mrs. Philips; it is more likely the result of his comparison of ancient and modern Platonics, which needs to be quoted at length:

> First, our Platoniques are generally of *different sexes;* whereas *Socrates* and his Darling, *Alcibiades* were both Masculine. Secondly, ours are commonly both *Young*, and in the Canicular or scortching years of life: but *Socrates* was *Ancient*, and superannuated for the incitements of wanton desires. Thirdly, *Ours* are generally far short of that Wisdome and those Virtues, that are requisite to engender the like Excellencies in others. Again, *Ours* pretend to love, because they would *Learne*, not Teach, and the Male Platonique (forsooth) is ever admiring and extolling the content he takes in contemplating the idea's of those rare Virtues, which he discovers daily in the Female; while she (Good modest Soul!) is as much transported with those perfections of Mind, she discerns in Him: when, indeed, those Virtues and Excellences are kept so close, that no person else can perceive any such in either of them. Lastly, Ours (especially the Women) are for the most part *Married* to others, and so ought to propagate Virtue, (if they have so much as to spare) rather in their Husbands and Children, than in Strangers: but, alas! those Relations are despised, in comparison of the Noble *Lover*, who alone serves to be made wiser and better. I could reckon up many other Differences more, but these are enough to let you see, what vast Disparity is betwixt the Platonique Love of the Ancients, and that of modern Puritan Lovers; and how little reason they have to usurp either the Example of *Socrates*, or auctority of *Plato*, for their patronage.[2]

This Platonic attitude toward love and marriage indicates the way in which the *précieuse* tradition influenced the social mode of Restoration comedy.[3] 'I hope, therefore,' concludes Charleton, 'the wise and virtuous will not be offended, if I take leave (without prejudice to that noble Amity, called Friendship) to suspect, that this Platonique Passion is but an honourable pretence to conceal a sensual Appetite, and is (in plain truth) cousin German at least to that Love, which made our Ephesian Matron so gentle and obliging to the Souldier.' While insisting on naturalism, Charleton does except 'that noble Amity, called Friendship' by means of which Mrs. Philips purified the Pla-

---

[1] Charleton, *op. cit.*, pp. 76-77.   [2] *Ibid.*, pp. 104-06.
[3] Cf. K. M. Lynch, *The Social Mode of Restoration Comedy* (New York, 1926), Chap. V.

tonic cult, though Bishop Jeremy Taylor found even that friend-ship less pure than Christian charity.[1] But the Restoration dramatists revealed the comedy of the whole cult when judged by the standard which Charleton employs.

Enough of *The Ephesian Matron* has been quoted to suggest the interest as well as the flavour of its satire, but the narrative vehicle cannot be said to live up to the ingenuity of its design. It is, nevertheless, an amusing work which conducts us into the spirit of Restoration comedy by satirizing not only the Platonic but also the Puritan lover, who defied the natural man by at best 'an honourable pretence.' Not a little of its verbal effect is indebted to the '*Carmination* or refinement' of the language by that 'Heroical Wit' whom Charleton saluted as the 'new flourishing Dr. Browne.'

[1] Cf. 'A Discourse of Friendship,' *Works* (London, 1864), i. 80-81.

INDEX

Adams, John, 43–62, 174
Addison, Joseph, 270
Agrippa, Cornelius, 183 n., 192 n.
Aristotle, 11, 12, 19 n., 20, 30,
    156, 162, 172 n.
Atterbury, Francis, 264–5
Aubrey, John, 257
Averroes, 13

Bacon, Anthony, 121
Bacon, Francis, 17–18, 22, 121,
    129, 186–7, 192, 195–200, 203–
    5, 208, 215, 221, 251
Bathurst, Ralph, 126
Beaumont, Sir John, 130 n., 256–7
Beaumont, Joseph, 134, 138, 139,
    140
Benlowes, Edward, 147
Berkenhead (Birkenhead), Sir
    John, 125, 179–80
Blount, Charles, 48 n., 155, 168 n.
Blount, Thomas, 45–6, 264 n.
Bodin, Jean, 19, 21
Brahe, Tycho, 10–11
Bramhall, John, 163–4
Briggs, Samson, 135, 136, 137,
    138, 139
Brown, R., 135, 137
Browne, Sir Thomas, 37, 38–40,
    148–9, 150, 154–7, 158, 175–6,
    197, 209
Bruno, Giordano, 13
Burnet, Gilbert, 129
Burton, Robert, 12–14, 102, 104,
    120, 219
Butler, Samuel, 147, 261–3

Bysshe, Edward, 245–6, 254

Campion, Thomas, 245, 255
Carew, Thomas, 123–4
Carleton, Thomas, 157–8
Cartwright, William, 64, 76,
    125–6, 266–7
Casaubon, Meric, 127, 216–18
Case, Dr. John, 19
Castiglione, Baldassare, 64, 76
Chapman, George, 122
Charleton, Walter, 162, 166–75,
    182, 235–7, 289–93
Charron, Pierre, 46, 193–5, 197–8
Cleveland, John, 125, 127–8, 129,
    132, 134, 137, 139
Cole, Thomas, 126
Copernicus, 12, 13, 34, 38, 41
Cornwallis, Sir William, 188
Cowley, Abraham, 37, 129 n.,
    284 n.
Crakanthorp, Richard, 162
Croll, Morris W., 63–4, 72, 75,
    121, 251–2
Cudworth, Ralph, 45 n., 163, 177
Cyprian, St., 21, 31

Daniel, Samuel, 245, 255
Davies, John (of Kidwelly), 245
Davies, Sir John, 161–2
Democritus, 13, 45, 150
Denham, Sir John, 249, 261–2,
    266–7
Descartes, René, 157, 167, 171
Digby, Sir Kenelm, 149–50, 162,
    209

295

Index

Index